IBERIAN AND LATIN AMERICAN STUDIES

Fractal Families in New Millennium
Narrative by Afro-Puerto Rican Woman

Series Editors

Professor David George (Swansea University)
Professor Paul Garner (University of Leeds)

Editorial Board

Samuel Amago (University of Virginia)
Roger Bartra (Universidad Autónoma de México)
Paul Castro (University of Glasgow)
Richard Cleminson (University of Leeds)
Catherine Davies (University of London)
Lloyd H. Davies (Swansea University)
Luisa-Elena Delgado (University of Illinois)
Maria Delgado (Central School of Speech and Drama, London)
Will Fowler (University of St Andrews)
David Gies (University of Virginia)
Gareth Walters (Swansea University)
Duncan Wheeler (University of Leeds)

Other titles in the series

Carmen Martín Gaite: Poetics, Visual Elements and Space
Ester Bautista Botello

The Spanish Anarchists of Northern Australia: Revolution in the Sugar Cane Fields
Robert Mason

Paulo Emilio Salles Gomes: On Brazil and Global Cinema
Maite Conde and Stephanie Dennison

The Tlatelolco Massacre, Mexico 1968, and the Emotional Triangle of Anger, Grief and Shame: iscourses of Truth(s)
Victoria Carpenter

The Darkening Nation: Race, Neoliberalism and Crisis in Argentina
Ignacio Aguiló

Catalan Culture: Experimentation, creative imagination and therelationship with Spain
Lloyd Hughes Davies, J. B. Hall and D. Gareth Walters

IBERIAN AND LATIN AMERICAN STUDIES

Fractal Families in New Millennium Narrative by Afro-Puerto Rican Women

Palabra de Mujer

JOHN T. MADDOX IV

UNIVERSITY OF WALES PRESS
2022

© John T. Maddox IV, 2022
Reprinted 2023

All rights reserved. No part of this book may be reproduced in any material form (including photocopying or storing it in any medium by electronic means and whether or not transiently or incidentally to some other use of this publication) without the written permission of the copyright owner. Applications for the copyright owner's written permission to reproduce any part of this publication should be addressed to the University of Wales Press, University Registry, King Edward VII Avenue, Cardiff CF10 3NS.

www.uwp.co.uk

British Library CIP
A catalogue record for this book is available from the British Library.

ISBN   978-1-78683-910-7
e-ISBN   978-1-78683-911-4

The right of John T. Maddox IV to be identified as author of this work has been asserted in accordance with sections 77 and 79 of the Copyright, Designs and Patents Act 1988.

Typeset by Mark Heslington Ltd, Scarborough, North Yorkshire
Printed on demand by CPI Group (UK) Ltd, Croydon, CR0 4YY

Contents

Series Editors' Foreword	vii
Acknowledgements	ix
Introduction: Fractal Families	1
1 Becoming Family: Mayra Santos Febres's *Fe en disfraz* and *La amante de Gardel*	43
2 Yolanda Arroyo Pizarro: *Cimarronas*, Love and Breaking the Silence	77
3 Yvonne Denis-Rosario: Fathers, Mothers, Fractals and Writing	102
4 Oshun and the *Palenque*-Plantation in *Daughters of the Stone*	128
Conclusion: Afro-Borinquén Today and Tomorrow	156
Appendix: Author Interviews	171
Notes	208
Glossary of Terms	211
Works Cited	218
Index	237

Series Editors' Foreword

Over recent decades the traditional 'languages and literatures' model in Spanish departments in universities in the United Kingdom has been superseded by a contextual, interdisciplinary and 'area studies' approach to the study of the culture, history, society and politics of the Hispanic and Lusophone worlds – categories that extend far beyond the confines of the Iberian Peninsula, not only in Latin America but also to Spanish-speaking and Lusophone Africa.

In response to these dynamic trends in research priorities and curriculum development, this series is designed to present both disciplinary and interdisciplinary research within the general field of Iberian and Latin American Studies, particularly studies that explore all aspects of Cultural Production (inter alia literature, film, music, dance, sport) in Spanish, Portuguese, Basque, Catalan, Galician and indigenous languages of Latin America. The series also aims to publish research in the History and Politics of the Hispanic and Lusophone worlds, at the level of both the region and the nation-state, as well as on Cultural Studies that explore the shifting terrains of gender, sexual, racial and postcolonial identities in those same regions.

Acknowledgements

I wish to thank the authors I study in this book, all of whom were gracious enough to sit down with me to talk about their work. Likewise, I wish to thank scholarly pioneers Marie Ramos Rosado and María Elba Torres Muñoz for their illuminating interviews. The University of Alabama at Birmingham supported my research with a CAS Dean's Humanities Grant and a Faculty Development Grant. John Moore and Charly Verstraet made important observations. Elena Deanda-Camacho, Rosemary Feal, Earl Fitz, Nicholas Jones, Ineke Phaf-Rheinburger, William Luis, Megan Jeanette Myers, Thomas Stephens and Benigno Trigo shaped important parts of this book through generous and careful readings. Thanks to Edward Friedman for his help with *Juliet of the Tropics* ('*La cuarterona*'). I am grateful to Don Goyo Acevedo, George Meléndez, Reinaldo Román, Mónica Ruiz and Laura Robledo for making Puerto Rico an important part of my life. Thank you to my father, J. Thomas Maddox III, for teaching me to value education, and *obrigado* to my wife Luciana Silva for her constant support and insightful questions. Regina and Joyce Maddox and my sisters Kay and Vicki showed me the importance of motherhood.

Introduction

Fractal Families

'racismolengua' (a María Reinat Pumarejo)	'racismolengua' (for María Reinat Pumarejo)
nuestro indiscutible legado racial	our inarguable racial legacy
nuestro esquema racial	our racial schema
lo negro es lo perverso	blackness is the perverse
lo oscuro	the obscure
lo malo	the bad
lo vergonzoso	the shameful
en cambio, lo blanco es santo	by contrast, whiteness is holy
inmaculado	immaculate
benevolente	benevolent
se denigra y no se degrada	it is denigrated and it is not degraded
se desprestigia	it is discredited
se mancha	it is stained
se humilla	it is humiliated
enblanquecidos nos superamos, nos elevamos	by whitening ourselves we overcome ourselves, we elevate ourselves
engrandecemos cualquier gesta con la blanquicidad	we aggrandise any exploit with whiteness
el negro de alma blanca	the Black man with a white soul
la mentirilla blanca	a little white lie
crimen de cuello blanco	white collar crime
'echar mano blanca'	'white magic'
ennegrecidos nos degradamos, somos escoria	when darkened we are degraded, we are filth
la negra maldad de Rafael Hernández y su 'Preciosa'	the black evil of Rafael Hernández and his 'Preciosa'
palabras que dan latigazos	words like lashes
palabras que carimban	words that brand us
negro día	black day
alma negra	black soul
lista negra	black list

la oveja negra de la familia	The black sheep of the family
las aguas negras	black waters
el mercado negro	black market
blackmail	blackmail
negra intención	black intentions
negro destino	black destiny
negrito	*negrito*
negra linda	Good-looking Black woman
negra inteligente	Smart Black woman
Ofendemos inconcientemente	We unconciously offend
pero ofendemos igual	but we still offend
Reciclamos el racismo	We recycle racism
lo perpetuamos	we perpetuate it

(Arroyo Pizarro, *Blancoides* 43–6)

This 2018 poem by one of the up-and-coming Black writers of Puerto Rico, Yolanda Arroyo Pizarro, exemplifies the recent rise of an Afrodescendant literature on the island and in the diaspora. Its title and thematics show the importance of language in creating and combating racism. The dedication to a Puerto Rican Black feminist who lived on the mainland for many years, Reinat Pumarejo, shows the transnational nature of Afro-Puerto Rican literature and the importance of anti-racist activism to its emergence. Her analysis of unconscious racism on the island, which communicates the general feeling of ostracisation on the 'Charming Island' more than the actual etymology of the terms, shows that oppression can take both subtle and not-so-subtle forms. Her love for the archipelago is evident in her allusion to 'Preciosa' by the 'Jíbarito', an unofficial national anthem for Borinquén (Ayala and Bernabe 167). The song romanticises the island's Spanish and Taíno histories, but it elides Black influence. It is focused on the *tirano* ('tyrant') whose *negra maldad* ('black wickedness') disrupts the harmony of the edenic island. Arroyo Pizarro, like the other authors of this book, evokes the past of enslavement that created the symbolic order in which she moves as an Afro-Boricua poet: words become whiplashes and sizzling slave brands, not only of the past but of today, every day. Black people are branded as 'perverts', hypersexualised and pathologised, just as the LGBTQ+ minority is labelled. Arroyo Pizarro's queer identity has no doubt influenced her recognition of the intersecting oppressive systems that have shaped her lived experience and her poetry. While the outside world may see her and her work as 'negroide', inferior to dominant society, a phenomenon she lampoons in her book title *Blancoides* (2018), she presents herself as a 'negra inteligente' who even has a Technology, Education and Design Talk ('Y tu abuela'). She invokes the tradition of Ismael Rivera, who, in 1978, recorded an ode to black Puerto Ricans, 'Las caras lindas (de mi gente negra)' ('The Beautiful Faces [of My Black People]') and to which she dedicated a book of narrative and drama, *Las caras lindas*, in 2020. Her pride in her Blackness, represented by the affectionate – or insulting, depending on the relationship – term *negrito*, is evident not only in her work but in that of several Puerto Rican authors of the new millennium. While the Caribbean island – one third of the Hispanic Antilles – has often defined itself relative to its political and cultural relationship with the United States since the 1898 invasion, these authors have decided to take on the new task of undoing centuries of oppression based on racism, sexism and heteronormativity. Their approach spans the island from its origins through to the diaspora and up to the present. They are problematising and transcending the notion of nation as a harmonious 'great family', since they, like the poet, are its rejected, animalised 'black sheep'. Yet they have formed a 'family of choice' like LGBTQ+ people often must do.

Since 2007, Afro-Puerto Rican women have been revising the foundational myths of the island and the diaspora to create a new vision of family as a national allegory that includes powerful Black women. Novelists Mayra Santos-Febres (b. 1966) and Dahlma Llanos-Figueroa (b. 1949) affirm Afro-Puerto Rican identity and tell its history, beginning with transatlantic slavery. I agree with Nieves López that it is historically important that so many Afrodescendant women are self-defining as such through literature (48). Santos-Febres uses sadomasochism and medicine to revisit slave history in the first book chapter on her novel *La amante de Gardel* ('*Gardel's Lover*', 2015), continuing a similar exploration of Black history, national identity and eroticism in the novel *Fe en disfraz* ('*Faith in Disguise*', 2009).[1] Short-story writers Arroyo Pizarro (b. 1970) and Yvonne Denis-Rosario (b. 1967) chronicle the struggle to create and preserve an empowering history of slavery and Black people on the island and in the diaspora.[2] Llanos-Figueroa's novel envisages a sugar plantation in which Afrodescendants are free and respected and a non-heteronormative 'great Puerto Rican family' in the present, granting diverse

Black families a right to the island homeland and the diaspora. All these authors return to the colonial hacienda to recover silenced or distorted Black voices from history, most of them female, but they also relate that foundational entanglement to later concerns, including those of today. To emphasise their role in creating national families with an affirming space for Blackness, I conclude with author interviews. These authors' modification of the definition of 'Blackness' affects how the Caribbean and diasporic peoples see themselves as a community that is at once one and multiple. To put it another way, these authors radically alter the 'great Puerto Rican family' to give greater agency to Afro-Puerto Ricans, particularly women, and include the Boricua diaspora in an ever-changing series of relations that I call the 'fractal family'. This paradigm is based on the decolonial, postmodern Black feminism of Santos-Febres. In a series of lectures she has developed the notion of a Caribbean that is an Afrocentric hybrid of wordviews, Western and non-Western, that recognises women as the centre of the family. Rejecting the patriarchal family and the plantation system that it bolstered, she proposes a social network that is similar to LGBTQ+ families of choice. While these communities are liberating, they also carry with them the violence wrought by both the maintenance and the dissolution of patriarchal, heteronormative, colonial and racist structures.

Today, Black women of Puerto Rico are writing a counter-narrative to the Puerto Rican family and nation that I call a 'fractal family'. In a constant state of becoming, it breaks up and goes in new directions that expand beyond the plantation and the island while maintaining individual diversity and opaqueness and interacting with the plantation. Concretely, all these Afrodescendant female prose writers represent Black families that may seem to begin with enslavement, but enslaved characters speak their point of view. The Black family and the Afro-Puerto Rican nation, for which it forms the basis in these works, are not structured in the same manner as the colonial plantation family. Beyond the narrative of the 'great family' lies its 'other'. These Black families that these authors create are matriarchal in structure. They include maroon communities that were considered a threat to the colony. They are part of the struggle for land rights. These families also include trades as an expression of creativity and a role in a community handed down and altered through the generations. These crafts include healing, such as midwifery, herbalism and spiritwork. The Afrodescendant family that they depict includes sex workers, both domestic and public, since enslavers often used Black and mulatta women for this function.[3] They include syncretic religious beliefs that extend the Black family to Africa and to a religious community on and beyond the archipelago. Enslavement and migration led to the expansion of these families to the United States and the rest of the Americas, incorporating other languages and rejecting linguistic purism. In these works, Afrodescent is a detour away from the past which led Puerto Rico to see itself as a whitened colonial nation. The 'fractal family' is a postmodern nationalism that advocates for cultural independence of the island in a transnational Caribbean framework. In this context, one does not have to choose between being 'Afro' and being 'Puerto Rican'. Like Pedreira before them, Santos-Febres and these new-millennium writers are creating and altering institutions that promote the ideology of Puerto Rican nationalism. Unlike him, they want the island and its diaspora to have a more complex, less hierarchical vision of themselves.

While Celis and Rivera consider Santos-Febres to be the most important female writer of Puerto Rico, mine is the first book that treats her as a theorist (17). No other study includes analyses of all these outstanding Afro-Puerto Rican writers, and Santos-Febres is the only writer among them with an extensive secondary bibliography of criticism on her work. She is the only novelist in the book who has a PhD in literature. She chairs the *Estudios Afrodiaspóricos y Racialidad* ('AfroDiasporic and Raciality Studies') Programme, the first on the island, which debuted in August 2021. Her vision will influence the future of the field. My interpretation of it comes from lectures that she gave from 2019 to 2021 on the 'fractal Caribbean'. The choice of imagery bears the influence of the visual artwork of Ballesta 9. A fractal is an irregular shape of which a part is the same shape as another that is larger or smaller than it ('fractal'). The particles of a snowflake are roughly the same form as the full flake ('fractal'). Santos-Febres summarises the concept as the '*uno-múltiple*' ('multiple-one') ('Fractal' 25:52). That is to say that an identity can be simultaneously individual yet part of a greater diaspora or repeating fractal. Another example is the shape of coastlines, making the paradigm highly relevant to the Caribbean imaginary, as is snow-covered New York City ('fractal'). 'Fractal' comes from the word 'broken', but Santos-Febres's pride in the Caribbean and Blackness evokes its other meaning 'shattered' ('fractal'). Shattered and scattered Caribbean and Black identities are represented by the families this book analyses.[4]

The Great Puerto Rican Family: Whitening Project, Black Sheep

Latin America emerged as a political, racial and literary construct, and Puerto Rico is part of that history. Omi and Winant refer to political events that create and shape the understanding of race as 'racialisation projects', and the Conquest, Latin American independence and eugenics are examples (3). Golden Age Spain and Portugal, which already focused on 'blood purity' due to the Reconquest, established a social pyramid based on *castas*, 'casts' or 'races' (Chasteen 85). Race justified the enslavement of Africans, who were seen as savages in need of Christianisation and tutelage (35).

The colonial system continued to influence the young republics of Latin America. White Creole Simón Bolívar, for example, considered the racial diversity of the region a barrier to unity and democracy (Helg 447). Cuba and Puerto Rico remained dependent on enslaved Africans for decades more than the rest of the Spanish colonies. The Dominican Republic's past of whitening discourse is influenced by its liberation from Haiti. Toussaint Louverture abolished slavery on the island in 1801, but in 1822 Haiti occupied the Dominican Republic, leading to resentment that would culminate in the twentieth-century dictatorship of Rafael Leonidas Trujillo, whose *hispanidad*, or identification with white Spain, informs national ideology to this day (Valdés, 'Centring' 13–14). During the nineteenth century, Cuba remained the 'Pearl of the Caribbean', where many slavocrats from Haiti joined the planter class on the island to create a new centre for the high-profit, labour-intensive sugar monocrop that persisted until 1886 (Léger 99). Puerto Rico's *hacendados* were likewise joined by Haitian planters, but their traffic in captives was on a smaller scale and less influential (Baralt, *Esclavos* 15). Partly as a result of the Bolivarian Wars, the Royal Spanish Decree of Graces (1815) encouraged Spaniards, loyalists and other Europeans to come to Puerto Rico for free land, where they joined the white Creole class (González, *Cuatro* 6). Spain only abolished slavery there in 1873.

The new republics sought to create new national identities through literature, and race informs them. In Argentina, works such as Sarmiento's essay *Facundo: Civilización y barbarie* ('*Facundo: Civilisation and Barbarism*', 1845) and his fellow partisan Echeverría's short story 'El matadero' ('The Slaughterhouse', 1871) exemplify the drive to urbanise, centralise and model the nation after Europe and the white United States. The eugenics-informed discourse of these founding fathers has apparently led to the nation 'forgetting' the Black roots of Buenos Aires, which recent studies of the national dance, or tango, have unearthed, as Fortes and Ceballos's documentary *Afroargentinos* (2003) shows. Santos-Febres continues the creation of counter-narratives to Argentina's racial and cultural homogeneity in *La amante de Gardel*. In Cuba, Luis has shown the centrality of enslavement to the formation of its national literature in *Literary Bondage: Slavery in Cuban Narrative* (1990). Del Monte formed a cadre of abolitionists to create a unique Cuban literature and a hoped-for Cuban nation with universal citizenship. They interviewed the 'slave poet' Juan Francisco Manzano, which formed the basis of Spanish America's only slave narrative (Luis, *Literary* 84). His circle deeply influenced Cirilo Villaverde, the author of Cuba's national novel *Cecilia Valdés* (1839, 1879, 1882) (Luis, *Literary* 100). This tragic novel has strong parallels with one written by Villaverde's fellow friend of Del Monte, Alejandro Tapia y Rivera (Ramos-Perea, *Tapia* 297). Ramos-Perea considers him the 'first Puerto Rican' (3). 'The Bard of Guamaní's' masterpiece, *La cuarterona* ('*Juliet of the Tropics*', 1867) is also a tale of star-crossed lovers that shows the racial barriers to creating a democratic, harmonious nation represented by a family allegory. Set in Havana, the protagonist Julia is a freeborn mulatta raised in the household of Carlos, the young enslaver. When he returns from study in Paris, he is smitten by her, but his mother forces him to marry Julia's white half sister Emilia to save the family fortune. Heartbroken, Julia commits suicide. As these examples show, race is central to the imaginary of these sister Caribbean nations. Family allegories of this kind are similar to what Sommer called 'foundational fictions' in her work of the same name (although Tapia was excluded), and which discusses whitening discourse in the Dominican Republic and Brazil, as well as other forms of racism in the context of new Latin American nations (Sommer 162).

Today, the 'great Puerto Rican family' is the local manifestation of a region-wide phenomenon of romantic plantation myths best known as 'racial democracy', a concept popularised by Freyre in his *Casa grande e senzala: Formação da família brasileira sob o regime de economia patriarcal* ('*The Masters and the Slaves: Formation of the Brazilian Family under the Patriarchal Economic Regime*', 1933). As the title suggests, the work depicts the region as uniquely benevolent to Black people, while retaining a plantation mentality that is also sexist. In Latin America the United States is often presented as the place where 'real' racism exists, regardless of what local realities show. However, romanticising the plantation is older than Freyre. Rodó's *Ariel* (1900) exemplifies how Latin American intellectuals argued that local elites were the only political force that could withstand advances from the United States, both at political and cultural levels. Vasconcelos idolised the Spanish, but he proposed whitening – and a cosmic race beyond whiteness – through *mestizaje*, a biological and cultural mixture (Ríos Ávila, *Raza* 153). In different ways, all three writers were part of masculinist, Eurocentric projects geared towards the creation of regional and national consciousnesses. Celis and Rivera recall that nationalist projects throughout Latin America imagined their communities as a patriarchal family, a tendency that even the writers of the boom of the 1960s–70s display (16).

Puerto Rico's 'great family' myth was deeply influenced by the US occupation, but it begins before the 1898 invasion. Suárez Findlay's *Imposing Decency* (2000) is very insightful and covers the period 1870–1920 (1). After the invasion, the local elites – many of them sugar-growing families – were struggling to form a white-Creole-defined national identity like the rest of Latin America that had already become independent from Spain. Honour, as defined by the elite, would provide identity and order (53). 'The family' was the reformers' central metaphor (57).[5] They claimed that the island would be whitened and 'civilised' through the morals of patriarchal white families (53). Overt oppression ceded to 'benevolent' liberal social reforms intended to create 'harmonious hierarchies' that legitimated elite rule (53–4). Especially in Ponce, Liberal Autonomism from Spain became part of a growing national consciousness (54). Liberals' paternalist ideology touched on race, sex and labour (55). To appease their party as well as conservative *hacendados*, they claimed that the island's character was essentially peaceful (55). They argued that, unlike other Latin American nations, their country would advance through legislation and harmonious, controlled racial mixture, not war, as was the case in Haiti and Cuba (55). Yet the Afrodescendants must be controlled, they said, since they were a threat to the white family due to their 'tempting' hypersexuality and laziness (56). The 'sons of Spain' were the only hope for redemption, the leaders of a 'disciplined march toward rational, de-Africanised virility' (56–7). Liberals also envisioned ideal labourers as white (58). They saw the education of women pertaining to all classes as a means of maintaining paternalist patriarchy, racism and whitening (59). Likewise, bourgeois feminists of the time excluded non-white women from their reformist vision of the great family (75, 108). The fear, persecution and disciplining of dark-skinned women was widespread among many populations (108).

This historical and cultural background informs the 1930s generation that formed the national canon of Puerto Rican letters based on the 'great family' myth. Antonio Pedreira and Tomás Blanco were the leaders of this literary movement. Janer considers Pedreira's foundational essay *Insularismo* ('*Insularism*', 1934) to represent a 'colonial nationalism': since it focused solely on culture, it allowed US colonialism to continue without a call for independence (2). It did not challenge the racism instituted by the Spaniards and their descendants but instead codified the 'great Puerto Rican family' metaphor for the nation through literature (18, 31). This family was to come together as a Puerto Rican 'race' to defend its culture from the Anglo-Saxons (31). Pedreira continued to create symbols to whiten the nation in *La actualidad del jíbaro* ('*The Peasant's Relevance*', 1935). Pedreira and the 1930s generation created the symbols and structures that are often considered synonymous with national culture, so it is understandable that critics since the 1970s look back to them to seek ways out from their blind spots and blatantly undemocratic thought.

Moreno's *Family Matters* (2012) uses an analysis of the 'great family' to write the first study of Puerto Rican literature that, like mine, includes the island and the diaspora and focuses on women (6).[6] She analyses writers, particularly women, who challenge the 'great family' myth (8). All the authors in my book are Afrodescendant women. Moreno sees in Pedreira and Blanco an effort to silence all women, a phenomenon that she sees continued in the national playwright René Marqués of the 1950s generation (17–8). This patriarchal plantation family was marked by 'racial democracy' (13). Those excluded from this vision – women, homosexuals and Black people – would challenge the oppressive silences of this family (13). Moreno shows that Pedreira was part of the second generation of the *hacendado* bourgeoisie who saw the monoculture system collapse during the Great Depression (31). While they lost economic power, they gained ideological influence through literature. They looked back to the nineteenth century with a nostalgia known as 'hispanophilia' to propose a cultural naturalism that could resist assimilation to US colonial culture (Moreno, *Family* 17). The house and family remained the central metaphor of the nation (Gelpí 5). Moreno notes that during the 1930s many Puerto Ricans left the island (which saw itself as undergoing a process of racial and cultural whitening) for the United States, where they were treated as non-white due to their skin colour and immigrant identities (41). Richardson observes the complications that this presented for Afro-Puerto Rican writers such as Pedro Pietri (73).

Yet Insularism had its dissidents. A foundational work that takes the 'great family' to task is islander Isabelo Zenón Cruz's *Narciso descubre su trasero* ('*Narcissus Discovers his Backside*', 1974), which details countless manifestations of racism in Puerto Rican culture. Fanon and US Black movements of the 1960s and 1970s inspired it (Rivera Casellas 22).[7] He challenges the 1930s generation for continuing the myth of the passive slave, promoting hispanophilia and degrading and erasing Black contributions to national culture (44–5). Santiago-Díaz argues that Zenón did not propose disintegration of the 'great family' but revealed the anti-Black beliefs of Insularist nationalism (73). Márquez notes how he deconstructs the myths of benign slavery and mild racism on the island and claims Blackness as central to understanding national culture (118, 120). Likewise, Afro-Puerto Ricans were to claim both the archipelago homeland and Black identity (Márquez 121). While all authors studied here reaffirm his focus on the island, Arroyo Pizarro and Llanos Figueroa represent West Africa as part of their translocal families (Márquez 123).

Rivera Casellas uses *Narciso* to show how Zenón broke with the folkloric, exotic representation of Afro-Puerto Ricans to focus on their lived experience and struggles (*Bajo* 25). In the 1930s, the alternative to Pedreira's romanticising of Puerto Rican white

Creoles, aside from Blanco's harmonious mixing of three races (Black, white, indigenous), was Luis Palés Matos's (1898–1959) festive representations of Black people on the island in his 'negroid' poetry (Rivera Casellas 21). Operación Serenidad ('Operation Serenity'), designed to 'protect' local culture from US influence, codified national culture as an arena where Blackness and racism were not discussed in a manner that challenged myths of harmony (Rivera Casellas 22).

González's *El país de cuatro pisos* ('*The Four-Storied Country*', 1980) challenged the elitist model of the Insularist family 'home'. He did not shy away from discussing Blackness (Santiago-Díaz 73). González notes that Black and mulatto islanders developed a national consciousness before 1815, when many European settlers came to the island (6). This is the moment when the island became the 'whitest of all the Antilles', as linguist Augusto Malaret later declared (Branche 151). As opposed to white Creoles defending the nation from US culture, González claimed that Afrodescendants used their democratic ideals to create a popular national culture alongside the hegemonic one (12).

Gelpí's *Literatura y paternalismo en Puerto Rico* ('*Literature and Paternalism in Puerto Rico*', 1992) charts the evolution of the 'great family' and its detractors in literature with a focus on gender and sexuality (131). Almost all Puerto Rican high schools teach *Insularismo*, so it is still part of negotiating the island's identity (925). His twin focus is Pedreira and playwright Marqués, the most influential voice of the 1950s generation (121). Paternalist national myths begin with Salvador Brau (1842–1912) and continue into the 1990s, the time when Gelpí writes his book. These paternalists in literature repeat the plantation hierarchy of the father as the most powerful and the rest as child-like inferiors: slaves, women and workers (131, 634). Gelpí criticises the exclusion of women from the national canon and the presentation of Julia de Burgos as an exception (141). Today, Black female authors are revisiting her as their precursor, including her biographer, Santos-Febres (*Yo* 17). Gelpí considers the theory of literary generations to be paternalist, since they often treat a 'caudillo' (Pedreira, Marqués) as an authoritarian father figure (161). They subordinate multiplicity to unity, unlike what I call a fractal family, which embraces disorder and heterogeneity (161, 172). Marqués explicitly states that Puerto Rican society is 'paternal o autoritario' ('paternal or authoritarian') ('Dócil' 172). Alongside it, for him, a 'matriarchal' pattern exists in literature at the level of the characters alongside *machismo* and the 'docile' men on the island that have ceded their power without conflict, promoting another convenient myth of harmony (175–6).

Gelpí sees in *Insularismo* (1934) a longing for an absent paternal figure (the plantation owners of the past), which Pedreira himself seeks to occupy (654). This attitude became central to the paternalism of the island's first elected Governor Luis Muñoz Marín, the Partido Democrático Popular ('pro-Commonwealth party') that he founded and the commonwealth status he negotiated (851). As the populist progress he led declined, female, LGBTQ+ and Nuyorican authors such as Nicholasa Mohr, alongside historians, broke with paternalism in the 1970s (702). For example, novelist Luis Rafael Sánchez satirises the national family in *La guaracha del Macho Camacho* ('*Macho Camacho's Beat*', 1976). For Pedreira, Puerto Rico was a sick, orphaned 'child' in need of healthy maturation (766, 823). His 'family' ruled the land – the *patria* – but Gelpí argues that authors who break with Insularism focus on the sea as a liberating space (1432). Arroyo continues this post-Insularist tradition when she notes that the 'great family' myth continues in the context of migration, and those who remain on the island exclude their diaspora kin ('Historias' 362). She observes that the latter must form new relationships and communities (362).

The Instituto de Cultura Puertorriqueña ('Puerto Rican Culture Institute'), founded in 1956, promoted a national vision intended to reconcile present and past conflicts of race and class (Moreno 39). It promoted a harmonious history of the mixture of the Black, white and indigenous races on the island (39). The 'great family' image was one of unity, not of redressing internal problems (39). This myth was aligned with national ideologies that came from every part of Latin America (Rangelova, *Gendered* 15).

García-Crespo notes the elitism and racism of *Insularismo*, and she sees how it shaped Puerto Rican identity from the 1930s to this day through literature and film (51). DIVEDCO spread this ideology to all levels of society in the 1950s and 1960s through schools and the media. Marqués was active in this government programme, touting the values of the patriarchal family as the symbol of the nation (Moreno 40). He called for Puerto Ricans who left the island to assimilate to the US mainstream but for those who stayed to zealously guard their culture (41). DIVEDCO revived the *jíbaro* or 'white peasant', which symbolised the nation for Manuel Alonso in the nineteenth century, as a romanticised patriarch (Moreno 42).

Ramos Rosado shows that Black women also dissented in the 1970s. For her, noting the roles of race and class, the decade was marked by the rise of women as both object and subject of literature (349–50). She broke critical ground with *La mujer negra en la literatura puertorriqueña* ('*Black Women in Puerto Rican Literature*', 1999), which she began in 1976 in consultation with Zenón (xix). Nonetheless, the critic maintains that the representations of Black women are caricatures incapable of liberating themselves or others in Luis Rafael Sánchez, Carmelo Rodríguez Torres, Rosario Ferré and Ana Lydia Vega (350, 356). She criticises the lack of Black female protagonists in Puerto Rican literature, something that the authors I study address. Ramos Rosado also decries stereotyped images of Black women as slaves, lovers and prostitutes (349). I wish to point out that the women in those roles have a history. They were dynamic individuals and part of a greater community. More recently, Ramos Rosado has called for a literature and history of the island – like these works – that end the erasure of Black history and the continuation of sexism (*Destellos* 114). The critic now teaches the first seminar on Afrodescendant women writers at the University of Puerto Rico's flagship campus Río Piedras (known as the Iupi [or UPR]), which includes all these writers, except the Latina Dahlma Llanos-Figueroa, who writes in English.

Compared to Ramos Rosado, Santiago-Díaz offers a much more positive reading of Rodríguez Torres, the subject of his *Escritura afropuertorriqueña y modernidad* ('*Afro-Puerto Rican Writing and Modernity*', 2007). To contextualise the Vieques native, he devotes a chapter to the racialisation project of the 1930s generation, which treated Blackness as a scapegoat for the nation's underdevelopment (35). It created the hegemony against which Rodríguez Torres rebelled in his self-conscious Black literature (36). Rodríguez Torres created a cosmopolitan Blackness that negotiates double consciousness and Afrocentrism, but with a genealogical element of finding extended family (37). Santiago-Díaz shows that, like Cangrejos (Santurce, San Juan), Vieques is a Black space due in part to a history of African captives taking refuge among their enslaver's enemies in the seventeenth and eighteenth centuries

(53). The Spanish founded San Mateo de Cangrejos in 1664 as a refuge for maroons from the British, Danish and Dutch empires, where they received land and freedom in exchange for becoming Catholic (González García 123). Cangrejos received rebels from the entire Caribbean until 1830 when Britain and France no longer practised slavery (187).

Santiago-Díaz and Rodríguez leap the *charco* ('puddle') between the island and the diaspora like I do, noting that, in the memoir *Down These Mean Streets* (1967), Afro-Nuyorican Piri Thomas is already challenging the 'great family' in Harlem. Writing in the United States in English, Thomas challenges the Insularist ideology that silences discussion of race on the island (1206). This affront came at a price, since his book was not translated into Spanish for decades and remained at the margins of a national Puerto Rican canon bent on whitening the national image (1215). His parents opted for 'honorary whiteness', anticipating today's 'colour blindness' in the mainland and the island, while the younger Thomas chose collective Blackness, writing in the context of Black Power (1218). Jiménez Román and Flores consider his memoir a 'psychological anatomy of the Afro-Latin@ paradox' and present him, along with the writers of the Nuyorican Poets Café, as pioneers of *Afrolatinidad* (9). The latter was also an affirmative space for queer Ricans, one where families of choice emerged among artists (Jaime 1). Their challenges to the intersecting marginalisations of Black and LGBTQ+ people are precursors to Frances Negrón-Muntaner's film *Brincando el Charco: Portrait of a Puerto Rican* (1994), which takes on these issues from a position of white Latina privilege.

In her study *Imaging the Great Puerto Rican Family* (2014), Lloréns shows the battling discourses over how to visually portray the nation as a racialised, gendered family. In the 1930s, island artists Miguel Pou and Oscar Colón Delgado began to portray Afro-Puerto Rican portraits intentionally, indicating a loosening of hispanophilia (xxv). From 1921–51, US photographers depicted *jíbaros* as mixed-race 'tropical whites', although Jack Delano produced (only) four images of Black *jíbaros* (xxv). These supplements represent Black cultural survival despite a national project focused on eradicating them from the national body (xxv). From 1948–70, Black people began to occupy the national imaginary through music, film and painting (xxvi). An example is Rafael Tufiño's painting 'Goyita' (1953), whom Lloréns reads as the island's Black grandmother (xxvi). Black social justice movements of the 1970s led to Loíza becoming the Black motherland of the island, reclaiming it from marginality and exoticism (xxvi). She shows how artists Lucecita Benítez, Sylvia del Villard and Carmen Belén Richardson gave Black people representation (xxvi). On the other hand, Myrna Báez's paintings show how maintaining whiteness informs upper-class women's imaginary of the 'great family' well into the 1990s (xxvii). Countering this discourse are artists such as those of the 1996 exhibition *Paréntesis: Ocho Artistas Negros Contemporáneos* ('*Parenthesis: Eight Black Contemporary Artists*') (xxvii).

In addition to Ramos Rosado, other Afro-Puerto Rican women have challenged racism among Puerto Ricans, regardless of how benevolent the community, or 'family', is presented. Ana Irma Rivera Lassén was accepted by the University of Puerto Rico at sixteen, where she founded, along with Mary Bird, Patricia Shahen, Alma Méndez and Nilda Aponte, Mujer Intégrate Ahora (MIA) ('Women, Unite Now!') in 1970 and remained active until its dissolution in 1979 (Mora Pérez 117). Rivera Lassén saw that even this feminist movement needed to make room for discussing the intersectionality of race and gender (118). She fought to separate church and state and for women's rights to divorce, abortion and mobility, altering the family and the nation (119). In 1974, despite resistance from other MIA members, Rivera Lassén came out as a lesbian and founded the Gay Pride movement on the island (119). She became the first Black and first lesbian president of the Colegio de Abogados y Abogadas de Puerto Rico ('Bar Association of Puerto Rico') and the first openly lesbian senator (120). Her legacy shows that race, gender and sexual orientation cannot be divorced from one another.

Paralleling Rivera Lassén, Marta Moreno Vega has worked for decades as an artist, a writer and an activist to create an affirming Black identity on the island that decries racist and sexist abuses from the plantation to today. Her memoir *When the Spirits Dance Mambo* (2004) shows the protagonist's turbulent family life alongside her discovery of African-American and Afro-Cuban identities in Harlem at places such as the Palladium nightclub. Another autobiographical work, *The Altar of My Soul* (2000), shows how her immersion in Afro-Cuban culture became the foundation of her newfound black identity and her cultural work as director of the Caribbean Cultural Centre African Diaspora Institute (CCCADI) and college professor. The foundation of her Afro-Puerto Rican identity is Moreno Vega's challenging of her family origins and 'great family' ideology by bonding with African-American and Cuban role models. As an adult, such activity develops through her adoption of Santería, the founding of the CCCADI and her remigration to Loíza to co-found the Casa Afro cultural *palenque* ('Nuyorican' 84). She lived in El Barrio during the time of the Young Lords, who had strong Black female leadership. Denise Oliver, for example, was a member of the Lords and the Black Panthers (Laó-Montes and Buggs 395). Today's transnational Afro-Boricua writers are continuing an important tradition that has not had as much visibility in literature in the past.

The 'Great Family': Its Dissidents at the Dawn of a New Millennium

By now, Duany considers Pedreira's notion of Puerto Rico as occupying the margins of the New World passé (178). He sees a transnational approach as important to showing how local events on the island interact globally 'on the edge' (or intersectionally) with issues of race, gender and ethnicity (178). According to Duany, 'The works of Santos-Febres and other writers of her generation profoundly disturb the paternalist, male-centred and some would say phallologocentric mode of representation in Puerto Rican culture', and Muñoz includes Arroyo Pizarro as part of that generation (Duany 184; Mendoza 1141).

Rangelova, in 2016, considers the 'great family' myth to be the dominant ideology on the island from 1950 to 2010, so it is arguably still the metaphorical structure that must be broken and re-built if Puerto Rico is to create a just, democratic vision of itself (*Gendered* 13). Rangelova sees, on the one hand, a cultural geography in feminist literature that disturbs the unity and cohesion of the patriarchal nation, while on the other hand, it challenges the hidden hierarchies of the nation of race, class, sexuality and gender (16, 28). She follows Lorde in arguing that to understand Black families we must broaden our definition of 'family' itself (30). Like Gelpí, Rangelova promotes feminist notions of nation and includes Santos-Febres's short stories and *Nuestra Señora de la Noche* ('*Our Lady of the Night*', 2008), which directly criticises the 'great family' as a grotesque construct (183). Rangelova observes how she uses the house to create non-patriarchal alternatives on the mainland to the home paradigm and adds the empowerment of women and Afrodescendants to new models of the nation (*Gendered* 84). The critic states that, for Marqués and 1950s generation writer Pedro Juan Soto, women's sex work and sex with married men are shameful things that break the family apart; however, I add that this work has always been part of the family and the nation, and has always been racialised (*Gendered* 19). Like me, Rangelova sees the brothel as a space of feminine agency (27).

Branche continues Pedro Juan Soto's line of thinking when he rejects the idea of an empowering bordello as an alternative to the 'great family' (155). In his essay comparing depictions of Isabel 'La Negra' Luberza Oppenheimer in *Nuestra Señora* and Rosario Ferré's 'Cuando las mujeres quieren a los hombres' ('When Women Love Men'), he holds that the story reaffirms racist stereotypes. In Ferré's version, the patriarch Ambrosio dies, leaving his widow Isabel the family estate. Surprisingly, she shares it with his lover, the madame Isabel 'La Negra' (155). Branche argues that while the story fuses the supposedly legitimate and illegitimate sides of Puerto Rican women's roles in the family (wife and prostitute), it continues plantation dichotomies (155). The paramour's last name is substituted by her race (155). While the white Isabel longs to be Black so that her husband will desire her, Ferré shows little attention to the racialised and gendered forces that led the Afrodescendant Luberza to this role (155). Instead of creating empathy for the so-called 'temptress', Ferré burdens her with allusions to the seductresses of history, including those imagined by Palés (155). Branche argues that 'Ferré's narrative joins the slavery era writers before her in a post-slavery episode of negative myth-making' (156). He considers the Afrodescendant Luberza's role as a gentle, maternal sexual initiator in the brothel to be an aberrational combination of sex slave and mammy fraught with the Oedipus complex (156). Since marriage to white enslavers and clients was barred for most Black lovers, Branche interprets the role as a deep, debasing objectification (157). Ultimately, he argues, Ferré reaffirms the wife-whore dichotomy of white and Black women, and prostitution is only a manifestation of these roles (157).

Even as we consider the brothel and the concubine as an extension of the Puerto Rican family in the project of creating a diverse nation, we must be wary of reaffirming the very racist stereotypes that we challenge. Having said that, we must also avoid moralising in a way that is racist and sexist in its own way: sex work is work, so if women use the oldest profession for pleasure and/or personal gain, we must consider those relationships as a part of Puerto Rican transnational history and family (Lawless). Like Branche, I read the *Noche/Fe/Amante* trilogy of historical fiction as a series of familial national allegories in which sex, craft and family perform national identity in opposition to Pedreira's 'great family' (160).

The Afro-Puerto Rican Family in the Age of Afrodescent and Intersectionality

Santos-Febres is a world-renowned writer of poetry and fiction, and she is also a Black feminist theorist, activist and editor who has provided leadership for critics interested in more encompassing notions of the national family. In her role as Executive Director of the Festival de la Palabra ('Festival of the Word'), Santo-Febres guest-edited a special issue of the *Afro-Hispanic Review* with Rivera Casellas in 2018 (10). They present Afro-Puerto Rico as part of the United Nations Decade for People of African Descent (2015–24), which has resulted in the term and political identity 'Afrodescendant' (10). Another important date is 2011, the UNESCO Year of African-Descended Peoples. Santos-Febres released *Fe* and *Nuestra Señora* before then. Rengifo notes that all Santos-Febres's novels give visibility to Black characters (511). The Boricua sees the term 'Afrodescendant' as a victory in the struggle for an affirming identity (11). In the midst of these comemorations, Hurricanes Irma and Maria ravaged Puerto Rico in 2017, revealing that the face of marginalisation was, as Santos-Febres puts it, 'mujer y negro' ('woman and Black') (11). Black, feminine identity is 'transnational', as is the island, for the writer (12). She rejects the hispanophilia of her university, the University of Puerto Rico (UPR) at Río Piedras, as connoted by the departmental name, 'Hispanic Studies' (12). She is justifiably critical – the direct heir of Insularism, Jaime Benítez of Hispanic Studies, implemented his mentor Pedreira's vision as UPR president until 1971 (Santiago-Díaz 123).

The special issue gives voice to the dissidents of this ideology. In 'Identity Practices', Lloréns-Torres uses interviews to show how Puerto Ricans today confront racial issues, and clearly the national 'family' has problems that must be addressed. Most Puerto Ricans see themselves as a harmonious mix of three races: they are Hispanic white (Spanish) and/or mixed race, and only a small minority is Black (29, 30). They believe the island displays 'racial democracy', unlike the racist United States (29). However, as Rivera Lassén has argued, Black womanhood is stigmatised from an early age ('Black Girls' 67). Many feel pressure to *mejorar la raza* ('improve the race') by marrying a white person and to *blanquearse* by appearing more 'whitened', for example, by straightening their hair (31–2). One can trace these ideologies directly to the plantation (30). Sadly, for someone to 'better' her race, another must 'spoil' their own, codifying Blackness as a source of shame (32). Contradictorily, most Puerto Ricans believe they have Black ancestry, yet they hide that Black 'grandmother' away, as Fortunato Vizcarrondo poetised (Lloréns, 'Identity' 37; Vizcarrondo 77). Santiago-Díaz claims that 'grandmother' too often occupies the 'kitchen' of the nation, like a hidden servant (*Escritura* 144). Blackness is confined to a slave past, not seen as part of the present (Abadía Rexach, 'Repiques' 24). Santiago-Díaz argues that, due to these beliefs, affirmation of Blackness cannot be its definition on the island since, for most, it is 'latent' and needs a stimulus to be made manifest (29). Since 2000 UNESCO-backed Latin American Afrodescent has provided that stimulus, and all the authors that I study display Black consciousness. Rivera Lassén claims that Afrodescent is specific to Latin America and the Caribbean, but I do not believe that we should carve up the diaspora by excluding African-Americans who have influenced all the writers I discuss ('Discriminaciones' 57).

In Puerto Rico, 'true' Black people are usually believed to be relegated to specific spaces and thus largely excluded from mainstream culture: Loíza, Guayama, Arroyo and Ponce (Lloréns, 'Identity' 39). San Antón is Ponce's most famous Black area (Santiago-Díaz 25), yet islanders often still see them as foreigners (39). The 'plantation family' metaphor is alive and well on the island. Rivera-Rideau et al. consider that the anti-Black attitudes, manifest in myths of whiteness or whitening *mestizaje* ('miscegenation'), have become 'common sense' (13). However, as my overview of critics shows, it is a view that no longer goes unchallenged.

Vargas-Ramos gathers a series of articles on race from the Centre for Puerto Rican Studies at the City University of New York on the topic, and the 'great family' remains an issue to be confronted. Jiménez Román argues that 'as with gender, sexuality and class, "race" is an issue that threatens the core beliefs of the "family" paradigm, the pillar of much of Puerto Rico's national rhetoric, both anticolonial and annexationist' ('Un hombre' 43). Boricuas see racism as an individual practice – supposedly espoused by a handful of ignorant whites – or, 'uppity Negroes', to use Jiménez Román's term (43). Black people who have demanded full membership of the 'great family' have been dismissed as 'overly sensitive' and disruptive (43).

Black identity in academia has existed since the dawn of the twentieth century. Ideas of the African diaspora and Black consciousness can be traced back to Afro-Nuyorican and cataloguer of the Harlem Renaissance, Arturo Alfonso Schomburg, as Jiménez Román, Flores and Valdés have shown (Jiménez Román and Flores 7; Valdés, *Diasporic* 1). Likewise, Laó-Montes has writen a genealogy of *Afrolatinidades*, or notions of African diaspora and identity in Latin America, since Fernando Ortiz and throughout the twentieth century (120).

However, Valero and Campos García show that the support of the United Nations has increased the visibility of Black populations. One can see its impact in academia, museums, governments and media, starting with the UNESCO Slave Route Project (1994), the Regional Conference of the Americas in Santiago de Chile (2000) and The United Nations Human Rights Council's World Conference against Racism, Racial Discrimination, Xenophobia and Related Forms of Intolerance in Durban, South Africa (2001). Santiago-2000 was the occasion when Black groups from throughout Latin America met and coined a term that is equivalent to 'Afrodescendant'. Along with encouraging usage of the prefix *afro-* to denote a Black identity within a national identity (*afropuertorriqueña*) or regional one (*afro-latinoamericana*), *afrodescendientes*, people with African heritage who exemplify *afrodescendencia* ('Afrodescent') found a new code to express who they are (Valero, 'Afroepistemología' 531–2, 539). The term affirms their diasporic nature and shared continent of origin, ostensibly in lieu of their skin colour, and alludes to a need to revise history to make visible the people descended from Africans in Latin America in the construction of modern-day political and cultural identities (533). De la Fuente considers it a transnational flourishing of consciousness and support (293). Kirschner et al. provide a decolonial genealogy of human rights in Latin America and praise the potential of the term and diaspora consciousness for coalition building across marginalised communities (14).

Santos-Febres continues the postmodern approach of Laó-Montes in that she seeks *afrodescendencias* (plural) or what he calls *afrolatinidades* (117). By contrast, Valero speaks of Afrodescent as a 'unifying experience' (534). She and García Campos refer to it as a 'permanent' and 'foundational' sense of identity ('Este libro' 65). García Campos claims that Afrodescent, by creating a transnational 'group self' through a politicised, 'strong' sense of identity, runs the risk of becoming essentialist (57). Both authors overlook the intersectionality of gender in constructing race and the role of Puerto Rico in Latin America, perhaps since it also is associated with the United States. Santos-Febres's notion of Afrodescent is much more fluid and fragmented. Attaining a postmodern conception of Afrodescent has the potential to be more liberating than previous notions of human rights, which too often centred on (white) 'man' as the universal human (Kirschner et al. 17).

Arguably, the intersectionality of race and gender in the struggle to assert human rights has existed since the time of African enslavement. Sojourner Truth famously asked 'Ain't I a woman?' at an 1851 Women's Convention in Akron, Ohio, noting that their movement had excluded Black women. bell hooks developed her poignant question into *Ain't I a Woman: Black Women and Feminism* (1981), a trailblazing text in intersectionality by showing the racialised and gendered barriers against which this population has struggled. It was a 'loveletter' that presented these women as beautiful, as leaders. Its accessible style targets a broader audience than straight, white, educated women (Goodman). She paved the way for queer theory by including sexual orientation in considerations of gender. In *All the Women are White, All the Blacks are Men but Some of Us are Brave* (1982), Hull et al. show that gender cannot be considered without including the factor of race and other aspects of identity and oppression. Crenshaw coined and theorised the term 'intersectionality' in a legal studies article in 1989, which noted the combination of race and gender in forming women's, and by extension, everyone's role in society with differing forms of privilege and oppression.

However, intersectionality already had a pioneer in Rivera Lassén. Calling for an Action Plan in Puerto Rico that parallels that of Durban, she closed her keynote at the First Afrodescent in Puerto Rico Congress in 2015 ('Dicriminaciones' 59). She affirms her Blackness and lesbian identities as sources of pride and strength. On the other hand, intersectionality allows us to see the powerful 'spiders' and 'webs' of history and politics (47). Networks of power intersect along the axes of race, ethnicity, sex, sexual orientation, gender identity, disability age, class and nationality (47). She claims that gender is more complex than masculine/feminine binaries, which supports Santos-Febres's and my own use of ideas from LGBTQ+ thinkers and communities to shed light on the thought and experiences of Black women, namely the performative nature of gender (47). Rivera Lassén challenges Crenshaw's linear thought, based on fixed identities, noting that different aspects of identity intersect in different ways (48). This ever-evolving 'spiderweb' is the place the subject resides, her 'casa' (28). Hence, she proposes the metaphor of the 'spider', the active creator of that web, for citizens instead of the victimised 'fly' (49). (One wonders why the spider does not eat the fly in this allegory, and what that would mean, but her emphasis is on agency.) She claims that by recognising the multiplicity of one's identities she can find empowerment (49). Santos-Febres speaks of something similar as the *uno-múltiple* of fractal identities. She argues for equity in human rights, not a one-size-fits-all approach, which I would call a national family of choice (51). This choice is important in a nation where Black people are disproportionately poor and where their social mobility is limited (50). Multiple identities demand representation in advocacy groups, such as Black women in feminism and lesbians in Afrodescent organisations (56). She reflects on Puerto Rican history as not entirely her own, at least not in how it has traditionally been taught (57). As an Afrodescendant, like Santos-Febres, her ancesters were brought to the island in captivity and called 'slaves' by Europeans and white Creoles (57). This other side of history, that of the captive and her kin, descendants of African peoples, must also be told and included in national and regional identity (57). The narratives of my study do just that.

In a personal interview, María Elba Torres Muñoz explained that she, Quiñones and the group now known as Congreso Afrodescendencia Puerto Rico ('Afrodescent Puerto Rico

Congress') worked to assemble the congress at the Iupi. In 2014 Torres Muñoz learned about the Decade of Afrodescent in Mexico and got to work creating the groundbreaking gathering recorded in the essays of *¡Negro, Negra!: Afirmación y Resistencia*, compiled by Léster Nurse Allende (2018), named for a poem by Rivera Lassén ('Negro, negra'). All the authors discussed here attended, and they read each other's work, so the events have taken steps towards creating a coherent group of translocal Black women writers. Although Irma and Maria had ravaged the island in 2017, the second congress was held in 2018. This gathering exemplified the synergy between Afro-Boricua scholarship, literature and community activism. It focused on reaching youth and the community through education about recognition, justice and development. These conferences were steps towards the new academic offerings in Black culture at the UPR. In a personal interview, Torres Muñoz claimed that the African diaspora needs a transdisciplinary approach to break with Eurocentric paradigms:

> Puerto Ricans, Afro-Latin Americans, have a reality and a discussion in their countries about their Blackness and their Africanity in their reality that is totally different than the US. We do not have – yes, we had insults, epithets, abuse, all that, but slavery in the US was different from Latin America. Our reality as Afro-Antilleans, Afro-Puerto Ricans, we have to define it and delineate it according to ourselves. It cannot be similar to what is happening in the US.

While Santos-Febres is more comfortable with the apparent 'contradictions' of being neither only African-American nor only Puerto Rican, Torres Muñoz's notion of Boricua nationalism ('for ourselves') and Latin American regionalism, shows the importance of paradigms like the fractal family, which is based on Caribbean reality.

Santos-Febres's idea of Blackness and Puerto Rican identity also links the island to the diaspora on the mainland. De la Fuente argues that this is necessary for the Puerto Rican diaspora, given the United States' entanglement with the island (293). Rivera-Rideau et al. deconstruct the Latinx/Latin American divide entirely in order to approach *afrolatinidad*, which I call Afrodescent (3). Its boundaries are constantly changing (8).

Afro-Puerto Ricans on the island are currently questioning their relationship with the colonisers. Generally, the two camps on the cultural side of this debate are the *puertorriqueñistas* and the *posmodernos* (Moreno 44). The former consider the island and its unique culture to be the true bearers of Puerto Rican identity. The latter include the diaspora, rejecting foundational metanarratives. Moreno claims that:

> while this study acknowledges the existence of a Puerto Rican nationality, it rejects the notion of a static and hegemonic Puerto Rican identity solely grounded in, and/or contingent on, *hispanismo* and the Spanish language. In fact, I would like to suggest that the *hispanismo*-, Spanish-language-, and island-centred discourse of the *puertorriqueñistas* constitutes a sort of ideological recycling that originated in the 1930s. (45)

Rangelova also notes the postmodern turn of the early twenty-first century to which Santos-Febres belongs; however, I disagree with her argument that postmodernism is anathema to nationalism (*Gendered* 83). Afro-Puerto Rican women novelists imagine a Puerto Rican family that allows for multiple languages to be in play, that challenge the model of the white or whitening patriarchy, and that present the nation in a postmodern manner that simultaneously allows for a decolonial, independent Puerto Rico.

I differ from Ramos-Perea's reading of the current generation of Black authors on the island: 'Ya el podrido y rancio posmodernismo agotó su ilegitimidad y su descompromiso palabrero. Ahora vale la urgencia' ('Now the rotten, rancid postmodernism exhausted its legitimacy and its babbling lack of commitment to anything. Right now, what counts is urgency') (Ramos-Perea, *Revista Boreales* journal cover). The struggle for self-representation and justice for Afro-Puerto Ricans, past and present, is commensurate with postmodern interpretations of family and nation, as I will show through their works.

Like their precursers, these writers are translocal Black feminists. Celis and Rivera note that, since her 1992 doctoral dissertation, Santos-Febres has advocated for a transnational approach to the island (22). Afro-Puerto Rican identity necessitates a translocal approach, which Sonia Álvarez et al. have theorised through their research group of *translocas* in *Feminist Politics of Translation in the Latin/a Américas* (2014). Black feminism approaches subjects like the Afro-Boricuas in this book as facing multiple forms of oppression, which they must repel both locally and globally from constantly changing positions across borders (2). In their collection,

Laó-Montes and Buggs embrace an intersectional, transnational, decolonial approach to Afro-Latinidad and Black feminism (381). They consider the 'Afro-Latin@s' of the present the clearest example of translocality (394). This coalition must respect differences, such as gender and class, and challenge social hierarchies that include heterosexism (382). This Afro-feminism is liberating and a 'project of affinity' – which Santos-Febres calls a 'family' (384). The diaspora is, for them, founded on racial violence, but it is also a cosmopolitan project of articulating multiple Afrodescendant histories (384). Thus, it must include a 'subalternist historiography' of Black women (386). Regarding epistemology, Black feminism can take the route of Caliban, who uses Western concepts to subvert modernity, or that of the Maroon, who uses non-Western concepts for the same end, such as diaspora religions (390). These authors do both. Gender and sexuality are not to be 'included in' but are constitutive of Black identity (385). Black feminisms should, they say, make marginalised subjectivities visible and a means of redefining all previous 'narratives of geography, memory, culture, and the self' that depose the national white or whitened patriarchs of old' – they should reject essentialisms (393). They argue that Black Studies and Latinx studies should not be considered too sharply distinct and opposed (394). Today, Santos-Febres is also wreaking havoc with Puerto Rican hierarchies, bringing multiple areas of identity together and creating a transnational dialogue between the Global North and South at one of their most visible intersections, the Black people of Borinquén.

The Fractal Family

My application of Santos-Febres's theory to literary fiction shares much with Ferly's *A Poetics of Relation: Caribbean Women Writing at the Millennium* (2012). She analyses female authors from hispanophone and francophone Antilles, noting that the Free Associated State has a uniquely strong female presence among its authors (1, 9). She challenges the island/diaspora binary (1). She notes that Santos-Febres subverts male-centred historical narratives of heroism and maintains ambivalence by noting the internal contradictions of her characters (56). Ferly observes that female Caribbean writers empower the subordinates of history (56). They challenge the notion of history as linear, masculinist filiation, following Glissant (14).[8]

Santos-Febres shares with Ferly a love of Glissant and a rejection of the plantation. At the Primer Congreso de Afrodescendencia en Puerto Rico ('First Afrodescent Congress in Puerto Rico'), Santos-Febres claimed in her speech 'Confesiones afropoéticas' ('Afropoetic Confesions') that she was afraid to be called a Black writer, reduced to an oddity like Sarah Baartman (1789–1815) (43), yet she had few role models (44). The 1930s white male Creole nationalist projects continue to dominate the Latin American literary canon (43). She determined to overcome her fear and follow role models like Burgos and Angelamaría Dávila (44). She sees a 'nueva cepa de mujeres' ('a new stock of women') who are unafraid, and which may mark a new moment in writing that breaks with the white Creole projects and all its colonial baggage (43). Now she sees herself as a woman who narrates 'fisuras en el tiempo, que crea alianzas con otros pensadores para poder imaginar todos juntos un mundo diferente' ('fissures in time, [who] creates alliances with other thinkers to be able to imagine together a different world') (45). Along with Arroyo Pizarro, Denis-Rosario and Llanos-Figueroa she is doing that. Those reimagined alliances are part of what I call the 'fractal family'.

As Celis and Rivera note, Santos-Febres's fiction and poetry challenge the 'great Puerto Rican family' (25). Additionally, she models her family paradigm for Puerto Rico on her own Black family. In her speech 'The Fractal Caribbean' (2019), the author shares her autobiography with professors at the University of Maryland, Baltimore County. She grew up in Carolina, Puerto Rico, the daughter of a Spanish teacher and a historian (11:50–12:00). Her brother self-treated for psychological and behavioural issues resulting partly from a learning disability until he died of an overdose (12:01–22) and her family fragmented (12:22–24). She travelled the world because of her writing, but she could not completely escape her origins or the confines of race, class and gender that formed her Black identity (13:00–08). Yet her traditional family's collapse left a void in her circle of personal relationships that was filled by her *barrio* ('neighbourhood'), part of a Caribbean tradition (13:50–14:00). Santos-Febres's extended family included neighbours and friends of multiple races and nationalities, and it extended from the island to New York and beyond (14:01–40). Puerto Rico's weak public institutions necessitate strong, often unconventional families 'beyond bloodlines' (14:48–50). Boricuas need them for economic, political and cultural survival (15:14). Eurocentric institutions have not protected the Caribbean nor have they displaced the *casas de abuelos* ('grandparents' houses') or *casas de santos* ('temples') (15:35–55). 'Home' means the patriarchal, white, mononuclear creole family on the surface (16:44), yet beneath that veneer, 'home' means 'community' for Santos-Febres (16:50–1). 'Family', for some, is biological and can be traced linearly through time (17:05); for the thinker, it is a system of relations 'much more like an activist organization' (17:10–13). Santos-Febres explores the tensions of linear Western thought with Caribbean thinkers of fractal (Afro-)Caribbean realities, beginning with Benítez Rojo (18:13). She recalls the creation of Caribbean Creole planter societies and maroon rebellions (19:04–08). Notions of 'history' and 'self' are not linear in the region, Santos-Febres claims, noting the unexpected events of Hurricane Maria and the ousting of corrupt, homophobic governor Ricardo Roselló (20:14–5, 20:40–6). She remembers how trauma is stored in the body and mind and passed between generations and among interconnected human communities (21:38–44). In her case, noting her connection to Blackness and Africa, she sought in Santería (Regla de Ocha) a means of coping with caring for her mother, who suffered and died from Alzheimer's disease (24:08–16). A 'maroon intellectual', she believes that Santería enhances postmodern theoretical approaches (24:40–51): 'at the centre of African diasporic religious practices, there is the oracle, the *uno-múltiple*, the system of binary language very close to computer programming, that behaves in variations' (25:52). The Ifá divination boards are an example (25:52), which Sánchez-Blake considers central to her poetics, along with the Orishas (188). The self is a system of relations, the theorist argues (26:35). In Santería, divinities are simultaneously one and multiple – one force with different manifestations (26:50). The deceased Ancestors are eternal and present in the mundane world, a spiritual family (28:27). For her, Glissant's *relation* is another example of the *uno-múltiple* and the centrality of inter-human relationships in the Caribbean (30:18–24; Glissant, *Poetics* 27). Literature, she feels, is not separate from community activism there: 'we writers have taken to the streets' (33:07–55).

This first speech is for intellectuals, but she also brings the 'fractal Caribbean' to a broader audience through the 'Afro-Saberes' lecture series of the Corredor Afro, a cultural centre in Loíza, Puerto Rico, co-founded by Moreno Vega and Maricruz Rivera Clemente. Black identity is inseparable from Caribbean identity for Santos-Febres, as she shows in her August 2020 'Caribe fractal y pensamiento afrodiaspórico' ('Fractal Caribbean and Afrodiasporic Thought'). The orator clarifies that she has never wanted to isolate the island from the rest of the Caribbean. She notes the influence of Moreno Vega in her theorisation of Afro-Caribbean thought, along with Mbembe, but his necropolitics is less consistent in her thought than her use of postmodern national allegory (17:00–10). Using the photographs of Ballesta 9, she illustrates how, in nature, fractals repeat and create new patterns, which for her represents Afro-Caribbean discourse (18:50–5). There are no hierarchies or linearity, no conflict between the individual and community identities, no time or *telos* (19:04). I disagree with the latter assertion, since she has goals: justice, representation and liberty. In the United States, when she studied there, those around her forced her to 'pick' between being 'Puerto Rican' or 'African-American' because the notion of 'Afro-Puerto Rican' effectively did not exist (28:10–13). Puerto Rican racialisation is, she reminds us, the product of the island's two colonisation projects, the Spanish and the United States, and the traumas of racism are repeated in Black families, including the denial of racism and the invisibilisation of Black people (29:37, 34:10/35:04).

What community, then, would be better for Puerto Ricans than the Insularist one? For the Iupi professor, Black reticular thought is the decolonial alternative to the origins and linearity of Eurocentrism, which is the basis of the patriarchal economy of ceding and inheriting property (37:10–18). Non-white, non-male, non-hetero, non-cis-gender people are excluded from this legitimacy of linear begetting (37:30–9). Even today, most Black people do not have titles to their land on the island, a barrier to FEMA repair funds in the wake of Maria (37:46–8). From Glissant she takes the 'desire for history' of invisibilised populations like Afro-Puerto Ricans whose excluded, silenced histories must be told because they are still being lived (38:22, 40:28–9; Glissant, *Caribbean* 77). Writers and community members must create spaces for that prophetic history to be articulated (41:42–3). It is like what the Akan people call *sankofa* – looking to history to imagine the future (41:58). It is a rejection of monolingualism, mono-ethnicity, hierarchies and monotheism (42:32, 44:30).

Crafting a Community, Performing a Self

Fractal Black families are building a space within the nation and the diaspora, showing that they have always had family crafts. In addition to general domestic labour, marronage and sex work, women created things, regardless of their externally imposed limitations. In *Writing Secrecy* (2013), Arroyo studies how Freemasons, an international, all-male society with wide and established networks in Puerto Rico, used the idea of 'craft' as a means to 'subjugated freedom' (7). In the organisation, men became part of a community through their work (7). Black women did too, in other contexts. Arroyo uses the Greek term for 'craft', *techné*, to describe the process. One displayed skill, or *techné*, in their/her/his profession, regardless of its prestige (agriculture, medicine) (7). For Socrates and Plato, *techné* means skills of the 'self': self-protection, bettering oneself and contributing to the community (7). Black women are creating characters that show their inherent worth through their mastery over crafts, over their sense of self and their care for their family/communities. Arroyo extends the 'craft' to writing and artistic skill, which all these authors and many of their characters display. The captive women of these books are creating an individual and collective identity while enslaved. By using their labours and skills for themselves and their families, they are subverting their instrumentalisation at the hands of their enslavers (Arroyo, *Writing* 8). They are building a land (and more) for themselves. In some ways, they are crafting a Puerto Rican collective that includes Afro-Boricuas in all their diversity.

One element of *techné* is assuming control over one's body. Santos-Febres focuses on the Black, female body, using her interpretation of Butler's *performance*, which the novelist takes up as using *travestismo* (drag, trans identity) as a means of consciously interpreting Black feminine gender and sexuality. Butler does not limit performance to *travestismo* – recently applying it to Black Lives Matter marches (2020). The theoretical concept is highly relevant to this book, and it certainly goes beyond gender to race and other areas of identity politics. The fact that the individual body is part of the fractal family of the Afro-Caribbean relates to the Black, female identity of Santos-Febres and all the authors I have considered. The performativity of gender and sexual identities dates back to Butler's *Gender Trouble* (1990) and *Bodies that Matter* (1993). In 2008, Debra Castillo applies Butler to Santos-Febres's breakthrough novel *Sirena Selena* in her introduction (xxv).

Santos-Febres's notion of *travestismo* indicates how deeply immersed she is in Puerto Rican culture, so Butler's work alone is not enough to elucidate her point of view. Much of the world came to know her as a novelist through *Sirena Selena vestida de pena* ('*Sirena Selena*', 2000), which depicts a Puerto Rican *travesti* who becomes a bolero performer in the Dominican Republic. These performative bodies are the Others of modernity (Celis and Rivera 20). Díaz (26) and Muñoz ('Travestismo' 71) interpret the *travestismo* of the work as a metaphor for Caribbean identity, and Rodríguez considers its queer bodies the simulacra of Caribbean culture in a transnational context (205). Rangelova argues that the novel claims no nationality, but I would reframe that approach to argue for a fluid, mobile nationality and identity in that work that connect with those I study here ('Nationalism' 76). The critic sees 'transvestites' (trans women and drag queens or *translocas*) as vehicles for 'transnational channels', but Santos-Febres's continued focus on her country has led me to conclude that we cannot leave aside the island's identity (76).

In 2004, Santos-Febres already views *travestismo* as a metaphor for the Caribbean, a place full of contradictions and fluid, wandering identities in metamorphosis (*Sobre* 121). For her, Caribbean *travestis* subvert not only gender norms but also those of race (127). She proposes Glissant's explosion of the national and the modern (129). This racial *travestismo* is a precursor to the fractal families of this book (130).

While writing *Sirena Selena*, Santos-Febres worked with the HIV/AIDS activist group Act-UP Puerto Rico, where she became part of the *ambiente* ('scene') at an LGBTQ+ club called the Danubio Azul (xiv). As Santos-Febres notes in 'Sobre cómo hacerse mujer' ('How to Become a Woman' 2003), that *ambiente* was a place where she learned about the conscious repetition and (re)creation of identity (*Sobre* 24). She learned to 'be feminine' as she wished to be by imitating her Black mother and her *travesti* friends – both drag queens and everyday trans people of the 'comunidad homosexual' ('gay community') (24). She learned that gender was a series of gestures, acts that she could control and deploy as she pleased (24–5). Unlike these 'feminine men' (who may identify as neither), the Black women of her family were strong, hard, fiery, boisterous, direct and demanding (25). Black women were not 'made' by society the way that white women were at the Catholic school where she was taught to be delicate, subtle and yet domestic (25). Black women worked with their hands and did not need a man to help – and if they had to, they kicked them out (25). They had to be stronger than their white bosses and their unreliable men (26). Her gay 'sisters' taught her to 'travestirse de mujer' in a creative, liberating way that transcends biological determinism in favour of a more complex, more self-determined identity (27–8).

The liberation of becoming more 'seductive' for Santos-Febres seems, at first glance, to contradict her essay 'El color de la seducción' (2001), in which she traces the figure of the 'negra promiscua' ('promiscuous Black woman') back to the plantation (*Sobre* 116). There, Black bodies were animalised and sold, not just for labour but for sex work and institutionalised rape (117–18). These 'degraded' women were simultaneously imagined to be responsible, as great temptresses, for the advances of their enslavers (119). This relationship modified membership of Black families to include white enslavers as 'amos, amantes, hermano-padres' ('masters, lovers, brother-fathers') and, no doubt, further combinations, unlike the modern conjugal nuclear family, though it has echoes in the structures perpetuated by poverty, racism and sexism (119). Santos-Febres notes that historical seductresses, lovers and sex workers sometimes used their wiles (while they were being used by men) to gain power (119). This story of race and power is written differently on the skin of every Caribbean person (120).

While Santos-Febres focuses on Black families, her 'fractal family' bears traces of performativity and the 'family of choice' that many LGBTQ+ individuals must form when their families of origin reject them. Gutiérrez Negrón has emphasised the heteronormative nature of the 'great family' notion of nation and shows how LGBTQ+ affirming writers such as Santos-Febres have worked to reject the oppression of the 1930s generation (171). Gelpí foresaw this in his readings of anti-Insularist writers such as Ramos Otero and queer characters in the ouvres of García Ramis and

Ferré (1462). Like these writers and characters, the 'family of choice' often lives outside the island due to intolerance in Borinquén (1540). García Ramis, in particular, sought a feminist family and nation that were not authoritarian (1578). These families are fluid to the point of being transitory (2032). They also include family members occupying the role of allies, such as the feminist women who supported Ramos Otero in the journal *Zona de Carga y Descarga* (Gelpí 2174). As in Santos-Febres's family, non-Afrodescendants have an important role to play in bringing justice to the archipelago and the diaspora.

LaFountain-Stokes has theorised identity, performance and community in *Translocas: The Politics of Puerto Rican Drag and Trans Performance* (2021). *Transformista* and *travesti* recall terms that have fallen out of favour in the United States, loosely corresponding to 'cross-dresser' and 'transvestite'. *Loca* ('madwoman') is a slur for men who are considered gay or effeminate (13). Yet LaFountain-Stokes creates new signifieds for these signifiers by considering trans and drag performers to be not only trans-*locas* but also trans-*local* – which is to say that they inhabit both local and international or, in the case of Puerto Rico, trans-colonial spaces (17). This includes Borinquén and the continental United States, which is home to roughly 2 million more Boricuas than the island (17). Insights from *translocas* further justify my integration of diaspora authors with island authors and present a notion of a translocal Afro-Puerto Rican family that complements Santos-Febres's.

Some readers of Constantine-Simms may ask why I choose to violate *The Greatest Taboo* (2001), the title of his landmark study on homophobia among African-Americans. One might ask, why use one minority's theory to interpret another's literature and, in some ways, lived experience? Should I use it only for LGBTQ+ Black people?[9] Why? I would counterargue that the Afro-Boricua writers of my study are imagining a democratic community that has yet to exist in its plenitude in Puerto Rico. Negrophobia and other phobias have yet to be overcome. Santos-Febres and Llanos-Figueroa are vocal queer allies, and Arroyo Pizarro is an out-of-the-closet *afrolesbiana*. It would be homophobic and transphobic of me not to consider these intersections of identity, and, having done so, I am convinced elements of *translocas* are a creative way to reimagine what has, for decades, been a cis-heteronormative, racist and patriarchal notion of nation and family.

LaFountain-Stokes's local theorisation makes it even more relevant to Puerto Rican studies. The intersectionality of sexuality, gender and race is central to the decolonisation projects for Puerto Rico and the world, so *translocas* must inform our understanding of the Afro-Puerto Rican fractal family put forth by these queer subjects and allies. Since the Conquest, Black bodies have been seen as 'perverse', 'illegitimate' or non-normative, just like those of LGBTQ+ people. Santos-Febres, in 'The Fractal Caribbean', views oppression intersectionally, declaring, in the wake of multiple recent police shootings of Black youths, that there is a war going on today against Black and non-binary people alike (50:34). Minorities are oppressed by many of the same forces, so it makes sense for them to be allies in seeking ways of imagining, theorising and looking for solutions.

LaFountain-Stokes devotes considerable attention to race and class in his readings of *transloca* performance. La Loca is also a figure from the iconic Fiestas de Santiago Apóstol ('The Feast of St James the Apostle') in Loíza, celebrated in late July (14). La Loca is a Black, apparently cis-heterosexual male performer who dons Blackface to pester passers-by during festivities in the street, although sometimes he is played by trans women and gay men (14). La Loca challenges the white Knights of St James, carnivalising the legend as the 'Moor Slayer' of the Reconquest (156). The author sees *transloca* displays like these as a means to hyper-visibilise race, gender and class on the stage or page (15). They even reverse the association of Santiago the Moor Killer with purity and goodness, which Ramos Rosado shows is an example of Eurocentrism (*Destellos* 111).

One example of translocal intersectionality for LaFountaine-Stokes is performer Javier Cardona's 'transloca drag of race' (*Translocas* 145). Most relevant to the novels in this study is the notion of 'Black masks for Black skin', a performance that makes visible a Black identity amidst the colonial context of whitening and invisibility on the one hand and oppressive stereotypes on the other. These are similar to the 'white masks' imposed by colonialism to which Fanon alludes, so LaFountaine-Stokes's reading of Cardona shows how one can be considered Black and still need to perform one's Black identity in an explicit manner, as all these authors do (136). Cardona's performance hypervisualises gender as well, since he appears in drag as two well-known female figures from the archipelago, a Black maid and a Black *santera* or *madama* ('spirit medium') (137). Like these authors, Cardona intervenes critically with these stereotypes (156). During the performance, he writes a counter-narrative to Snow White (as a symbol of white oppression and the ideal of culturally whitening oneself) in which he becomes the Black-clad Evil Queen (144). Quoting the character's catch phrase, 'espejito, espejito' ('mirror, mirror, on the wall'), Cardona evokes the mirror as a fractured image of the self. He shows a looking glass to himself and to the audience (147). The critic ties this mirror, this fractured vision of subjectivity, to those of Lacan's mirror stage, Zenón's *Narciso* and González's 'En el fondo del caño hay un negrito' ('At the Bottom of the Channel, There's a Little Black Boy', 1972). Like the *espejito*, however, the authors of *Fractal Families* cobble together the fragments of identity that have survived whitening discourse to create a Black, female, fractal identity that is scattered and that grows into new forms.

While Cordona's performance illuminates how these women novelists give visibility to race and gender, LaFountaine-Stokes coins the phrase 'transloca drag of poverty', which theorises the stage personae of Erika López, Holly Woodlawn and Monica Beverly Hillz (*Translocas* 70). Likewise, class, a theme in all the works that I study here, intersects with race, gender and sexual orientation. It is a contributing factor to splitting and reassembling communities. Rangelova has shown the cultural effects of the 'feminisation of poverty' on the island (*Gendered* 10). The *transloca* performers are part of the same phenomenon as *Sirena Selena*, which depicts the intersection of homosexuality and transgender identity with frequent homelessness and poverty – 'street queens' (74, 77). LaFountain-Stokes ties these to the 'houses' of *translocas* who would be otherwise homeless, led by 'mothers' in a matriarchal family of choice (77). In turn, these houses bear parallels with the houses of Santería (LaFountain-Stokes 75). They are fractal families, following Santos-Febres's definition. These scattered houses, places of relative stability not based on genealogy, are the alternative to the plantation house, the classic setting of the 'great family' (Gelpí 1656). They are also a place where eroticism flows freely, unlike the repressed setting of the classic patriarchal home, which had exceptions for the deviations of men (Gelpí 1970). 'Houses', both street queen and *santera*, are a model of family that Ríos Ávila does not consider when he argues that all things queer are enemies of the family and the nation ('Queer' 1135). They merely necessitate different models.

Afro-Puerto Rican Families: Born Enslaved

Just as LGBTQ+ families need interpretive innovation, Afro-Boricua collectives also necessitate new concepts of family. After abolition in 1873, most Black and mixed-race families were different from most white upper-class families. While workers were not always listed with a Black identity, the impact of slavery in this plantation-based and port-based economy is undeniable. Suárez Findlay gives an overview of these families and their frequently fluid structures. In Ponce, the focus of her study, race, gender and national politics were intertwined with the family (2). Often, national projects to impose respectability justified policing and persecuting women of colour (3). She notes that 'Liberal Autonomists, bourgeois feminists, working-class radicals of both sexes and Afro-Puerto Rican political activists all forged their ever-changing senses of themselves – their differences from and affinities with others – *as* they created discourses and often *through* the discourses themselves' (italics in original, 5). 'Decency' and sexual norms were highly gendered and racialised between 1870 and 1920 (7). Respectability informed national projects to erase differences and create internal cohesion (9). Alternatively, it is a method of repression and exclusion (9).

Crespo depicts the roles of Afro-Puerto Rican women from the eighteenth century to 1930. Having a female domestic worker was common, and enslaved Black women were preferred before abolition (227). They cooked, cleaned and cared for the enslavers' animals and children (227). Physical punishments were cruel, and rape was a method of control (227). Daughters of captives sexually initiated the enslavers' sons. Often, sexual abuse was blamed on the women and called 'prostitution' or 'concubinage' (227). One-third of laundresses were enslaved (228). At the turn of the twentieth century, twice as many Black women worked outside the home for pay as did white women, so being in the public sphere and labouring was stigmatised and associated with Blackness (226).

This history illuminates Santos-Febres's lived experience. The women of her 'clan' were uniquely strong. While her mother was a teacher, most Black women on the island often did domestic manual labour – they did not have the luxury of being frail. Many were either sex workers or stereotyped as such, even being persecuted by state and local campaigns focused on decency (Suárez Findlay 78). Those wishing to create a stable social order often considered working-class women prostitutes, frequently without evidence (78). Those considered 'decent' (married, not promiscuous) were de-Africanised, while the reverse was true for the labourers (78). Yet they had agency.

Popular classes of the nineteenth century, most of whom were Afrodescendants by today's definitions, despite having predictable gender roles, expected 'decent' men to provide financially for their wives or at least not to leave them to be the sole breadwinners (Suárez Findlay 125). If they did not, it was acceptable for women to seek another consensual monogamous union (119). Women knew that marrying in the Church under Spain was a life sentence, even if the male partner was poor, reckless, lazy or abusive (114). When the United States arrived, 'Americanisation' meant seemingly benevolent, 'civilising' means of homogenising families. Half the babies on the island in 1898 were born out of wedlock, and to the segregated Americans there seemed to be extensive miscegenation that needed to be policed (118–19). To make marriage attractive to women, it was popularised through divorce laws (121). Eighty-five percent of women's divorce petitions from 1902–20 charged men with abandonment (130). Thus, the United States presented itself as a civiliser (121). However, neither divorce nor marriage provided widespread familial constancy or a homogeneous culture (134) – 'Stability without justice was an empty ideal' (134). Like the changes in marriage that Suárez Findlay describes, the 'fractal Puerto Rican family' should be a family of choice, not one of oppression, and it opens the Boricua community to justice when permanence is absent or restricting.

This Book

Fractal Familes is about Afro-Boricua novelists and short-story writers who, since 2007, have been rewriting the origins and history of Borinquén. They are imagining a counter-narrative to the 'great Puerto Rican family' that includes increased Black, female agency.

They return to the plantation to recover what they imagine to be the enslaved's point of view, most of them female, but they do not leave that history trapped in the past. They relate it to today's concerns of continued racial prejudice and sexism.

They imagine the Puerto Rican archipelago as at once based in the island and scattered in the diaspora, an *uno-múltiple*. Santos-Febres proposes a family of choice, one that is not based on blood, borders and hetero-patriarchy but on performative, fluid identities that the subject can choose (Santos-Febres, 'Caribe' 37:11–13). The Afro-Puerto Rican nation-family allegory is not structured in the same manner as the colonial plantation family allegory. It is matriarchal, it is marked by marronage, and it includes the pursuit of land rights. Its crafts, healing, midwifery, sex work, traditional medicine and manipulating vital forces of the spirits, are a font of creativity and a sense of community that is handed down through generations. These *techné*, as Arroyo calls them, are an alternative to the colonially imposed notions of honour that justified so much oppression in the name of family (7). These writers are reforming institutions that promote the ideology of Puerto Rican nationalism. They also make the interpretation of the island and its diaspora a more complex, less hierarchical vision of themselves. This community is a repeating, irregular, unpredictable shape or fractal.

These authors are not the first to criticise Pedreira, the Insularists, or, later, Marqués's allegories of the national family. Flores, Gelpí, Moreno, Lloréns and other critics have shown that the 'great family' was oppressive and exclusionary. It was a racist, sexist, conformist, colonial cultural nationalism that justified the local elite. The 1930s generation codified it in literature, the 1950s generation promoted a popularist version of it and the 1970s generation challenged it, focusing on gender and sexuality.

After Pedreira, the 'great family' included a whitening myth of cultural and racial mestizaje. On the mainland, Afro-Puerto Ricans such as Schomburg, Thomas, the Young Lords, the poets of the Nuyorican Poets Café and Moreno Vega formed affirmative Black identities, which, sometimes, intersect with femininity and queerness. On the archipelago, Vizcarrondo, Rodríguez Torres, Ismael Rivera, Rivera Lassén, Zenón and Ramos Rosado have all demonstrated self-conscious Black identities in their writing. They form part of the *uno-múltiple* of the transnational Puerto Rican family, as are the oft-overlooked maroons, mediums, Orishas and ancestors of the past.

These Black feminists have overcome prejudice not only from those who support patriarchy but also from white feminists. They are continuing a legacy of intersectionality that spans the Caribbean and at least two centuries. From Truth to hooks, Hull and Krenshaw, gender and sexuality have informed Black womanhood among African-Americans. In Latin America, since 2000, Afrodescent as a political identity has increased Black consciousness, but it must be nuanced with other aspects of identity, as Rivera Lassén argues ('Discriminaciones' 59). Race intersects with national identity, and the fractal family that these authors form is one that, while *posmoderno*, remains independentist, granting Black ownership to the land of the island, in some ways for the first time in Afro-Boricua history. Such independentism can be postmodern in part because it is based on the transnational theories of the Caribbean developed by Benítez Rojo, Glissant and now Santos-Febres. Both LGBTQ+ families and Afro-Boricua networks need interpretive innovation as one reimagines the translocal nation as a family. Today, intersectionality, along with performativity, has created theories like those of *transloca* LaFountain-Stokes, who has Caribbeanised the notions of performance that Butler pioneered. Black femininity has constantly been formed by racialised stereotypes regarding legitimacy and promiscuity. Hence, the concubine and the sex worker also form part of an Afro-Boricua notion of family, which is the basis of the new national allegory of the fractal family.

Chapter 1 considers the fractal families of Santos-Febres's two latest novels, *Fe en disfraz* (2009) and *La amante de Gardel* (2015). Looking back on the history of slavery and racism, two researchers – one an Afro-Venezuelan female, the other a 'white' Puerto Rican male – engage in kinky sex, eroticised by tales of master-slave encounters, in *Fe*. In *La amante*, an Afro-Puerto Rican looks back on the family craft, taking stock of her personal history – including a formational affair with Carlos Gardel – and that of her family lineage of healers.[10] Both works deal with the Orishas, the enslaved ancestors, maternal figures, lovers and sexual relations between those of unequal power (Black superior and white subordinate, famous white musician and unknown Black student). Both subvert myths of master-slave harmony, once in the boom town of

Diamantina, Brazil, and again in the port city of Cartagena de Indias. These far-flung settings contribute to an anti-plantation, anti-Insularist notion of the Caribbean as a fractal that repeats beyond the Antilles. Both works challenge colonial Christian traditions through ritual – Fe and her lover celebrate the body on Samhain and Micaela is reborn on Holy Week, becoming a Western nurse who controls others' reproduction. Her brief exchange with Gardel, affected by her spiritual mother Oshun, causes her to abandon the body for a life of the mind. The melancholic Gardel proves to be a son of the sea goddess Yemaya, brought into the Caribbean by African healing rituals. Both women have a family craft: Fe is from a long line of illegitimate lovers, many of them forced, while Micaela's family secret is the potentially poisonous *corazón de viento* ('wind heart') plant, which treats syphilis and unwanted pregnancy. Both Micaela and Fe are examples of Black women in white spaces – the early twentieth century hospital and the early twenty-first century research institute. What they do not present is a means of creating lasting Black communities in those spaces. Their affairs yield no fruit, no filiation.

These two fictional texts and Santos-Febres's fractal Caribbean raise questions. Apart from identifying with the sexuality of Fe and Micaela, how can one follow them? The continued sexualisation of Afrodescendant women continues stereotypes rooted in plantation sex. In addition, neither 'historical novel' is entirely true – Chica da Silva was, in part, an *arriviste*, and Fe and Micaela can be considered the same. Postmodernism has the issue of muddying the waters between history and fiction, and the result can be the neglect of a past that remains to be studied.

Chapter 2 focuses on Arroyo Pizarro's *cimarronas* ('female maroons') who exemplify the painful splitting and healing of fractal families and identities. She is a queer Afro-Puerto Rican atheist writing about enslaved women in *las Negras* (*Black Women*, 2012) and the Black families that it best exemplifies in her work. The author's choice of female maroons breaks with the long-standing masculinist image of the figure. As women, they have bonds with their families that are different from men's: an African captive recalls her lioness-like mother in Africa while on the slave ship; a Black midwife kills enslavers and enslaved as they are born; and an enslaved woman kills the white captor who rapes her. African villages, which functioned as families, are traumatically dismantled. These stories are a frontal assault on the harmonious hacienda, and they also seem to borrow from Toni Morrison's *Beloved* (1987), showing the shared bonds of African-Americans and Afro-Latinxs. Arroyo Pizarro uses the metaphor of these slave rebels interchangeably with the neologism *ancestra* ('female ancestor') to inspire Black women on the island to write stories that represent their identities through creative writing and archival research on slavery.

However, Arroyo Pizarro seems compelled in *las Negras* to choose only two sides of her complex identity: Afrodescendant and female. She repeats the gesture in her Technology Education and Design Talk (2016), in which she presents herself as a mother recalling her grandmother in order to create a better world for her daughter, an alternative filiation. She never mentions her sexual orientation, the trait that defines so much of her fiction and activism, or her wife. Likewise, homosexuality is absent from these stories and only appears on the plantation as a form of rape inflicted on a captive in a poem from that period. Likewise, her atheism conflicts with the aesthetic of deified African Ancestors. It distances her from Moreno Vega and Santos-Febres's practitioner perspectives, but it also gives her creative freedom to resignify spirits. To her credit, her fragmentary narratives and poems in her more recent work move towards a more inclusive fractal family in which the queer, Black, feminine and Puerto Rican intersect more freely, though her queer characters do not have the historical depth that her Black ones do. Her work with the Cátedra de Saberes Queer ('Queer Knowledges Study Group') will no doubt lead to new representations of (Afro-)Queer Borinquén.

The most iconic Puerto Rican painting is *El velorio* ('*The Wake*', 1893), and like its painter Francisco Oller (1833–1917), Yvonne Denis-Rosario uses death and funerals to represent fractal families, as discussed in Chapter 3. In *Capá prieto* (2009), a Black female researcher's return for her father's funeral leads to the discovery of documents about eighteenth-century Black soldiers of Cangrejos who fought off the English, showing that it was not only white patriarchs who founded and 'protected' the national family. The white Creoles and their institutions consistently endeavoured to take land away from poor Black people, including the police murder of Adolfina Villanueva Osorio in Loíza to create a Catholic retreat on her land. Her killing comes indirectly from the plantation, since her family received that territory from an enslaver. Death brings family back from the mainland, showing the fractal nature of the island. The collection honours Black women primarily as maternal figures, such as the Nuyorican children's librarian Pura Belpré and an alternative, matriarchal filiation of Black women dating back to the nineteenth-century Black educator Rafael Cordero y Medina. The matrifocal Black line is a foil for the white male lineage of a rich white family that dreams of its Black wet nurses in an act of debt and contrition. Denis-Rosario's expansive portraits of Afro-Puerto Ricans depict Black families, but they all seem heteronormative.

Chapter 4 analyses the fractal Caribbean and the subversion of plantation filiation in Afro-Latina Llanos-Figueroa's *Daughters of the Stone* (2009) to subvert the great family myth. The novel tells of five generations of Oshun's daughters, who gradually lose their family's craft of healing magic but gain a sense of connection to the land. Nonetheless, when the enslaver bequeaths the family estate to the second generation, she uses Oshun's magic to ensure the territory becomes her land, torturing then healing members of the white Criollo elite. The matriarch thus deconstructs the plantation/*quilombo* binary, creating an Afro-Puerto Rican utopian plantation that colonial officials surely would have assailed mercilessly. The relationship between the Black family, the land and the house Africanises the plantation and makes it egalitarian. This utopia creates an Afro-Caribbean notion of historical time since abolition and the US invasion are not mentioned. Oshun's power is more destructive in this novel than in Valdés's theorisation, since the goddess allows for enslavement, torture, arson, hurricanes and family collapse as punishments for disobedience (*Daughters* 1). Hence, she is more like an African goddess, who is not always benevolent. The family of *Daughters* instrumentalise the goddess's rage, creativity, sexuality, storytelling and healing. The storm that destroys the plantation supplants key moments in national history such as abolition and the War of 1898, keeping the focus on Afrodescendant communities. Alongside this alternative to filiation lies silenced trauma: rape, torture, death and shock that give the lie to the harmonious plantation myth (Glissant, *Caribbean* 73). The intergenerational trauma evokes elements of Toni Morrison's *Beloved* (1987), as well as plantation-set works by Ferré and Zeno Gandía. The novel begins to heal this silence through storytelling, which Glissant considers central to the Afro-Caribbean (*Poetics* 68). The novel's detours to the *palenque*-plantation form a new fractal as the narrator and latest daughter of the stone discovers a new family that includes space for a lesbian mentor, lover and daughter of Oshun. The final, Latina protagonist's remigration to the island are intriguing as well, since one must ask, why did the author exclude so much of Afro-Latinx New York?

My conclusion is a synopsis of this study's main arguments. I remind readers not to forget the trauma involved in creating the fractal family, often trauma rooted in slavery. Hence, we must use *sankofa*, the habit of memory, to continue developing this postmodern notion of family that undoes some of the damage the Insularists and the 1950s generation wrought under Pedreira and Marqués.

These authors are prolific, and the works analysed here are only a sample of their oeuvre, which spans literary criticism, drama and television (Denis Rosario), poetry (all of them except Llanos-Figueroa) and literature for children and young adults (Arroyo Pizarro). The Black Latinas Know collective is fostering and advocating for women who are informed readers of these Black Latina artists, and I recognise the need for a more diverse group of writers as well as scholars that are more representative of the Americas.

Just as these women are making themselves heard in new spaces, it is only fair to give them the last word on their fiction. My book ends with an appendix of interviews in English. The authors talk about the works studied here as well as their challenges and hopes for the future of the island, the Puerto Rican diaspora, and the fractal bonds between them.

Chapter 1
Becoming Family: Mayra Santos Febres's *Fe en disfraz* and *La amante de Gardel*

In addition to being a theoretician and leader of the Programa de Estudios Afrodiaspóricos y Racialidad ('Afrodiasporic and Raciality Studies') at the University of Puerto Rico in Río Piedras, Mayra Santos-Febres is, primarily, a writer (C and AL). Her two latest historical novels, *Fe en disfraz* (2009) and *La amante de Gardel* (2015), fracture the plantation family and create in its stead a fractal family from its pieces. The plantation family, allegorised as the harmonious 'great Puerto Rican family', is feudal and hierarchical. Slave-based, it is racist. Ruled by a *pater familias*, it is sexist. Insular (and, later, Insularist), it is isolated and static. It is intended to yield fruit constantly for those at the top of the family hierarchy, and it is designed to pass property – land, servants and goods – to a legitimate heir through filiation, both concrete and abstract (linear thought). Santos-Febres tears the plantation apart like a bodice and flings it far and wide. The snowflakes of New York and Chicago both have fractals like the Caribbean coastline. One must not forget that the Young Lords Party was born and thrived in both these US metropolises (Eaton-Martínez 109). Both works focus on love affairs that result in unorthodox familial relationships that subvert the 'great family' myth. Weldt-Basson considers *Fe* a negotiation with a national trauma, but the trauma of enslavement is transnational ('Memoria' 196). Rivera Acevedo argues that it abandons the Insularist tale of the *hacendado* and the *jíbaro* fighting off the US imperialists (73). Diana Gumbar considers *Fe*'s open discussion of racial discrimination a disturbance of the 'great family'

(58). Supporting my 'family of choice' notion of the nation, Santos-Febres builds on the narrative tradition of sadomasochism in Puerto Rican literature, which includes Ramos Otero's 'Vida ejemplar del esclavo y el señor' (1975) and Ferré's 'De tu lado al Paraíso' (1976) (Gelpí 2346). This chapter will show how Santos-Febres imagines Martín Tirado, a Puerto Rican researcher who is seduced by his Afro-Venezuelan supervisor as they research the history of enslaved Latin American women in Chicago. She reveals herself to him, she reveals Martín to himself, and, through this relationship, they create a new kind of community. Then, I show how the women of *La amante* create their own international community and family of choice, and how they reveal a Black side to the iconic tango singer of the most Europeanised countries of Latin America, Argentina and Uruguay. In both cases, though, I note the limitations of Santos-Febres's fictional families. Is there too much emphasis on white characters? Can the reader follow the models of these contradictory anti-heroes and achieve justice? Postmodernism is liberating in many ways, but does it come at the expense of the limited historical record that we have of the enslaved? While I consider *Fe* to be a historical novel, it is more of a contemplation on how individuals relate to history than a reproduction of historical events. Peñaranda-Angulo calls it 'naming the forgotten' through fiction (112). The only historical character of the novel seems to be Chica da Silva, presented here as Xica da Silva, her persona in a 1970s Brazilian film (Diegues). The characters speak to how the West in general and the island in particular relate to the effects of the past upon the present.

The narrator is the white, cis-male webmaster Tirado. He is the personification of the humanities at the dawn of the new millennium, and he is Puerto Rican. He is working with his supervisor, Fernanda 'Fe' Verdejo, on a database of testimonies of enslaved women at the University of Chicago. His position is relevant to the plot, since, historically, he is the 'objective' voice of authority and reason. He is subordinate to the knowledge and power of a Black woman to whom he becomes attracted. His objectivity is as questionable as his sex life, since both are fraught with echoes of colonialism, just like the 1930s generation.

The Patriarchal Voice: Martín

Martín is a traditional 'Caribbean white' or person seeking to be white as Santos-Febres puts it (*Sobre* 128). He is unaware of any Black family and, if he were, he would likely feel pressure to deny them. At the beginning of the novel, he is engaged to a white Puerto Rican cis-woman named Agnes (35). They are in a long-distance relationship due to travel for professional opportunities, much like many academics, including Santos-Febres herself, who left the island for Cornell University (Celis and Rivera 22). He is a graduate of the commonwealth's flagship at Río Piedras and *boricua de pura cepa* ('authentic Boricua'). Like the *criollistas*, he evokes the colonial past, and he identifies with the Spaniards (Weldt-Basson, 'Memoria' 196). Weldt-Basson is concerned that this depiction is a stereotype, but Santos-Febres reveals his repressed Black identity and his negotiation with the past – not a simplistic celebration of it like the Insularists' ('Memoria' 198). He has an illegitimate affair of unequal power relations, like many Creole whites, with the Afro-Latina Fe, although the power dynamic is much more fluid, given her control over him and his career. Their relationship opens up a new awareness about himself, and it is only after he begins to have sex with Fe that his consciousness is opened to traumas that he seems to have repressed.

Despite having read multiple accounts of rape at the hands of Creole whites, Martín is disturbed to learn that he is likely among their ranks. At a college Halloween party, he shows up dressed as Don Juan Tenorio, the (in)famous 'Burlador de Sevilla', as he was called in his debut appearance, penned by Tirso de Molina circa 1616. *Burlar* can mean 'to fool' or 'to rape'. Don Juan's relationships occur among partners of unequal power and sometimes can be seen as rape by contemporary definitions of consent. Part of the questionability of consent is the lies that he tells to get his way, the *burlas* or 'tricks'. He became an archetype of the men who use multiple women for sex, and patriarchal cultures have celebrated him as a sign of virility for centuries. Ironically, by recalling a costumed performance of the *burlador*, Martín gains greater insight to himself: he most likely deeply hurt a woman at that party, but he may never quite know what happened. He recalls every detail of his costume, like historians do for Spanish-descended men, but the woman he seduces is a blur (96). He makes out that she is dressed as Marie Antoinette (97). The morning after, he remembers her shouts, unsure if they are from pleasure or pain, and he discovers blood on the sheets, perhaps from her lost hymen, from his unwanted thrusts, or both (97). Uncloaking the repressed memory of his first *conquista* ('seduction', 'conquest') recalls the unease of the violent traditions of the plantation he continues in the twentieth and twenty-first centuries. He re-enters his sadistic moral grey zone when he reads about the sexual assaults upon Black women during the colonial period (41). He is aroused by the texts of these women as well as by the curt messages from his illegitimate lover, Fe, who reveals to him that these Black women are part of her – they look just like her. Also, Fe looks like his first lover/victim. During their erotic play, she dresses like the eighteenth-century mulatta double of Marie Antoinette – Chica da Silva, reinscribing the traumatic memory of Martín, yet revealing different traumas – those of enslavement. During their erotic play, she has him cut into her, splitting her flesh with a blade forged in Toledo, Castille's original capital and its most famous steel works (109). The blade mixes their blood and, as in the case of his first *burla* in 1984, he can no longer tell the body from which it came (111).

The becoming Other between Martín and Fe reveals a side of himself that he likely did not expect (Casamayor-Cisneros 148). Santiago-Díaz claims self-reference is commonplace in all Western Black literature (108). Fe, who has assumed the role of dominatrix, gives him specific orders for ablutions before their encounters (19). In one moment, he sees himself reading in a mirror, feeling that his white skin, whitened further by distance from the sunny Caribbean, is a 'wound' (19). How could occupying the top of a (neo-)colonial hierarchy be painful? It is so because he has purged his memory of key members of his family. Casamayor-Cisneros claims that Fe has 'penetrated' his white psyche, splitting open a (feminised) wound and revealing his unconscious secrets (147). Evoking Vizcarrondo, he sees in his flat nose the memory of his repressed 'Black grandmother', those African ancestors that one denies in order to climb hierarchies rooted in the plantation (19). Like the blade, it rewrites his colonial reflection – and self-image – from 1984 (96). Naturally, Lacan's mirror stage – entering or re-entering the Symbolic Order – comes to mind, but 'En el fondo del Caño' by José Luis González is more relevant (González 94). Like the three mentions of a mirror in *Fe*, there are three times the protagonist and poor 'negrito' Melodía sees his reflection in the story, leading to an open ending. The reflection that the child sees invites him, apparently, into the turgid water of the aquatic slum he inhabits. The child either drowns or otherwise 'se fue a buscarlo' ('went to go find him') (94). A more optimistic reading is that he went to find himself, for himself – he became an independent Black subject. Zenón's title *Narciso descubre su trasero* ('*Narcissus Discovers His Backside*', 1975) is also relevant to this mirror stage of racial consciousness. The fragmented images and sensations that he experiences while performing his love affair with the Black woman reveals a side of himself that before was a blur. It is a part of his psyche that fills and heals the wound of his repressive whiteness. Part of sloughing off his old self is abandoning his predictable relationship with Agnes, who is a hispanophile in her own right, a linguist who studies in Seville (18). They were to have a child together and pass down their white privilege (18). He escapes to her during spring break, which is Holy Week in Puerto Rico, but love is not resurrected amidst the colonial-Catholic surroundings on the island (65). In fact, he learns that she is sleeping with her dissertation director and the two go their separate ways (71). She remains on the island, insular and colonial like the Insularists. He embraces Fe on Halloween, a parallel holiday of death and rebirth.

Fe: The Other of the Colony, Then and Now

However, the novel would be incomplete if it were merely a self-help book for white men. I disagree with Méndez Panedas when she claims that Martín 'humanises' Fe (429). She does that on her own (429). He learns, as the title indicates, that Fe is just as much the novel's protagonist and Martín's double who splits and reforms his relationships with himself and his family. Peñaranda-Angulo sees the novel as a decolonial feminist 'herstory' (110). Her homeland of Venezuela, like Puerto Rico, was highly dependent on the United States until Hugo Chávez ushered in an era of socialist bolivarism in alliance with Cuba. (Post-)Independentists like Santos-Febres often look to Cuba in solidarity due to this shared history. Arroyo Pizarro was also impressed by Venezuela's Afrodescendant scholars and embraced the nation's anti-imperialist stance (*Tongas* 9). One must consider that Venezuela's society had not reached the collapse that one witnessed in 2021, so it was easier for Santos-Febres to overlook the shortcomings of *bolivarismo*. However, she creates a protagonist working to decolonise herself, ironically by using the opportunities afforded by the US empire.

Fe's research calls to her attention 'Xica da Silva', the enslaved *parda* ('mixed race Afro-Brazilian') who rose to be the mistress of her master João Fernandes de Oliveira's estate in eighteenth-century Minas Gerais. Until the new millennium, she was held up as an example of Brazil's 'racial democracy', since she was depicted as a seductress who became the *de facto* wife of one of the richest men in the colony (Furtado 8; Zito Araújo 980). Fe identifies with her, largely because she has reached almost the top of an empire's hierarchy, and others perceive her as the 'Xica que Manda' ('Boss Xica'), Silva's nickname (Furtado 6838).

Santos-Febres does not go far into Silva's biography. Despite negotiating a level of power that would be unthinkable in the British colonies, Silva was a unique case, and hers did not come without suffering. Most white men in her time married white women, but there was a shortage in the Minas Gerais diamond boomtown where she lived (Furtado 265). Her captor likely chose her partly due to her light skin as a mixed-race *parda*, reaffirming the colonial pigmentocracy (1179). She was descended from women of the Mina coast in Africa, who were known among enslavers for their beauty – and relatively light skin (1179). One could say that she rose to a life of being 'almost' white in terms of privilege and perception. Valladares-Ruiz, Rivera Casellas ('La poética' 113) and Casamayor-Cisneros associate the novel with Judith Butler's performance theory, but I see Fe dressed as Chica as *transloca* – performative, subversive and translocal (592; LaFountain-Stokes, *Translocas* 143). Arce sees her personification of Silva as a subversive 'travestismo', but she claims that wearing the clothing was a violation of laws prohibiting Black women from wearing such dress (235). Boss Xica did not have that issue as a powerful, land-owning woman whose status came with opulence. She was carried to church on Sundays in a sedan chair by captives, and she freely wore the finest garments (1566).

Nonetheless, her relationship with her enslaver was that of a concubine, not a wife – a privilege usually reserved for white women. Marriage at the time, permitted only between equals in the colonial hierarchy, was meant to produce heirs and to bequeath estates (2822, 2884). Non-white women, who vastly outnumbered white men, were used for sexual pleasure (2843). Many used their enslaver's attentions to negotiate privileges for themselves and their children (2853). Upon her manumission as his concubine, Chica gave João nine girls and four boys over sixteen years (2916). He made them all heirs, and they received an education befitting their class, even if they were not fully 'legitimate' (2916).

Despite achieving great power, she had a hard life up to that point. She was born in a slave barracks and treated like a 'small adult' who was to work and received no special treatment as a child (1170, 3441). She likely lost her virginity at the age of twelve (2762). Despite her ambition, she had no pretensions of overthrowing the system that facilitated her rise to power. She freed only one of her 104 (or more) captives, reaffirming her power and status, perhaps to the dismay of readers hoping for Black solidarity (3459, 3569). Since she was in charge of a diamond mine, most were men (3569). She was a woman full of contradictions and, no doubt, she experienced traumas throughout her life. It is difficult to make her into a hero, unlike the beloved maroon figure of the Caribbean. She was a woman who survived and, in a sense, thrived in a brutally oppressive system with parallels to the haciendas of the Caribbean – and, in some ways, parallels with US academia, a white-dominant and often Eurocentric space.

Fe has risen to the heights of her hierarchy. She is leading cutting-edge research into enslaved women of Latin America. This topic is uniquely important in the region since it has only two 'official' slave narratives: Juan Francisco Manzano's of Cuba and Mahommah Gardo Baquaqua's of Brazil. In the Iberian Atlantic, one must look to other records to find the life stories of enslaved Africans, as Rosario Mendez Panedas shows in her article (425). Therefore, Rangelova's reading of *Fe* as a 'neo-slave narrative' needs to be contextualised this way – the abysmal lack of 'slave narratives' on which to base one's novel (150). As Santos-Febres notes in her interview at the end of this book, she is aware of the lack of Latin American slave narratives.[1]

Fe is being driven to do this great work by something she does not reveal to Martín until they are having sex. Her work is, at first glance, ascetic. She travels to Minas Gerais, and there she finds Silva's descendants. Her female progeny embody contradictory personae: nuns who end up being *putas* ('whores') (24). Fe goes through a similar process with historical materials – including a dress worn by Chica da Silva, which had been stored away for generations, a hidden heirloom, a source of pride for the status it represented, and a source of shame for the role as 'concubine' it portrayed (25). It seems 'cursed' to the nuns in that every time one of them wears it, they leave the monastic order, never married, always 'illegal' in their relationships with men (78). This confirms Santiago-Díaz's argument that Black people have always occupied an illegitimate role in the 'great family' myth (60). For Fe, as it seemed to Santos-Febres, her own sexuality seems shameful, a form of being 'too feminine' in ascetic academia (*Sobre* 27). Fe makes the dress into *techné* through performance – she uses the pain of its metal harness to open wounds during sex like the blade from Toledo (57). In doing so, she is forming a kind of family tie to this lineage of fallen 'Madonna-whores', these Afrodescendant women who have lived in illegitimacy and the contradictions Black women face in colonial society (Arce 233). Yet she breaks up the linear filiation of the family through her relationship with Martín. The 'mask' Fe puts on, here the dress of Chica da Silva, allows her to see something new in the mirror: her past.

Fe overcomes the ascetic individualism that allowed her to rise in academia by embracing her hidden pain. Like Martín's, Fe's repressed trauma is presented with a header, as if both were slave testimonies (Weldt-Basson, 'Memoria' 194). The setting is 1985 in Maracaibo. Fe's grandmother sent her to a Catholic boarding school to protect her from the advances of the 'señoritingos del litoral' ('young lords of the coast'), which recalls colonial relationships between white enslavers and Black or mixed-race women (88). The coastline ties the country to the Caribbean, since the maritime life created a society similar to San Juan's. The 'real world' intruded into the monastery when Fe's mother, who is pledged to be a nun, is impregnated at fourteen (88). The solution was to marry her off to a cousin and leave the illegitimate Fe under her grandmother's care. The family is matrilineal, but the grandmother is raising the granddaughter due to unexplained interruptions in the family line (87).

Throughout history, Black families often have these interruptions, necessitating a family of choice and non-linearity. Santos-Febres's description of her nuclear family, the basis for her 'fractal Caribbean', is an example. Branche already notes the matrilineal structure of Black families when describing Luberza's apprenticeship as a washerwoman, a traditionally Black and female vocation on the island, in *Nuestra Señora*:

> the care and concern ... speak to a larger issue of community and collaboration that is both transgernational and translocal. The co-mothering (*comadrismo*) of which she is the recipient is the gendered expression of Afro-diasporan slavery and postslavery practices of mutual recognition and solidarity, which I have called elsewhere *malungaje*. (163)

The latter term refers to a kind of 'brotherhood' or Black solidarity formed during the Middle Passage (163). Branche sees them as part of a *malunga* ('Black') family, but the fractal family that I am arguing for includes non-Black allies and is not separate from the nation or its diaspora (164). Like Santos-Febres, he looks beyond bloodlines, oppressive identities and inheritace of property to the networks formed by crafts and mutual support on and off the island (163). The translocal elements that Branche mentions are Isabela's biological mother, who is an immigrant from the Anglophone Antilles and Benítez Rojo's objectification, in his view, of maternal Afro-Cuban woman (163). In Martinique, Chamoiseau considers the matrifocal nature of Black families crucial to life in the Caribbean: 'since slavery, the symbolic father was the master ... the family was structured around the mother, the grandmother and women – that's the foundation' (Chamoiseau and Morgan 445). African-American families, as the now infamous 1965 Moynihan Report shows, also are deeply affected by matrilineal family structures. Spillers's classic rebuttal to it, 'Mama's Baby, Papa's Maybe', considers, as many readers might today, that it blames the victims of racist sexual exploitation, Black women (67). She criticises the report for portraying Black families as frozen in time, not evolving due to historically conditioned power dynamics (66). Spillers notes that, until recently, many Black families have been seen as illegitimate, which disturbs inheritance of property in patriarchal systems (65). González Echevarría shows that, since colonial times, Latin American literature has been marked by a quest for legitimacy through writing (109). Yet Santos-Febres imagines a community for Puerto Rico, its diaspora, and the greater African Diaspora that includes elements that were formally deemed illegitimate, namely Black women and their families.

When enslaved, women were often sexually abused and sometimes separated from their families. After abolition, former captives often served similar roles, working as servants and concubines. As Suárez Findlay has shown, in 1898, half the babies in Puerto Rico were born out of wedlock, which was particularly common among the poor (118–19). Women of the latter class tended to cohabit with men to have a supplementary income, although they usually worked outside the home (121). Divorce allowed women to sue for abandonment and seek other partners to offset their financial struggle to survive (130). Migration from the country to San Juan and to US urban centres like New York has also added to this fragmentation for all Puerto Ricans. As Santos-Febres shows, mass incarceration has further separated Black families (personal interview). In all these cases, Black women have faced barriers to maintaining stability, unity and legitimacy, despite the fact that some Black families may be highly patriarchal and/or stable today.

Families often carry racialised, intergenerational traumas. Fe repeats her mother's 'disgrace' at the same school, foreshadowed by her being given her mother's name: María Fernanda (88). Like her mother, she is a 'first' – the only Black woman in a school for whites, a legacy of being the 'first' in her group that she shares with Silva and Santos-Febres, and one she would take to the heights of prestige in Chicago (89). Her grandmother, for her *quince*, assigns her a dress (not unlike Silva's) and a white partner with good financial prospects in the US empire as a future petroleum engineer (89). (Here, one sees a wink to Chávez for nationalising the oil.) The cousin's godson and *señorito* Aníbal rapes Fe, making her part of the family tradition of 'fallen' Black women – who had few prospects to rise in colonial hierarchy. Fe reframes her bloody loss of virginity (with parallels to Martín's induction as a potential rapist), focusing on the pleasure that she felt. That pleasure returns when she has masochistic sex with Martín. She becomes a part of history, at one with the adolescent self that she repressed, and is in control (Valladares-Ruiz 599). She is assuming that pleasure for herself, not the white man, as her ancestors did (Peñaranda-Angulo 107). The 'craft' of meticulously controlling the balance of pleasure and pain creates a relationship with the past that is free from shame. It is no coincidence that these pleasures of the flesh occur in a hotel room alongside a table, the symbolic centre not only of nourishment and ritual but also of family and the home (Gelpí 2388; Santos-Febres, *Fe* 19). Fe welcomes him at a table, while his fiancée tells him she is sleeping with her adviser at one o'clock in a restaurant, representing 'family' as transitory both in its constitution and dissolution (70). Unlike the home of the hacienda, the stable, confining place for white women and the all-but inescapable space for enslaved women, the hotel room is a place of becoming Other in the form of sexual theatre. It does not pretend to remain static, but to return through cycles and rituals like the holiday it celebrates, Samhain. Their family is chosen, not imposed upon them, although Fe is in control.

The Afrodescendant nun in Brazil who gives Silva's dress to Fe is, despite being 'married to Christ' and a 'sister', utterly alone (78). Surely, Fe felt the same way in her own near monasticism in the university. Yet she has her own mirror stage moment when she tells Martín that the enslaved women they are researching look just like her (53). They are her sisters, mothers and grandmothers. They are fractal because she chooses them and they are scattered across the Americas. Their stories are like hers, but they scatter in different directions depending on their context, making them 'translocal' (Celis 133) 'places of memory' (Valladares-Ruiz 587). Rangelova notes that for Fe, as for many Afrodescendants, their ancestors had no nation ('Writing' 154). Yet there are patterns in the chaos: Black women have faced racialised and gendered violence from the beginning, but they have survived to tell their stories. Writing allows Fe to create this family for the first time, and her psychosexual *techné* creates a new sense of self for the future with this family behind her. Arce claims the space between the settings of each violent narrative provides emotional distance from them for the reader, but I disagree – they unite a diaspora through shared pleasures and forms of pain (239). The technology of today provides a *techné* to create new notions of community with the past. The family members she discovers practice *techné* that form the models for other Black families in *La amante*. One is a *curandera* or healer who makes love potions, while the other is accused of the racialised crime of prostitution, as Peñaranda-Angulo notes (107–8). The testimony of the captive Diamantina presents a fertile Black body that is healthier than those of the 'pure' white women of the time, who were sexually repressed and, in her case, infertile (108). She thus inverts the 'great family's' demonisation of Black women's sexuality, which was considered without familial honour (Branche 150).

Fractal Genealogy: Against Filiation

I concur with Schulenburg's view that the researchers' relationship is 'erotic' in the sense that Bataille gave the term: chaotic, violent, transgressive, unproductive play (117). Elsewhere, Santos-Febres argues that Bataille's theories of eroticism do not apply to Black women because they viewed sex as work (*Sobre* 84–5). She claims that Black women had no taboos to transgress (84). I disagree – even the enslaved were hybrid subjects. One had to learn Spanish and convert to Christianity to have any hope of ascending hierarchies. With no transgression, there is no eroticism, and Black women – like all of us in the West – have a sense of transgression that Santos-Febres shows is formed by colonial Catholicism. Desacralising a nun – even if she does it herself – is sacrilege, and the 'everyday use' of Silva's dress is an academic sacrilege that damages an irreplaceable artefact. The performance evokes Alice Walker's short story 'Everyday Use' (1973), in which a rural African-American mother wants to give an ornate quilt she made to her illiterate daughter who lives with her instead of the one who left for college. The effete young woman believes it should hang on display as an artefact (Walker). Santos-Febres rejects 'museuficación' of Black culture, as Gumbar argues (62). In Santos-Febres's novel, the lovers defile the dress for pleasure, self-discovery and creativity.

Their family is erotic. At no point is reproduction mentioned. Fe is forty years old or older and has no children. She may be menopausal or she may be using contraception. She has control over her body that none of her predecessors had during their affairs/assaults. The researcher is creating a role for Black women that lies, in some ways, beyond the sex slave and the Mammy, and she is bucking the stereotype – be it 'Welfare Queen' or hyper-reproductive slave – that Black women reproduce excessively (Jones 329). She is learning and feeling, not producing a filiation. In this work, she breaks with the nineteenth-century model of filiation and fraternity, a rupture Rubén Ríos Ávila already sees in *Nuestra Señora* ('Virgen' 72).

Fe's fractal family scatters geographically and into the past. Her tale of learning is not a traditional coming-of-age story that takes place chronologically during adolescence. She is not a child and she has no children, which breaks with Pedreira's notion of the nation as a child and youth as the hope for building the nation (*Insularismo* 757–66). The only future Santos-Febres mentions is Martín's anticipation of their next encounter at the end of the novel (115).

However, the 'everyday use' of Silva's dress is not every day – it is every Samhain. African paganism is subdued and the presence of European paganism is at the fore. The absence of explicit depiction of African deities is telling – Santos-Febres's theory includes the *uno-múltiple* (multiple-one) that she has based on syncretic Yoruba religions. The pagan roots of Halloween – a commercialised and often superficial holiday exported to Latin America via the United States – show Martín another side of European history. They rediscover Black *brujas* ('healers, poisoners') on this so-called Noche de Brujas ('Witches Night'), named for Anglo-Saxon witches. They see that 'Civilisation', a concept of the West, has its own polytheistic faiths and its own histories that lie buried beneath the surfaces of the present. The costumes of today can reveal this part of the West through a kind of performance, just like Silva's palimpsest-dress. One can find implicit African imagery in the gown as well. It is imbued with multiple meanings – a vain, temperamental, beautiful, seductive Black woman who loves lakes – even the often frozen Lake Michigan – like Fe can be seen as a daughter of Oshun, a spiritual progeny that she shares with Micaela, Gardel's lover and Dahlma Llanos-Figueroa's characters (Moreno Vega, *Altar* 89, 104). She is the goddess of mirrors, a common element of Santos-Febres that the author associates with eroticism and self-discovery (Weldt-Basson, 'Marginalised' 177).

Part of the ritual performance of Halloween for this couple is, in some ways, a fleeting removal of their mask-like identities by assuming new masks like La Loca of Loíza. Casamayor-Cisneros believes silences in identity performance reveal the un-colonised body and that the moments between performing our identities are opportunities to break up previous narratives of race, gender and sexuality (144). Their shared secret is akin to the family secret of *La amante*.

Does It Work for the Reader, Though?

The novel has silences and problems. What are Black women, as a group, to do according to Santos-Febres? Generally speaking, they can discover their history, create community and stop denying elements of their past in order to assimilate to the dominant culture of the day and climb social hierarchies. I disagree with Rangelova when she dismisses office sex with subordinates as merely Martín attempting to present himself as rational ('Writing' 156). She blames him, the subordinate, for the affair instead of holding Fe accountable for her actions. What Fe is doing is unethical. Bosses should not sleep with underlings. Researchers should not steal and destroy artefacts. Fe is an anti-hero, not a role model. If there is a didactic side to the text, the details of its lesson are hard to implement. What if the uncolonised, silent pulsations of the body that Casamayor-Cisneros praises, like the quest for *jouissance* of the poststructuralists, are simply not a satisfying means of implementing social justice (149)? Then she must choose a different performance, her own fractal. Víctor Figueroa claims the affective and sexual elements of the process that the characters enact is inherently a 'struggle for liberation'. Yes, it is, but for how long? The *carnivalesque* side of *jouissance* is, by its nature, transitory.

Sex is a passing pleasure and has parallels with the temporary escape from abuse that is the hair salon in Santos-Febres's story 'Hebra rota' (Rangelova, *Gendered* 145). The 'great family' home, in the tale, is a site of gendered and racialised domestic abuse, which the protagonist Yetsaida escapes for moments in solidarity with other women but to which she returns afterward (147). After having her hair straightened and escaping her racist, violent father, she goes home due to a lack of options (151). At the young age that the story depicts, she can only dream of permanent escape (151). Likewise, Víctor Figueroa admits that Fe is 'still' oppressed by racism and sexism. Fe is a dominatrix, not a dictator. Her power is psychological, nothing like the manifold violence of the enslavers, so she is not occupying their position but reinterpreting and adapting it. Her change is mental, sexual and academic, but she is still a Black woman confined by a white-dominated West.

Ramos Rosado criticises Santos-Febres's sexualisation of Black women (personal interview). In other contexts, Santos-Febres also criticises the reduction of Black women to sex objects, yet Fe is, at best, a 'sex subject' (*Sobre* 116). Another issue with her erotic aesthetic, which Arce presents as a positive, is that, by arousing the ideal reader, the author is toppling the receptor's sense of moral superiority (238). In the 'fractal Caribbean', there is no right or wrong ('Fractal' 28:30). While this ambiguity is intriguing, one cannot lead an anti-racist project by taking a relativist stance on slave rape. Why change anything about racism and sexism if one's values are no better than those of the enslavers? Other critics argue that the novel inverts or transcends the colonial legacy in interracial relationships (Peñaranda-Angulo 105; Rivera Acevedo 83; Rivera Casellas, *Bajo* 103; Rangelova, 'Writing' 157). I do not believe that Fe completely transcends the trope of the 'tragic mulatta' trapped between white and non-white worlds that Rivera Casellas traces back to Cecilia Valdés and Julia from *La cuarterona* (1867) so much as updates it in the context of US academia (*Bajo* 78: 'La poética' 100). Fe's family, formed with Martín, is an erotic one that builds on the sense of institutionalised transgression, which formed over centuries of concubinage, as Arce argues (230). I see the opposite of what Casamayor-Cisneros does, which is that she escapes fate by having sex with Martín and destroying the dress (156). They surely go back to work the next day, more aware but in the same positionality. Víctor Figueroa claims that their desire for one another is enough to create an unforeseen, perverse liberation project, but desire needs articulation and praxis.

Before turning to *La amante*, I wish to point out, again, that the only figure portrayed with any attention to the historical record is 'Xica da Silva', whose name is spelled as it was never used when Silva was alive. Valladares-Ruiz considers the novel a postmodern questioning of history (587). The fractal Caribbean represents a postmodern outlook. There is no absolute truth. Casamayor-Cisneros asks, though, if it is enough to study the historical record to understand what enslaved women survived (143). Yet without the historical record, Santos-Febres is not giving voice to the enslaved, as Weldt-Basson claims, but creating her own ideas of what they might have said ('Memoria' 187). It is unclear how much of the novel is simply Santos-Febres's imagination, which creates its own silencing of enslaved women, since their ideas may have had little or nothing to do with how she presents them.

If Afro-Puerto Rican women are seeking their past, and there are precious few written fragments (and oral memory, archaeological evidence, and other sources), why ignore the few stories that are documented? It is likely that Santos-Febres wrote this book alongside the Cátedra de Mujeres Ancestrales de Puerto Rico ('Ancestral Women of Puerto Rico Writing Group'). If not, she certainly used the same methodology that Arroyo Pizarro, the group leader, uses (personal interview, 2016). She consults unpublished archives and published historiography, and then she uses her creative licence as a writer to craft characters that appeal to contemporary audiences. If Santos-Febres must turn these stories into hard-core pornography – with knives, rusty metal, blood and semen, sometimes in public – to sell books, are readers more interested in the sensual mulatta trope than the stories of actual mulattas? Since the novel's publication, there are more of these stories available, like the enslaved Afro-Puerto Rican Juana Agripina's court testimony, edited by Carmelo Rosario Natal in 2013 (1) and Benito Massó in 2016 (1).

As the historical record is revised to give more range to the voices of Black women, readers may have to settle for more subtle pleasures, like those of reading family scrapbooks, than detailed accounts of hot sex and brutal rape. Juana Agripina was more interested in gaining legal freedom than talking about coitus. Santos-Febres's goals seem to be to tantalise and entertain as much as to inform and reflect on history and memory.

This section has shown how Santos-Febres imagines lovers of unequal positionalities as they research the history of Latin America's enslaved Africans. They create a new kind of community through self-discovery. They reveal the impact of the past on the present. The Afro-Venezuelan's relationship to the United States is ambivalent in Chicago, since she comes from Chávez's anti-imperialist nation. She parallels Puerto Rico's transnational love-hate relationship with the empire. Yet the novel reveals other postcolonial traumas. Martín, the white Creole male, ceases to represent the objective voice of authority, succumbing to Fe and repressed elements of himself, the abject elements of the Insularist 'great family'. Through a sexual kink, Martín discovers his ambiguous relationship to racist rapists of the past. Fe revisits her traumas though sadomasochism. Mirror imagery allows them to reflect on themselves and history, which the lack of Latin American slave narratives has exacerbated. Writing finds and creates family and identity in the novel. Erotic in a Batailléan sense, balancing pleasure and pain, this short novel creates a relationship with the past that is free from shame. Its allegory is not focused on reproduction of bodies or of oppressive systems. That history involves matters of legitimacy and violence in sexual encounters and family formation. Often, rediscovering the Black side of Afro-Puerto Rican history involves tracing matrilineal narratives and noting their frequent restrictions to 'Madonna-whore' binaries as well as racist stereotypes and limitations, such as the work women do.

The novel reveals a fractal family, one of choice, one with Afrodescent, one with Orishas and ancestors, one that is *transloca* in its queer kink and transnational setting, but one that is not perfect. Santos-Febres overlooks inconvenient elements of Silva's life, how she confirmed her status quo, how she did not liberate enslaved Africans, her illegitimate relationship with her lover. While sex seems to liberate Fe from a parallel role in white-privileging academia, its fleeting nature ultimately does little to change today's status quo. Fe is an anti-hero focused on pleasure, not justice, since she sleeps with her subordinate. She is a 'sex subject' who fails to dismantle the academic constraints that confine her as a Black, female immigrant in any sense other than the discovery of her lost family of enslaved 'sisters' and 'foremothers'. Yet even these discoveries lack veracity, since the only historically documented story is that of Silva.

La amante de Gardel: Melancholy and Mother Oshun

Santos-Febres continues her Afrodiasporic, cosmopolitan imagination of Puerto Rico in *La amante de Gardel* (2015). As in the preceding novella, she focuses on Black women and family. They seem to be the conclusion of a trilogy of historical novels, or novels that reflect on history, that begins with *Nuestra Señora de la Noche* (2008), which was written at the same time as *Fe en disfraz* (2009) (Rivera Casellas *Bajo* 98). Like the daughters of 'Xica que Manda' ('Boss Xica'), the 2015 text presents a new matrilineal yet fractal family history for the protagonist who represents Puerto Rico, Micaela Thorné, and, in my interpretation, casts that family as spiritual daughters of Oshun. After exploring European paganism in *Fe*, Santos-Febres is embracing her own non-Western beliefs, and they are clearly present in the plot. Unlike *Daughters of the Stone*, however, the deities Oya and Yemaya, along with events that allude to Changó and Oya, also structure the destinies of the characters. It is a bittersweet transnational romance between the most famous tango singer of all time and an Afrodescendant woman who wants to be more modern than her precursors. The complex allegory relates a melancholic history of the Puerto Rican nation in which the future is unclear and undetermined. I focus on the Orishas, connecting them to other discourses, like that of Arroyo's Derridean reading of the Caribbean. In this way, the text is a combination of worldviews focused on nostalgia, death and destruction. I interrogate how closely the nation is to follow its model for the future.

Oshun is the Yoruba deity of love, sexuality and fertility (González-Wippler 104). She also governs wealth and marriage (104). Goddess of rivers and fresh water, she is closer to the earth than to the sea, the domain of the melancholy mother Yemaya (Valdés, *Daughters* 11). Oshun is beautiful and creative but vain, vengeful and stubborn (González-Wippler 107). She can be a healer, but she is also associated with death (González-Wippler 106–7). Her symbols are honey, herbs, sewing, lace, jewellery, perfume, combs and mirrors, and her colours are white and yellow or gold (González-Wippler 104–5; Moreno Vega, *Altar* 87). She rules the lower body, so she can heal the stomach, womb and genitals (González-Wippler 110).

As with *Daughters* and other works analysed in this book, *La amante* tells of a matrilineal yet scattered family: the enslaved African Mercuriana de los Llanos Yabó, María Luisa Yabó Candelaria, Julia Yabó, Clementina Yabó and Clementina de los Llanos Yabó, also known as Mano Santa ('Holy Hand') (30). Allusions to this lineage are scattered throughout the book, but it is evident when Mano Santa prays to the female ancestors to heal Gardel of his secret illness – syphilis (30). She prays to 'corazón de cielo, corazón de nube, corazón de viento' ('sky heart, cloud heart, wind heart') (30). She combines the powers of her feminine ancestors with the powers of Olorun (sky, cloud) and wind, the domain of Oya. Despite these other forces' influence in temporarily healing the ailing superstar, it is clear that all of the Llanos Yabó clan are daughters of Oshun. There is little mention of the men in the family – Micaela's father was a printer, but by the time of the novel, twenty-seven days around Holy Week in 1935, he has gone far away (19). Micaela longs to do the same (19). She comes from Campo Alegre, a slum near Santurce, San Marcos de Cangrejos, Puerto Rico, where she lives with her grandmother, Mano Santa (18). Her mother, Adelina de los Llanos, is absent, but in the narrator-protagonist's dreams, she looks down upon her daughter, the darkest-skinned of three daughters, and she spurns the traditions of Clementina de los Llanos Yabó for being 'primitive' (77). She and her daughter Nicolasa have very light skin, and her other daughter Adelina is dark but stunningly beautiful (77). They are not a part of this Santería lineage, but they represent those who forget it, since the daughters are unwitting daughters of Oshun: the mother for her sewing ability (110); the daughter Adelina for her beauty; and Nicolasa for her talent as a musician (77). Micaela feels shame for her Blackness and for her grandmother's traditions, represented by devouring and slobbering the blue *corazón de viento* ('wind heart') medicine in her dream. The novel relates how she negotiates with and overcomes that shame. She does this by finding a mentor, Dr Martha Roberts y Romeu, who guides her through nursing school and then pre-medical studies at the School of Tropical Medicine in San Juan. Because of being her protégé, Micaela receives a scholarship to Johns Hopkins University and becomes a pioneering specialist in women's reproductive health, like her spiritual mother (185). Nonetheless, that support comes at a price: revealing the family secret of how to make birth control from the miraculous *corazón de viento*. Unveiling the secret makes it fractal and evolving, as opposed to hiding it, which made it filial – static and linear.

The secret craft has parallels with Arroyo's *Writing Secrecy in Caribbean Freemasonry* (2013). Writing under the influence of Derrida, she expounds upon the theme of the secret craft among Freemasons, including Afro-Caribbean and Nuyorican lodge members. She notes that secrecy is essential to Mason rituals. Along with the French philosopher, she considers the 'locus of the secret' to be 'an autobiographical place' (1). Writing, on the other hand, typically discloses secrets (1). Thorné is telling her family secrets, her own, and those of Gardel, assuming huge risks but also creating her own Afro-Puerto Rican identity and her own version of her nation's history in an Atlantic context. It creates community and intersubjectivity, such as her lineage and her becoming Other with Gardel, which begins in a literal trance the couple share when she administers him the *corazón de viento* and spends the night by his side to ensure that it does not poison him (31). Thorné is also cultivating the family craft (medicine), which Arroyo calls *techné* (9).

While Santos-Febres is writing about an almost all-female Black community, the secret and *techné* are also central to her novel. The *corazón de viento* exemplifies both. Keeping control of this knowledge has given her ancestors power, influence and a pragmatic, if vilified, role in various communities for centuries (70). This secret understanding is clearly the gift of Oshun. It is used in different doses and moments as birth control or abortion, giving women control over their maternity and hence their bodies and lives. It is highly coveted by Dr Martha Roberts de Romeu, since she is working with scientists to develop a Western form of birth control for the island (50). Since US medical advances improved infant mortality rates and life spans, the island became 'overpopulated' (42). Dr Roberts is working to climb the social ladder. She was a pioneer who received a scholarship to Johns Hopkins since there were no medical schools on the archipelago. Like Oshun, Dr Roberts and Micaela are highly interested in money and fame that come from taming the *corazón de viento* (195). They work at the Negociado de Salubridad e Higiene Materna ('Maternal Health and Hygiene Clinic' – a *negocio* 'business' of health), which pays and certifies *comadronas* ('midwives') to oversee birthing at hospitals (50). Dr Roberts hopes to discover the secret of the herb in the process. She negotiates with Mano Santa to discover the untold element of distilling a tincture from the herb, but she refuses to relinquish her sacred knowledge (183). The grandmother eventually arranges a scholarship for Micaela to go to Johns Hopkins as well, leading the young woman to think that she did it on her own (187). Micaela eventually betrays the secret to Dr Roberts and thus becomes much like her: the first woman to tie fallopian tubes, along with other achievements in reproductive health (195).

Like Dr Roberts, the Llanos Yabó lineage has always faced problems with the 'inquisición' ('Inquisition') – the Church, one of the pillars of the colony (51). Dr Roberts must avoid abortion – a secret left to *comadronas* like Mano Santa – and present her research as attempts to make women more fertile (51). The Church supports the sexual double standard that makes male birth control – which Mano Santa offers to make – a completely unrealistic endeavour in the mind of Dr Roberts (80). Regla de Ocha practitioners have had to hide Oshun behind the mask of Our Lady of Charity in the Caribbean for fear of the Inquisition. Mercuriana becomes a maroon because her captors deliver her to the Holy Office in Cartagena de Indias, Colombia for being a *bruja* ('witch') (71). Llanos Yabó's fictional life parallels the testimony of Ana de Mena (1608–?), who was imprisoned for witchcraft in Cartagena but was born in Puerto Rico (Crespo Vargas 14). Their crimes are gendered and so are their punishments. As Llanos Yabó flees, the healer imagines the horrifying *araña de hierro*, sharp plyers used to tear off the breasts of women believed to have slept with the devil in exchange for magical powers (70; *La Verdad*). Having sex with the diseased and womanising Gardel could also put Micaela in this category. The image of opening and altering a woman's body with the Inquisition's instruments foreshadows the investigation and manifold violence of forceps in cutting Fallopian tubes, sterilising women. Mercuriana attempts to flee to a *palenque*, but the path is too well known, so she hides with the Zenú Indians along the Sinú River (70). This encounter is the beginning of a syncretic *techné*, an Afro-indigenous way of knowing born out of intercultural exchange. They notice that the plant grows only along the riverbed – the domain of Oshun (70). Dr Roberts is engaging in a more ruthless form of combining medicinal knowledge, but one can see her investigations in folk remedies as a continuation of this exchange. Christianity is also part of Mano Santa's ritual to forgive Micaela for 'betraying' her secret to Dr Roberts just before her death. She takes her on a tour of churches, praying penitence at each one (187). This ritual coincides with Holy Thursday, which commemorates Judas and Peter's betrayal of Christ (187). Tradition holds that Judas's betrayal resulted in the death and resurrection of Christ, and that Peter, despite his disloyalty, would become the first Pope. Hence, the holiday leitmotif of this novel, like *Fe*'s focus on Halloween, is Holy Week. Micaela finds herself in a similar role as a traitor who preserves and promotes a tradition. Unlike Dr Roberts, she treats her grandmother's medicine as sacred, and she combines her traditional understanding of it with Western historical accounts of its discovery. She uses chemistry to study it and the US occupation and empire to promote it (195). *Corazón de viento* and Mano Santa die, but they are reborn.

A *Palenque* of One's Own

Arroyo's Derridean insights show how these daughters of Oshun continue the Afro-Boricua tradition of feminine *marronage* (*Writing* 1). I might add that Derrida's musing on the Greek term *pharmakon*, which means both 'medicine' and 'poison', also informs the danger and blessing of *corazón de viento* (70). Jáuregui applies the two terms to the Latin American context by dividing the Classical concept into *medicina* ('political resistance, healing') and *midecina* ('political submission, death') on the part of Amerindians (68). His object of study is the representation of indigenous peoples in Miguel Carvajal's *Las cortes de la Muerte* ('*The Court of Death*', 1557) and their negotiations with the colonisers (68). In Santos-Febres's work, medicine and poison are also in tension with one another, and *corazón de viento* can be either or both. The medicine brings Micaela and Gardel together in secret – she accompanies her grandmother to his side, walking through the corridors reserved for Black service workers (27). The young woman spends the night with him (31). It is not for sex, as many believe, but for assurance that the medicine will not kill him. When her grandmother dies of tuberculosis, she asks for the tincture to numb herself as she passes on (14). When Micaela reveals the secret of the medicine, she creates two vials of the mixture: one for Dr Roberts and for science; the other for herself (184–5). She has the choice to use the tincture to treat Gardel for his ailment once the initial dose wears off after twenty-seven days (193). Like the craft, she inherits her grandmother's small ranch, called La Doradilla, the feminine equivalent of the town Dorado, where it is located and that means 'golden' or territory of Oshun, which has parallels with Llanos-Figueroa's La Caridad (67). Decades later, Micaela takes the poison on the ranch (197). The novel is a confession of her secrets before death. The tincture gives her a new life, a rebirth as a medical doctor, very different from the poor women she treats (50). Then, it gives her control over her own life as it ends. She narrates the novel at that moment between healing, nostalgia and the release of death, like Scheherazade. When her story ends, so does she.

Unlike Mano Santa, Oshun is not forgiving, and her vengeance seems to seal the characters' fates. Oshun gives Micaela a life filled with love because of her relationship with her grandmother. However, on the other hand, Micaela loses her mother and her sisters because they do not believe in the goddess (77–8). They also 'exile' the girl to La Doradilla because her Blackness brings them shame (77). They ignore her beauty, the realm of the deity. The remedy brings the Zorzal Criollo to the island and into her arms, but he ultimately abandons them. Ramos Cobián, the owner of the Paramount Theatre and a handler of Gardel, dies of cancer shortly after insulting Mano Santa's remedies as *brujería* ('witchery') (158). If Ramos Cobián is the overt disbeliever, Gardel is the arrogant, passive heretic. He engages in a twenty-seven-day affair with Micaela, taking her on tour with him across the island (15, 85). Ultimately, shame of Puerto Rico drives her to leave the island – abandoning her origins in a neighbourhood that nobody ever leaves – which may also have angered her vain spiritual mother (19, 179).

Sex work also relates to the goddess of female sexuality. Ramos Cobián appears in the hotel room where the couple had slept the night before, awakening her and dismissing her with a wad of cash as though she were a sex worker (159). Once again, the transitory hotel/motel substitutes the house as the setting of a love relationship, fragmenting the 'great family' model (Figueroa, 'Desiring'; Rangelova, Gendered 35). Gardel has also prostituted himself with a rich, married white woman for fame and money on the island (160). His friends call him a *cafisho* ('gigolo') (Santos-Febres, *La amante* 145; Maddox and Stephens 96). He never apologises or asks for further treatment. Micaela and/or the goddess condemn him to continued suffering with syphilis. She has the chance to give him the second vial of *corazón de viento*, but she decides to keep it for herself. Gardel dies in a mysterious plane accident that incinerates his 'hermanos' ('brothers'), the stories of whom the novel develops (15, 144). The rage of the sister-concubine of fire god Changó would explain such a death. One could see Micaela's blessing and curse of having no children and no men after Gardel, her only lover, as the fate administered by the jealous Oshun for betraying her secrets to the west for the sake of money, for Micaela's *corazón de vento* ('money heart'), another Deriddean wordplay of *viento* ('wind') and *vento* ('money' in Lunfardo) (155). She lives mostly alone and she dies in solitude (197). Having become pure mind (researcher, doctor, writer), Micaela even feels melancholy and divorced from her body, the realm of the goddess. Oshun's powers inform how she approaches her *transloca* performance of Black femininity while facing poverty, a performance that she shares with Gardel's past life (LaFountain-Stoke 70).

Yemaya, Melancholy and Brotherhood

Yoruba traditions associate melancholy with the sea. The novel opens with a quote from the Roman poet Tibullus: 'Ahora, bajo nuestro dueño Júpiter, muertes continuas y heridas, ahora el mar, ahora mil senderos inesperados para morir' ('Now, under our owner Jupiter, continuous death and wounds, now the sea, now a thousand unexpected paths to die') (9). Unlike the patriarchal Roman tradition, Oshun is working with Yemaya, the sad mother of the oceans, to control the destinies of these characters. *Corazón de viento* comes from the Sinú River in Colombia, which issues into the Caribbean. It flourishes in Puerto Rico along the banks of the Loíza River by the coast of Puerto Rico, according to the 1793 account of André Pierre Ledru (148). It grows wild in La Doradilla, which lies on Puerto Rico's Río de la Plata, a semantic link between the tiny island and the Southern Cone (77, 80). *Corazón* grows where it is exposed to salt and fresh water (Yemaya and Oshun). While Oshun's colour is gold, the tint of money, Yemaya's is transparent blue, the colour of the *corazón* tincture (69). If Tibullus associated the sea with death, Mano Santa associates it with putrefaction, both literal and figurative. *Corazón de viento* is not merely a wildflower, it is the fungus growing on it as well (69). The symbiosis of beauty and rot, brought nearly to boiling point, is what creates the magic potion (183). The symbiosis of the grotesque and the aesthetic is what creates this novel about suffering, disease, creation and love.

Gardel is like a sad song of the sea. When they make love, 'se virtió' ('he poured') himself into her and, later, she uses the same verb to describe her body when he performs oral sex on her. Their minds and bodies are flowing together in an extended trance. He is the illegitimate son of a washerwoman from France (99). Raised between Montevideo and the Abasto area of Buenos Aires, he is certainly an Atlantic Creole of a sort, a Zorzal Criollo (Berlin 39). His wandering the Atlantic as an ambassador of the most European of Latin American nations, Argentina, ironically makes him like the subjects of the Black Atlantic, deconstructing the

Afro-Caribbean and the Europeanised River Plate. His story overlaps that of the illiterate genius of the guitar, his lost 'brother', el Negro Ricardo, who joins him in forming the Black roots of the tango until he feels he is not being credited for his work and leaves the group. There are also clear racial tensions between Gardel's musical mentor Isidoro 'el Tano' Vidal and his Black colleague, which likely relates to the fact that 'el Tano' denies his own mixed-race heritage beneath the veneer of being *napolitano* ('Neapolitan') – not unlike Martín Tirado (Santos-Febres, *La amante*, 99; Maddox and Stephens 507). El Zorzal's sexual initiation is with La Valeriana, a sex worker who is either a 'Gypsy' or a Lebanese woman (100). He tells Micaela that the woman who taught him to have intercourse and to sing is 'una mina tan oscura como vos' ('a woman as dark as you') (94). He has an open partnership with her and the Tano, so the trio leave him with both the flower of his voice and the rot of syphilis (101). While Micaela insists the disease has not passed to her, it is clear she claims no other lover than Gardel. Clearly, he has infected her mind – like syphilis – since he begins to call her by his name, Morocho, or in her case Morocha, beginning with their first sexual encounter (115). While he gains the nickname for his dark hair (like that of a Moor), she acquires it due to her skin (as a *morena*). Whether or not he literally contaminates her, he is a source of infection and lust, a combination embodied in the nineteenth century by women of African descent, such as Cecilia Valdés and Julia from Alejandro Tapia y Rivera's *La Cuarterona* (1867) (Santos-Febres, *Sobre* 87). The Black women of this text make Puerto Rico not a 'sick' country, as it had been for Zeno Gandía and Pedreira, but a place of healing for itself and for other countries such as Argentina that see themselves as (only) white (Gelpí 207). As with *Fe*, this bildungsroman results in growth and learning that begins with Micaela's youth, but her learning does not result in reproduction and many of the lessons she learns come many years later (Gelpí 766).

The voyages through the sea, Yemaya's territory, are also part of deconstructing the Black Atlantic and the Western, Eurocentric world in the novel. Gardel brings a highly cosmopolitan yet melancholic aesthetic to the tiny island with his tango and habanera performances. His music is a stark contrast to the *jíbaro* music of the time in Puerto Rico and the upbeat salsa music that has come to dominate the international image of the island. His tour of the island as part of Latin America reaffirms its place there, not merely as part of the United States. His voyage to Paris presents it as a Madame where he must serve as a gigolo to an influential woman to break into the scene of the self-proclaimed cultural capital of the world (154–5). Like the healers of Micaela's family, the Pope prohibits his music while he is in Paris (155). Conquering New York is a similar process, a Dama de Hierro ('Iron Maiden') (164). As in his affairs with Micaela and Guillermina, the opening doors of the feminised city, like the real women's open arms and bodies, bring him ever closer to death – and he brings them along due to his beauty and his disease (160). Like many Black and mulatta women on the archipelago throughout history, Gardel is the illegitimate lover of the rich Guillermina (160). The narrator describes his sexual initiation with Valeriana as 'sangre entre las piernas' ('blood between his legs') as if it were menstrual bleeding (101). He even drinks the tea she does for menstrual cramps – *hojas de poleo* ('pennyroyal leaves') – thinking it is like yerba mate (69; 146). As the Zorzal and the Morocha make love, she reflects '¿Aquello que se dio entre nosotros fue un espejismo de palabras contra el mar?' ('Was that thing that happened between us a mirage of words on the sea?') (90). She notes that her body smells like the sea and that he becomes *acuoso* ('watery') (115). She insists: 'me hacía yo mujer con Gardel encima, ondeando como un mar dulce, de repente encabritado ... La certeza de una muerte compartida' ('I became a woman with Gardel on top of me, undulating like a sweet sea, suddenly bucking ... The certainty of a shared death') (115). Their passion is marine and melancholic like Yemaya, and they begin becoming Other. Gardel is white, but he is marginalised and meandering, and in a novel that constantly deconstructs Black-white, Western and non-Western categories, he becomes less and less a Eurocentric figure. By the end of her tale, the Zorzal Criollo is part of Micaela's fractal family.

His voyages parallel those of historically marginalised groups. Clearly, his struggle to break into the music scene of the Barrio Latino of Paris and later the Barrio Latino of New York has strong parallels with the struggling Boricuas and other Latinxs attempting to make their way in the United States. The Great Migration of Puerto Ricans began in 1935, and Gardel finds himself among them. It was shortly after the Harlem Renaissance, when Black women were defining themselves in an urban setting *en masse* for the first time, since they had left their former homes in the countryside (Rivera Casellas, *Bajo* 96). That same year Pedreira, Blanco and the 1930s generation imagined the 'great family' as a plantation rooted in an insular island. His coming to Puerto Rico, even as the white Zorzal Criollo, blows the plantation apart, revealing hidden histories in both the Black and white characters.

His voyage parallels another journey north: that of Mercuriana and her daughters. He tells Morocha that 'es linda esta Isla tuya … tan linda como vos' ('this Island of yours is beautiful … as beautiful as you') and, on his part, he brings her 'su pedacito de mundo a estos recodos olvidados' ('his little piece of the world in these forgotten bends in the road') (111). Santos-Febres is deconstructing the Black-Puerto Rican binary and the Black-Latin American binary. After Gardel's many journeys, he embarks on a road trip across the island with the young Afrodescendant by his side, showing her 'esta Isla tuya' ('this Island of yours'), distinguishing her from the poor Black people in the slum of Campo Alegre, who have never left the town where they were born (19). Her movement between rural La Doradilla, the slums of San Juan and the US metropole makes her a sort of Black *jíbara* who makes the journey many Puerto Ricans did to improve their lot, such as in Marqués's *La carreta* (*The Oxcart*, 1953).

In other transnational Afro-Caribbean imagery, Micaela shares desires with other island-women. Gardel gains passage into the Parisian music scene when a hurricane devastates the often-overlooked French colony (now Department) of Martinique, once again tying his beauty to death and decay (153). Gardel leaves behind a Haitian mistress and a Cuban lover who both commit suicide by setting themselves on fire (11). Micaela opts for a slower death, a *medicina/midecina* that keeps her alive but with which she ultimately longs to kill herself (11). Haiti and Cuba realised the most influential revolutions of their centuries. The Haitian Revolution represented the defeat of Napoleon by a coalition of enslaved and free Afrodescendants. The Cuban Revolution expelled the Batista government that had the backing of the United States during the Cold War. Yet both revolutions produced nations that have suffered great poverty and seen many dashed hopes as the years have passed. They burned in Changó's fire, not unlike how Gardel burned in his plane crash (11). Puerto Rico never realised its independence, and even Pedro Albizu Campos's appearance in the novel is only to remind the world that genocidal characters such as Cornelius Rhoads (1898–1959) have populated US medicine on the island (170). Albizu Campos leaked a secret personal letter from Rhoads elaborating his racist sentiments towards the islanders: 'lo que esta isla necesita no es trabajo de medicina social, sino un tsunami o algo que extermine a toda la población ... He hecho todo lo que he podido para adelantar el proceso de su exterminio; matando a ocho y trasplantando cáncer a algunos más' ('what this island needs is not social medicine work, but a tsunami or something to exterminate the entire population ... I have done everything I can to accelerate the process of their extermination; killing eight and transplanting cancer to a few others') (170–1). There is no sign of revolution or independence in the novel, here is only a melancholic, lonely lament for a sometimes horrifying, sometimes beautiful but always fleeting past and uncertainty about the future.

Sad Voices of the Mulatta-Antilles

Santos-Febres is also deconstructing the Puerto Rican-cosmopolitan binary with Micaela in opposition to Insularism. Her beauty places her in the tradition of the Island-Mulattas of Luis Palés Matos, whose *Tuntún de Pasa y Grifería* (*Tuntún of Kinks and Nappiness*, 1937) would be released two years after the death of Gardel. While it is clear that Micaela represents Puerto Rico in Santos-Febres's transnational romance, it is also clear that she represents the cosmopolitan, undeniably African coastline of the island in the tradition of the 'Mulata-Antilla', as in Palés's poem (82). If Palés presents islands and women as objects of desire, Santos-Febres presents them as suffering women who often love and lose – a more dynamic, melancholic vision of lands defined by the sea. In some ways, Palés broke with the Insularists by representing Black subjects, speech and customs in his poetry. In others, he reaffirmed their racism (his *negrista* poetry's initial rejection on the island), while elsewhere, like his endorsement by Blanco as an example of racial harmony on the island, he became a symbol of racial harmony that silences lived racism (Rivera Casellas, *Bajo* 20). Perivolaris considers his poetry a continuation of the harmonious 'great family' narrative (90). Branche claims Palés treated Black people as aberrations on the island and indulged in plantation fantasies by depicting Black bodies and folklore superficially, presenting Black people in subservient roles and even as foreigners (152–3). This exclusion is also part of the 'great family' myth (Santiago-Díaz 71). Gelpí observes that he transcended the boundaries of the island and connected it with the Caribbean (2801). Ríos Ávila deconstructs the Pedreira/Palés binary, noting that both make literature write the nation, be it a whitened colony or part of the mulatto Antilles (*Raza* 121). He says Pedreira imagines the soul of the family while Palés remembers its body, emphasising Blackness and femininity, the foci of Santos-Febres (*Raza* 123, 128). Yet his depictions are intentionally superficial (130). Ríos Ávila argues that Palés shows how the Caribbean *defracta* ('diffracts') the illusions of totalising discourses held both by US and Latin American thinkers, revealing the chaotic performativity of identity (*Raza* 158). Without abandoning the literary patriarch's carnivalesque eroticism, Santos-Febres represents a much more realistic, nuanced Afro-Caribbean woman's life, which Palés concealed beneath a veil of folklore, but she follows his lead in extending her settings beyond the island.

The Family Today

In 2015, the island's economy was in shambles, as it is today, so the novel's focus on finances reflects its political context. As Micaela faces her individual life and death, she is left wondering what it means to be a woman once she can choose not to bear fruit as well as choosing the time of her own demise. If the poverty and provinciality of the countryside (idealised by Insularism) is not enough for her, if the journey of the *jíbara* to the metropole (studying at Johns Hopkins) and back is not enough for her as René Marqués expected it to be, if cosmopolitanism presents itself as a fleeting relationship (the affair with Gardel), then what is Puerto Rico to do? When will it no longer be a developing nation that cannot be a nation? When will the world cease to turn its back on the island as it falls into multiple forms of depression – economic, cultural and psychological? Her Puerto Rico is melancholic and its identity undetermined. Like Dr Roberts, it has ambition and mobility, but it does not know what it wants. As Peñaranda-Angulo argues in her reading of *Fe*, discovering and reflecting upon history through higher education is a 'puerta hacia la libertad' ('door to freedom'), but I think Santos-Febres does not clearly show how to go through it (113).

The book ends with a series of existential questions for the island in general and for Black women in particular, personified by Micaela (197). What is clear is that the answer must be sought by a fractal combination of Western and non-Western ways of thinking community and the body. She ties the journeys of Mercuriana, Micaela and Gardel to the travels of Enlightenment-era European explorers. She does this to invert their colonial gaze. Referring to Mano Santa, she recalls that such explorers treated people like her grandmother as part of the flora and fauna of the lands they discovered, animalising them and making them objects of study (34). Alexander von Humboldt, for example, found his way to Cartagena and meets José Celestino Mutis (1732–1808), who is gathering plants like those of the indigenous people that Mercuriana finds before (71). Unfortunately, that expedition also crumbled (72). Humboldt continues his journey to Cuba, where he observes that the island is 'al mismo tiempo, metrópoli y colonia' ('at once metropole and colony') (72). He notices that Havana is as developed and enlightened as Europe, but that its countryside is as untamed as the Orinoco (72). She wonders if that seeming contradiction defines the whole Caribbean – that *curanderas* ('healers') operate alongside science (72). Micaela longs to find the secret of *corazón de viento* in his complete works, but there are none on the island – she must leave the limits of Insularism and the rejection of modernity. She ultimately finds *corazón de viento* when Gardel's secretary brings her a book that was being given away along with the others they brought her for entertainment (147). The author, Ledru, is also a lost French traveller who finds himself on Puerto Rico's tiny Isla de Cabras ('Goat Island') and then in Vacía Talega and Loíza (148). In these places, he finds Taínos growing *corazón de viento* (148). The enlightenment discovery of a healing plant in the mecca of Puerto Rican traditional Black culture inspires Micaela to improve herself and continue her family's tradition on the world stage through providing birth control (148). She breathes sacred energy into the plant and recalls her ancestors, even as she prepares it in a modern laboratory (182–3).

Undertakings great and small come and go. Perhaps fertility and sexuality are not the solutions to the island's problems now, so

Oshun is not the goddess to call upon. Yemaya is a mother of origins, of the past, of bittersweet sadness. The goddess of cemeteries who guards the boundaries between living and dead, Oya, is also goddess of storms and the winds of change. The breeze that blows ships off course, like those of Humboldt and Ledru, like the human breath that is the catalyst for *corazón de viento*, like that which has brought storms to the island for centuries has also cleared the way for new beginnings (184). Gardel dies a few years before the cure for his syphilis, penicillin, is perfected (196). *Corazón de viento* falls out of fashion once a Western birth control pill is invented (196). Micaela has chosen death, though she is not yet dead. She, and the island that she represents, are full of nostalgia for the optimism of the past. Yet she does not know what form her rebirth (if any) may take. All factors point to her being the fall of the House of Llanos Yabó because she has not had a child. Yet the novel is about both embracing and transcending the female body. She has embraced the mind. If the reader avoids Micaela's solipsism and toxic nostalgia, they/he/she can find a way out of the labyrinth of a Puerto Rico that continues to sink into decadence. The reader can imagine new families and a new nation with Afro and indigenous Boricuas that is representational and empowering for its three foundational groups as well as its relationship with the United States and the world.

This beautiful allegory, like *Fe*, has problematic elements. In 1937, the 'Euthanasia Law' (136) was passed on the island, leading to 34 per cent of women being sterilised between 1940 and 1960, as Luz Nereida Lebrón shows in the only published essay on the novel (444). If one has not seen Ana María García's documentary *La operación* (1982), one is not aware of the 'neo-Malthusian' history of family planning in Puerto Rico (García, 'Not' 38). During Operation Bootstrap, the US and local governments worked to convince women to have tubal ligation, resulting in the sterilisation of over one-third of the female population (García, 'Not' 38).

Arguably, Santos-Febres is showing how women used contraception to control their own lives, but it is clear that this programme was actually taking autonomy away from women, forcing them to reduce their family size. They would not have faced this treatment had they been rich, white and/or from the mainland.

Like Fe, Micaela cannot reverse this history, so she creates pleasure from the pain, but the reader cannot do so without informing herself about the broader history of family planning and colonial sterilisation. She poses a more nuanced question: would so many women have chosen sterilisation – informed or otherwise – had they had access to *corazón de viento*? Temporary birth control was difficult to access, and many women felt pressured to stop reproducing and work outside the home (García, 'Not' 38). Fertility is the centre of African faiths. Micaela is an *arriviste* who facilitates the appropriation of Black knowledge by the colonial government. She is no better (or worse) than Chica da Silva, who enslaved 104 Black workers. However, she has a responsibility for her actions that the reader inherits and interprets. She does not protect the opaque nature of Caribbean subjects, as Glissant might say (*Poetics* 189). That opacity allows for other fractals of knowledge and practice to develop under the relative control of Black subjects. Scholars of Afrodescent must ask when revelation is empowering to Black subjects and when allowing them to keep their secrets and their silences is most appropriate. Black subjects must have autonomy to decide.

La amante, like *Fe*, is an ambivalent family allegory of Puerto Rican history without clear directives for the future. Thorné's family of choice includes the Orishas, which in some cases are deified ancestors (Changó) and all of which are a familial pantheon (mothers, daughters, etc.). I have traced the *techné* of healing and destruction to Oshun and Yemaya, each of which personify loose equivalents to Derrida's philosophical *pharmakon*, which is at once medicine and poison. The family is matrifocal yet scattered. Writing is also a craft that Micaela cultivates, following her absent father. Sex work, Oshun's domain, is another family craft that links her to Gardel. Oshun could also be punishing her for betraying her secrets to the West for the sake of money, for Micaela's *corazón de vento* ('money heart'), another Deriddean wordplay of *viento* ('wind') and *vento* ('money' in Lunfardo) (155). The colours of the novel, gold and blue, represent the interplay of the two mothers who govern the plot, proud Oshun and sad Yemaya.

Micaela feels shame for her Afrodescent and for the blue *corazón de viento* ('wind heart'). Ultimately, shame of Puerto Rico drives her from the island, which may also have angered her spiritual mother Oshun. By negotiating with (neo-)colonial structures, she gains a formal education and succeeds in her career. Revealing the secret makes it fractal and evolving, as opposed to keeping it secret, which made it filial – static and linear. It creates community and intersubjectivity through her becoming Other with Gardel, her mirror image when one considers their parallel Atlantic voyages. The novel also reunites his story with that of his lost 'brothers,' el Negro Ricardo and the Tano, who may also be Afrodescendant. Through the transmission of a disease that can be interpreted as the curse of colonialism, the African diaspora is tied to other diasporas: Italians, Roma and Latinxs. The Black women of this text make Puerto Rico not a 'sick' country, but a place of healing through affirmative Blackness. *La amante* deconstructs the Black-Puerto Rican binary and the Black-Latin American binary, building on Palés's island-Mulattas. While she offers no definite solutions, Santos-Febres proffers fractal combinations of Western and non-Western ways of thinking about community and the body. She ties the journeys of Mercuriana, Micaela and Gardel to those of European scientists and explorers to invert their colonial gaze as she did with Palés.

Reproduction and control over it beg serious questions. Beginning around the time that the novel is set, in 1937, Puerto Rico, under US sovereignty, implemented its 'Euthanasia Law', leading to more than one-third of the island's women being sterilised. Arguably, Santos-Febres is showing how women used contraception to control their own lives, but it is clear that this programme was actually taking control away from them. Yet would so many women have chosen sterilisation had they had access to *corazón de viento*? Sometimes keeping secrets about Black cultures maintains their alterity and grants them more agency than communicating traditions to the outside world.

Conclusion

In both novels, white, male protagonists radically change alongside equally important Afrodescendant female protagonists in what Glissant would call a *rélation* (*Poetics* 27). Their becoming Other unveils elements of the Afrodescendant identity of both partners and their families. They come together by choice to explore their bodies. However, the author could have explored women's roles, ideas and history further if she had spent less time writing about white men. Micaela does not need a white, male double to represent Afro-Puerto Rico in the 1930s: the double might be another Black woman, like the nun Montse, who reveals a different side of Black, female identity in *Nuestra Señora* (264). Ramos Rosado observes that she is the *madrina* ('godmother') who is part of a non-traditional family, perhaps a syncretic one (*Destellos* 125). Close friends who care for others' children as well as madames and fixers receive this title (125). Weldt-Basson shows that the white male continues to be the 'narrative axis' and Montse's madness is not empowering ('White' 142). The white male is no doubt a double that allows her to create an aesthetics of Rélation between the West and its Other, but I fear that the white people take up too much of the text (Celis and Rivera 20; Irizarry 224).

Alternatively, Miguel Rosenzvit's novel *Fiebre negra* (*Black Fever*, 2008) is a Black-white love story set in the Black community of Buenos Aires in the mid-nineteenth century that city officials trapped and allowed to die from yellow fever in 1871. What would have happened if the love story connecting Puerto Rico to Argentina had taken an Afrodescendant woman into the forgotten Black area in the capital of a country that too often believes it has no Black people? The information is in George Reid Andrews's 1980 history and the documentary *Afroargentinos* (Jorge Fortes and Diego Ceballos, 2003). Weldt-Basson compares *Fe* to Argentine novelist Ana Gloria Moya's *Cielo de tambores* (*Drum Sky*, 2002), which dramatises the forgotten Afro-Argentinian fighters for national independence and has a Black, female narrator ('Memoria' 188–9). Arguably, the fact that Gardel was born in Toulouse and part of the novel is set in France contributed to *La amante* being awarded the National Pharmacy Academy Grand Prize in Literature in 2020 (MetroPR). Josephine Baker in Brazil and Parisian negrophilia's contributions to the birth of samba are two connections between France and Afro-Latin America that Shaw has studied in depth (1). *La amante* does not need *Gardel*.

Santos-Febres's penchant for dark, complex, erotic allegory informed by literary theory continues in the short stories of Arroyo Pizarro. Her lived experience as an atheist Black lesbian activist in Puerto Rico exemplify how biography influences text and reception. Clearly occupying a different positionality than the 1930s generation, she repeats and alters images of the slave ship, the hacienda and the Spanish Inquisition prison, creating insurgent yet suffering female protagonists.

Chapter 2
Yolanda Arroyo Pizarro: *Cimarronas*, Love and Breaking the Silence

Yolanda Arroyo Pizarro writes new foundational myths for Puerto Rico based on *cimarronas*, Black female rebels, that are counter-narratives to the 1898 US foundation and the hispanophile, Insularist family. Dávila Gonçalves notices this rupture, connecting Arroyo Pizarro to Santos-Febres, but she does not propose the new family model I am creating (38). Arroyo Pizarro corrects the exclusion of queer and Black subjects from the nation (Mendoza 1139). Her writing, seen as a whole, is a fractal family portrait. As a Black, out-of-the-closet lesbian who married a 'white guerrera negra' ('white Black warrior woman') poet-activist Zulma Oliveras Vega, she has formed a family of choice (*Negras*, trans. Alejandro Álvarez Nieves 7). Their ceremony in 2015 was the first same-sex wedding on the island (Melo). To marry, she and Oliveras Vega joined the case Conde-Vidal versus Rius-Armendariz, which began on 25 March 2014. Their marriage followed Arroyo Pizarro's divorce from the father of her daughter, Aurora, so the formation and reformation of families is rarely easy or painless (Acevedo, interview 125). While Arroyo Pizarro's grandmother nurtured little Yolanda and bolstered the girl's self-esteem, the author's mother abandoned her, a loss the author believes drives her writing (127). Her thematics have evolved to depict both Blackness and queerness in compelling ways. Mendoza has compared her work on enslaved women to *Fe* (1142). She lives on the archipelago, but her dialogue with North America and the rest of the Caribbean has been constant. Her challenges to a homogeneous, insular Puerto

Rican identity have been unrelenting since her *Los documentados* ('*The Documented*', 2004), which is about Dominican immigrants to the island. However, her first novel *Caparazones* (2010) and her collective anthologies of *Cachaperismos: Poesía y narrativa lesboerótica* ('*Dike Stuff: Lesbian Erotic Poetry and Narrative*', 2010, 2012) show that she created a lesbian persona, selecting which facet of her identity to emphasise (LaFountain-Stokes, 'Recent' 520). A gifted speaker and activist, she has had to perform her identities in public settings and declare the nature of the communities to which she belongs. As Arriaga-Arando argues, she uses Glissant's Caribbean discourse to break with the Insularism of the 1930s that still holds sway over race, gender and sexuality (197). She is part of the fractal Caribbean, and the new national/diaspora families that she creates and depicts are giving visibility to Black women of multiple identities going back to the enslavement period.

The textual interplay between Arroyo Pizarro's *Saeta: The Poems* (2011), the short-story collection *las Negras* (2012) and her more recent works portray Black women's familial bonds with Africa and each other through the liminal natures of love, death and violence. The short stories are the centrepiece of this chapter. The author considers *las Negras* to be the work she had the most difficulty writing, since it is a product of lived racism, so the splitting of the Afro-Boricua family is once again a painful one, and its melancholy is ever-present (Fuster Lavín, interview 116). She relates it to the first time she learned in school that, despite slavery, there were still exemplary Black people on the island (116). The first edition of *las Negras* is a triptych of stories in which the slave ship, the prison and the plantation are the primary settings. 'Wanwe' depicts the shattered bonds of family and faith suffered during the Middle Passage, 'Matronas' refashions the 'turn towards death' into a uniquely feminine form of rebellion, and 'Saeta' erects an antiplantation personified by a female maroon. Ramos Rosado considers the three stories a portrait of the many contributions Black women made to Puerto Rico as well as the forms of *marronage* they used to empower themselves ('Mayra' 207). This narrative cycle appears to be ongoing, as her Technology, Education and Design talk (2016), her poetry collection *Blancoides* (2018) and her prose in *Afrohistoria* (2018) show. Material from the poetry collection also contextualises the narrative works and allows one to visualise the author's evolution as a Black writer.

Arroyo Pizarro: Family and Biographical Elements in Her Black Poetry and Narrative

Saeta: The Poems is her first extended written work devoted solely to Afro-Boricua identity. In her acknowledgements, she gives explicit reasons for the new focus:

> this book was made possible thanks to René Thomas, Director of Black Cultural Centre at Purdue University in West Lafayette, IN. I was very happy to have instructed a group of students in a Creative Writing Workshop Taller de Mujer Negra Cimarrona Puertorriqueña on October 2011 in San Juan, Puerto Rico ... Gracias por recordarme que soy afro puertorriqueña' ('Thank you for reminding me that I am Afro-Puerto Rican'). (7)

Clearly, US Black academic culture had reached out to her and, in a broader sense, to the island. I do not mean to say that Arroyo Pizarro is uncritically copying US imports – on the contrary, she refers to US 'African [American] Studies' as a product of the 'colono ejemplar por excelencia' ('exemplary colonist par excellence') (63). She claims that it should be adjusted to Puerto Rico's history (63). The author's use of diaspora discourse has another origin in Latin America, as she notes not only in the term 'afro-puertorriqueña', but also in the title of the story that follows her poems: 'Sin raza, una historia de bullying en el colegio: Reflexión en torno al 2011: Año Internacional de los Afrodescendientes' ('No Race, a Story of School Bullying: Reflection Regarding 2011: International Year of Afrodescendants') (125). Her diaspora framework is 'international' due to the UNESCO commemoration, and it became even more international through the essay's translation into French (127). Arroyo Pizarro was disappointed that Puerto Rico did virtually nothing to commemorate the 2011 International Year for People of African Descent, in contrast with the 2012 Primer Foro Internacional de Afrodescendencia y Descolonización de la Memoria ('First International Forum of Afrodescent and Decolonisation of Memory'), in Caracas. Ironically, at this event, they discussed her book in an academic setting before her homeland (*Afrohistoria* 59). While it is common on the island to claim that any complaint of racism inicates an inferiority complex, Venezuela was discussing 'afroreparaciones' ('reparations for enslavement') (61). Arroyo Pizarro, longing to start a similar discussion on the archipelago, notes that one cannot contemplate reparations if one does not understand their immersion in a society that is mixed-race due to the brutality of slavery and colonisation (62). Her ouvre creates sustained Afro-Boricua visibility.

Reversing the cultural erasure and distortion of Blackness is important for her relationship with her daughter, Aurora, as her acknowledgements exhibit: 'a Aurora, gran Negra cimarrona de mi casta / por haberse parido de mi cuerpo' ('to Aurora, great Black maroon woman of my blood, / for giving birth to herself from my own body') (*las Negras* 13; *Negras*, trans. Álvarez Nieves 7). Aurora is also the point of departure for Arroyo Pizarro's Technology, Education and Design talk, in which she takes literally the rhetorical question poet Fortunato Vizcarrondo asks, '¿Y tu abuela, dónde está?' ('What about your grandmother? Where is she?'). The poem is teasing white or mulatto islanders that overlook their Black ancestry so as to appear whiter (Vizcarrondo 77). On the other hand, she argues that Aurora should know that side of her family and be proud of it. In the Cátedra de Mujeres Negras Ancestrales ('Ancestral Black Women's Study Group'), Arroyo Pizarro teaches Afro-Puerto Ricans of varied ages how to use archival research to rediscover their family roots, including their enslaved ancestors. The *cimarrona* is also a reaction to Arroyo Pizarro's trials with whitening discourse. Ramos Rosado argues that Arroyo Pizarro contributes meaningfully to history by representing female maroons, which canonical literary and historical accounts excluded ('Mayra' 206).

According to the account 'Sin raza' ('No Race'), the problem Arroyo Pizarro faced as a child was not that she did not have a race, but that she was racialised (*Afrohistoria* 74). In another essay, she recalls that her nickname was 'Bembetrueno' ('Black Thunder Lips') (7). If the teacher mentioned the word 'Africa', if classmates got close enough to her curly hair, if she came out of the bathroom during recess or break, her classmates taunted her – and, apparently, only her – for being Black (*Saeta* 126). She expresses her sympathy and solidarity with a girl who recently faced a prison sentence for fighting back when students bullied her for being Black. Like her, other girls need heroines, strength and love as Black women (5–6).

Arroyo Pizarro was part of an extreme minority attending an institution with colonial roots. Most students are presumably white or whitened and descended from Spanish and/or US colonisers. The school – Colegio San Vicente Ferrer – is Catholic, tying it further to the colonial discourses that she discusses in the poems and short stories (*Saeta* 125). However, racism goes beyond the classroom: she prays to 'dios' ('god') every night to wake up white, presumably to have peace (126). Her own grandmother, who raised her, told her that she was born white but that she was accidentally dyed Black when she fell into a cup of coffee (126). As whimsical as it sounds, this story merely repeats the negative associations of Blackness as a 'stain' that cursed little Yolanda, who struggled to remove it. The author expresses continued discomfort with the quest to be 'white' or 'Black' enough, even as she creates a new definition of 'Afro-Puerto Rican' for herself (127). 'Sin raza', which shares the coffee origin myth with her TED talk, entwines her quest to rediscover her Black family – her grandmother and beyond – her Black self and her new and sometimes combative identity as an atheist. Taking the Catholic Church to task for its crimes during colonialism is part of her own fight for freedom from her alienating origins as a little Black girl, fear and pain that she must still recall today as a successful writer. The author is striving to find and create models not of victims but of fighters with control, strength and a plan. Their characterisation often displays an affirmative African identity and Black solidarity, and the protagonists are women. This emphasis, which is total in the short stories, is a narrative innovation in Puerto Rican letters on the island – no other work gives such primacy to Black women's voices. In *las Negras* and *Saeta*, the diaspora is formed as families are torn apart and communities are re-formed in Puerto Rico.

Wanwe Loses and Regains Her Family

The short story 'Wanwe' emphasises matriarchal familial structures, much like the author's own, and it charts the disintegration of African families. The story is set in a slave ship embarking on the Middle Passage. The title character, an enslaved Namib woman, is witness to the torture and death of a woman who attempts to escape the enslavers while being canoed to the ship (26, 39). Wanwe flashes back to the *ureoré* ritual that bound women in Africa and to the memories before her and her mother's capture, a time when she focused on growing up and selecting a male partner.

From what I can tell, the *ureoré* ritual is her artistic creation, not the result of an ethnographic study. According to a note in the text:

> In the *ureoré* ceremony, girls who grow up together, like sisters, sleep very close to one another, forming a line that connects them by their shoulders. When the grownups aren't looking ... the girls play *ureoré* with the boys. If the grownups catch [*sic*] them, they would all be punished, because the shoulder game is for females – forbidden to males. (*Negras*, trans. Álvarez Nieves 35)

In the story, the ritual symbolises an idealised feminine Africa. I do not interpret it as lesbian eroticism, as Falconí Trávez does ('Puerto Rico', 60). It is a circle that the inevitability of enslavement breaks, since the narrator is recalling it after her kidnapping. Rituals like these were central to many African women's life cycles and, they believed, their ability to have children (Sweet, *Recreating* 61). The entire Namibian village that she describes has women at its heart, which is likely to be similar to the reality of many women on the continent. The protagonist's mother helps her select a husband by her twenty-ninth cycle (Arroyo Pizarro, *las Negras* 36–7). Paralleling the *ureoré*, the cycle part of *Saeta: The Poems*, is (roughly) structured as a side-by-side triptych in Spanish and Swahili. 'Menstruo / hedhi' ('menstruation') and 'óvulo / yai' ('ovum') are the longest sections, and the third, 'pre menstrual / kabla ya hedhi' ('premenstrual') consists entirely of an epigraph from the final stanza of Julia de Burgos's 'A Julia de Burgos' ('To Julia de Burgos') (21, 63, 123). Arroyo Pizarro is using the cyclic female body and matrifocal (yet scattered and reconstituted) families to create an oppositional history to colonisation and slavery. Menstruation is associated with uniquely female experiences, as in the poem 'nuestro brujo sabe convertirse' ('our shaman knows how to turn into'), in which there is an African ritual drum that only menstruating women can play (*Saeta* 42). Arraiga-Arando considers describing menstruation here and depicting women warriors in 'Matronas' as examples of 'lesbian language', yet no lesbians appear in either (201). His observation that menstruation ties her to Oshun is astute, and I say it is another example of the spiritual aesthetic of fractal families (203).

Her mother, a huntress who takes her children alongside her but who protects them, exemplifies the imaginary tribe's matriarchy.

The choice of the hunting mother relates to the Nigerian proverb on which she based the collection: 'Hasta que los leones tengan sus propios historiadores, la historia de la caza siempre glorificará al cazador' ('Until lions have their own historians, the history of the hunt will always glorify the hunter') (*Afrohistoria* 47). Famously, it is the lioness that hunts for her young and her pride, so this metaphor is appropriate for creating a matriarchal tribal culture in the work. It is an empowering variation on the dehumanising animalisation of the enslaved. The lioness-mother also represents a lost, silenced, but inspirational African past (Falconí Trávez, 'Puerto Rico' 61).

The author claims that the lion is the metaphor of two figures she considers central to her own poetics. The 'lions' of history are the 'Ancestras', a neologism she created for Black female 'Ancestors', a word that is masculine in standard Spanish ('ancestro'). She alters the term to highlight the performative matrilinearity of her project. It also alludes to Yoruba-based religions that involve spirit possession by deified ancestors (Moreno Vega, *Altar* 281). The author is more interested in the trope of 'Ancestras' as a means to 'narrar mis carencias y obsesiones' ('narrate my lack and my obsessions') (78). Arroyo Pizarro, however, is opposed to venerating Afro-Caribbean deities (Acevedo, interview 142). The writer is not obliged to a mimetic representation of historical events, so she uses the metaphor of trance in a manner similar to the poetic muse. In workshops, she tells her Black creative writing students to allow an enslaved spirit to inhabit their bodies, becoming an 'avatar' that tells the 'true' history of slavery (*Afrohistoria* 52). Hence, 'family' relates to historical groups, religion (and its adaptation as metaphor) and the creative process like it does for Santos-Febres. The corporeal aspect of trance religions makes them an apt metaphor for dance, too. The female troupe las Kalalusas adapted choreography for 'Wanwe' as Afro-Dominicans, an identity that bravely confronts the dictatorial legacy of Trujillismo's authoritarian *hispanidad* whitening discourse during the Dominican Día de la Mujer Afro ('Day of the Afrodescendant Woman') 2014 (*Afrohistoria* 54).

In 'Wanwe', during the African mother's hunt, enslavers from another tribe come to take her and her children before selling them to Europeans on the coast. The story of a mother's capture, repeated millions of times over history, transcends the individual character's trials and unifies the three-part narrative. In the final story of *las Negras*, 'Saeta', the protagonist Tshanwe dreams of her home in Namibia among the Namaqua (117). She blows a whistle that signifies there is an animal too great to overcome in the first story (44). In the third, the sound is to call women to war, but it only brings with it the sensation of loneliness on the plantation (118). As she puts it, only the frogs hear her, which in the worldview of the characters is a symbol of the 'frog in the moon' from the first story of *las Negras*, which sees the injustices of the world (51). Tshanwe turns the symbol of enslavement – the whistle – into a battle cry that reunites African women in a collective struggle against enslavement. The anti-plantation or *palenque* community ethos that the whistle's call represents stands in contrast to the desiccated Africa left behind by slavery: 'Rivers have turned to sand. Water currents are no more than muddy, infected holes … Now this land has an overabundance of dearth; her daughters have been taken away' (*Negras*, trans. Álvarez Nieves 130). A dead Africa, the source of Puerto Rico's plantation labour, gives the lie to the harmonious Puerto Rican hacienda painted by early twentieth-century fantasies and its hypocritical family values.

The book is not a historical study, but it points to a deeper message: that one of the primary traumas of the Middle Passage was the destruction of families. Puerto Rico was part of the greater network of the slave trade that the Portuguese dominated in the Iberian empires. Sweet follows the biography of captive Domingos Álvares from Dahomey to Brazil and then to Lisbon during the eighteenth century. The impact of captivity on Álvares, like the African women depicted in *las Negras*, while it would leave anyone disturbed, was filtered through his Dahomeyan worldview (Sweet, *Domingos* 68). According to the historian:

> Some of the enslaved probably found the isolation and uprooting from family to be unbearably traumatic. In stable societies of the Gbe-speaking region, an individual's social identity was defined largely by his or her place among family and kin. Wealth, power and prestige were measured primarily in people, not land or money. Thus, a premium was placed on enlarging the kinship unit – through polygamous marriages, childbirth, adoption and even the enslavement of outsiders … In short, a person was a person only insofar as he was a member of a kinship group, and the kin group was defined by the number and quality of people in its ranks. (Sweet, *Domingos* 68)

Hence, beyond the struggle to recall a lost homeland, like Ndizi does in 'Matronas', African characters are struggling to piece together a sense of self through a collectivist cultural value of which the isolation and alienation of enslavement reminded them daily (69). 'Family' meant 'village' for many African peoples. 'Under these trying circumstances, new communities mimicked patterns of reciprocity that characterised natal kinship units' (Sweet, *Domingos* 69). In Arroyo Pizarro's poem 'Separated from Our Blood', a captive leaves the slave ship in the New World to find herself so alienated that her literal 'blood taste[s] different' (33). In *Recreating Africa* (2003), and exemplified by losing the *ureoré* game, Sweet goes into detail:

> To be removed from the kinship network was to alter the life cycle in ways that are unimaginable to most Westerners. The meanings of the markers that define the human life span – birth, childhood, adolescence, marriage, child-rearing, old age and dying – were all radically transformed. (*Recreating* 58)

The *bozal* (African-born, unassimilated) women of *las Negras* form new communities through collective pain (like Wanwe watching a woman's earrings torn out before she is hanged, and another thrown to the sharks while alive) and aggression (killing the enslavers in the stories that follow).

The author has poetic licence to play with eras and origins, and so she chooses the Namaqua, a Namibian indigenous people who were massacred alongside the Herero women warriors, not during the Transatlantic slave trade but under the Germans in the twentieth century. Rejecting a single origin is rejecting filiation like Glissant. Arroyo Pizarro is proposing two opposing origin myths for Black women in Puerto Rico, each beginning with 'el primer recuerdo pudiera haber sido' ('the first memory could have been') (*las Negras*, my trans. 25). The first is the ship that made her a transatlantic slave; the other, playing on the ambiguity of the subjunctive verb *pudiera*, was her kidnapping by a rival group of Africans in her village (43). This second origin is one that incorporates more of the worldview of a person raised on the African continent and a story of rupture, anger and marronage. Falconí Trávez has noticed the theme of resistance throughout the work ('De cuerpos' 139). Gilroy sees a 'turn towards death' as a form of rebellion in the Anglophone slave narrative tradition, in which Afrodescendants saw death as deliverance from the living death of slavery (63). Dávila Gonçalves perceives the conflict of Eros (life/sex) and Thanatos (death) in her work (40). Arroyo Pizarro is writing against the Puerto Rican myth of the harmonious plantation in which the enslaved were a beloved part of the family. She is giving them agency through violence, even when that violence reaches the extreme of remorselessly killing newborns. The depiction of this violence denaturalises its sanitised depiction in the literary canon and emphasises the Black body, as Falconí Trávez argues ('De cuerpos,' 137, 141).

'Wanwe' ties the loss of family and the recreation of it to an analogous relationship with religion. For many African peoples, religion *is* family in a literal sense. Ancestors are objects of worship, deities are merely very ancient and powerful ancestors and living elders are fonts of wisdom because they are closer to the spirit realm. 'Wanwe' is the beginning of a progression of doubt into atheism that culminates in a refashioning of African myth in the final story. Assuming that 'Sin raza' ('No Race') is autobiographical, it is understandable that the author is abandoning the faith that failed her, Catholicism, when she prayed for relief from racist bullying. Fundamentalist Protestantism, almost universally homophobic, likely did not fit her, either, which is why, since 1998, she has stopped using the pseudonym Gabriela Soyna (*Afrohistoria* 81). She uses her birth name to publish what she believes is her true identity: Black, atheist and queer.

In the case of Wanwe, she is horrified that she watches a woman die from illness without receiving an important death ritual from her community (34). Beyond dehumanising the woman, this silence tears at the collectivist identity of each enslaved person on the ship. In the absence of a sense of self, Wanwe longs to die so that she can return to her ancestors (27). Death is an escape – not a journey to the afterlife. 'Ancestral beings do not liberate them. They do not appear, despite the women's summons. The new deities do not listen either ... Orún, Olódùmare, Bàbá, Ìyá and the goddesses who are still on Earth do not appear' (*Negras*, trans. Álvarez Nieves 57). One wonders by a Namibian from southern Africa is thinking of Yoruba gods from many miles north, but the message is greater than the historical truth: enslavement provoked a religious crisis in the enslaved. Clearly, these future Afro-Puerto Ricans do not see Christianity as part of their national essence as the Insularists did but as part of a brutal colonial system.

'Saeta': Return of the Arrow

Arroyo Pizarro had already published 'Saeta', the short story, before *las Negras* in *Ojos de luna* (*Moon Eyes*, 2007), but the author clearly felt it belonged alongside these other stories of enslavement and struggle. It takes aim at the benevolent, patriarchal hacienda myth, erecting a feminine anti-plantation personified by the *cimarrona*. Ramos Rosado considers it important that she depicts the sexual violence of enslavement ('Mayra' 207). Count Georgino Pizarro rapes Tshanwe, a *bozal* he names 'Teresa,' while Jwaabi ('Juana') watches and awaits her 'turn' (trans. Álvarez Nieves 103). The young master Gregorio's dog dies, so he cries 'He's dead, and no one knows why' (109). Tshanwe finds an Amerindian arrowhead in the dog's body and keeps it as an amulet (110). Early one morning, the master takes her and Jwaabi to the shed where he keeps his archery equipment for hunting. He rapes them again, but this time Tshanwe takes his bow and arrow, recalling women warriors of the Namaqua (115–6). Continuing cruel rituals, the master's sons Trino and Gregorio stab her, almost fatally (123). She fights back, so the enslaver beats her, apparently to death (125). He orders male captives to bury her, but it rains, so they leave her body exposed. She escapes, perhaps with the help of the spirits of the Namaqua warriors (130). The white males go out for target practice the next day, shooting their arrows into the forest (131). One arrow returns, killing Don Georgino (131).

The author shakes the notion of the 'peaceful' plantation from the first page. It begins *in media res* with the rape scene. Throughout the plot, there are doubles. First, the captor assaults Tshanwe while Jwaabi watches; then, he reverses their roles. The plantation owner is drunk constantly, so his violent acts are accompanied by his psychological and emotional loss of control; he repudiates the notion of the benevolent patriarch. First, he wrestles with his son, which results in the boy punching him in the face and making him bleed. The master's fallibility is an opening for Tshanwe to strike. The symmetry of this back and forth culminates in the cathartic moment when Tshanwe kills him, ending the cycle of violence. The sexual violence of the plantation is part of how Tshanwe learns language, including her Christian name, 'Teresa'. The violence culminates in a resignification of 'no one knows why'. In the last line, she applies the phrase she learned because of the dog's death

– apparently at the hands of indigenous maroons – to the vengeance of killing the alcoholic *pater familias* with one well-placed shot. Her arrow bears the Amerindian arrowhead, and it is like a boomerang that mysteriously fires back at the shots of the masters.

A fractal reading of the retaliation keeps in mind Glissant's image of arrow nomadism. Ríos Ávila sees in the Caribbean a constant non-linear movement of thought that changes the goal-orientated path of filiation, conquest or 'straight shooting' ('Pájaro' 59). The zigzag of the Count's arrow, first lost then abruptly returning, represents a plantation gone awry and a family of warriors that has formed (*las Negras* 130). That *manigua* ('forest/sacred space/slave rebel stronghold') is beginning the long, meandering process of destroying and reforming the rigid structures of the colony.

In 'Saeta', the *bozal* Tshanwe cannot speak Spanish and would usually be treated like an 'idiot', a term for which *bozal* is now a synonym (Maddox and Stephens 83). Yet I agree with Rivera Casellas that speaking primarily the tongue of her mother breaks up the monolingual world that the hispanophile master attempts to impose and is a source of resistance (109). Her discovery of the master's mortality evokes Gonzalo Fernández de Oviedo's 1532 account in which the Taínos discover that the Spaniards are not gods, which results in the indigenous rebelling and killing the invaders under Chief Hatuey (Rodríguez López 14). Luz Angélica Kirschner et al. consider Hatuey part of a decolonial genealogy of human rights in Latin America (4). Hidalgo de Jesús sees the story's conclusion as Tshanwe growing from victim to executioner, assuming agency (*Mujeres* 314).

Reason is not opposed to all faiths equally in Arroyo Pizarro's work, because they help her imagine. The author's rejection of Christianity in the book does not extend to a complete rejection of African religions because these myths exist to enhance the health of the faithful, not to hold them back with prohibitions (28). The narrator relates how an invisible (and perhaps inexistent) shaman brings her back to life after death (as opposed to awaiting the Christian heaven) with the power of the warrior women of Namaqua, her ancestors (129). This 'embrujo' ('spell'), this use of an arcane, incomprehensible *bozal* language, is, for the implicit author, a manipulation of superstition to pragmatic ends, which the author considers central to the tryptic: 'cuerpo, armas y venganza' ('body, weapons and vengeance') (*Afrohistoria* 88). It supports her right to just war.

There are two possible causes for the 'resurrection' of the rebel, spirits or human obliviousness. Dávila Gonçalves notes how the ending breaks with the realist aesthetic of the exposition and development of the plot (55). The story's return to myth speaks to Arroyo Pizarro's uniqueness as an atheist writing in the Afro-Latin American tradition (personal interview). She refers to herself as an 'atea militante' ('militant atheist'), which has drawn accusations of 'Eurocentrism' and even 'hispanismo' from those who believe in African spirits (*Afrohistoria* 29). She counterargues that she views Regla de Ocha and similar diaspora faiths as examples of stigmatised cultural resistance and survival (*Afrohistoria* 12). She also suggests that Black people should renounce Christianity out of sheer 'dignidad' ('dignity') after its repeated justification of slavery (29). Atheism is a form of decolonisation for her (31). Aesthetically, the return of spirits after a graphic apparent death is another element that she shares with Morrison's *Beloved*, which Brown calls 'a collective anger steeped in the melancholy of the bereft', regardless of one's belief or disbelief (*Repeating* 104).

In *Afrohistoria*, the author reflects on the role of the *cimarrona* ('female maroon') in her writing, which she argues is a creative historiography. When she writes, she writes from 'ira' ('rage') at the injustices of history (48). She sees the *cimarronas* of history as proof that her 'bisabuelos' ('great-grandparents') were not 'sumisos o dóciles' ('submissive and docile') as she was taught in school, rejecting Marqués's imagery (48). She wants to show both their historical contributions and their attempts to escape (50). She goes so far as to claim that women held a 'papel protagónico' ('active role') in the majority of slave uprisings, although evidence for that is scarce (51). Evoking the *cimarrona* figure reflects her current role as an activist that is facing multiple forms of oppression head on: patriarchy, racism and heteronormativity, so it is no wonder she is looking to people who fight a Goliath-like system and form just parallel structures. *Cimarronas* seem to be founding something from nothing, just like Arroyo Pizarro must feel as she looks to the island's hegemonic literary and historical traditions: there are no slave narratives and few slave biographies in either (53). She claims that resistance is the only correct ideological place from which one can write about Black women (63, 81). She expressly wants to memorialise enslaved Black women without victimising them (83). For Arroyo Pizarro, to be *cimarrona* was to be seditious, creative, freedom-seeking, hardworking and in control of one's destiny (62). She labours to show that *afropuertorriqueñas* are 'hijas del heroísmo' ('daughters of heroism'), once again linking family to identity, nationality and disorder (*Afrohistoria* 94). This desire has driven her since 1998, when she adopted the pseudonym Gabriela Soyna while she was still a fundamentalist Christian (*Afrohistoria* 81). 'Soyna' composed the lines that would become the epigraph to *las Negras*: an ode to the omnipresence of *cimarronas* that led slave uprisings throughout Puerto Rican history (*Afrohistoria* 81). Hence, before she found the rebels in history, she willed them into being for herself and for other Black women as an empowering foundational narrative. The author has already brought to light the case of Mayagüez, Puerto Rico, where most captives were females, where women worked the fields and where more than one-third of the enslavers were female (97). She is deepening our understanding of Puerto Rican women's role in history and linking them to the rest of the Americas. Yet her insights are not 'specific' to the Caribbean, as Hidalgo de Jesús argues ('Mujer' 5; Arroyo Pizarro, personal interview).

Arroyo Pizarro is innovatively adding female protagonists to the long literary tradition of Spanish American maroons and *palenques*, as she notes in *Afrohistoria* (61). Glissant considers maroons to be not only historical runaway slaves but also cultural resistance towards European-American culture and the formation of new communities (*Poetics* xxii). Historians themselves, even when they began to write histories of marginalised groups in Latin America, tended to focus on those who took a direct approach to rebelling against the slave system. The most iconic example of these histories is Miguel Barnet's *Cimarrón* (*Biography of a Runaway Slave*, 1966), composed primarily of interviews with former maroon and *mambí* (Cuban independence infantryman) Esteban Montejo. Since the Cuban Revolution had recently triumphed, there was a new emphasis on telling the story of the oppressed and rebellious, and so Montejo's narrative became the first *testimonio*, the genre of 'anti-literature' that the Cuban Casa de las Américas came to celebrate in its awards and publishing in the 1970s (Sklodowska 1). Furtado notes that this kind of approach dominated until the 1980s, when other historiography on slave history became common

(559). Researchers such as Barnet are purveyors of the 'thing-Zumbi' binomial, in which the enslaved must be fighters or otherwise studies treat them as if enslavement completely objectified them (559). Furtado, in her study on Chica da Silva, notes that these approaches tended to emphasise male rebels. Often, captive women negotiated with enslavers more than taking direct action against them, since patriarchy enjoined them to remain with their children and to seek better futures for them (580). Arroyo Pizarro notes the negotiations of concubines like 'Teresa', but she frames them in the language of struggle and emphasises physical confrontation as a challenge to an intolerable, unjust system. At the most carnal level, Arroyo Pizarro gives the example of sex workers not allowing clients to kiss them on the mouth – women have agency to struggle and bargain, even in the most oppressive circumstances (personal interview).

Arroyo Pizarro challenges the masculinist nature of the thing-Zumbi paradigm by adding a female protagonist, Tshanwe, who must negotiate with her rapist for a time, but who ultimately takes the fight to him. In this way, she adds to prose what Krudas Cubensi do in their song 'Oye se busca' ('Hey, I'm Looking For'): *cimarronas* and rebels (Arroyo Pizarro, *Afrohistoria* 9). In *Afrohistoria*, she links the Puerto Rican *cimarronas* to female warriors from throughout the Caribbean like the Mulatresse Solitude of Guadeloupe and the Garífunas of Guatemala (*Afrohistoria* 92–3, 132). This international solidarity is supported by the influence of Moreno Vega, whom she met at a book talk on her *Women Warriors of the Afro-Latina Diaspora* (2012), and who works to denounce 'el racismo cifrado en la debilidad de la mujer' ('racism coded as women's weakness') (115). On the other hand, Arroyo Pizarro makes the problematic claim that she is giving 'voz' ('voice') to these women, which will always be driven by her own 'carencias y obesiones' ('lack and obsessions') (99). She is not limited to evidence as a historian would be, but we must recall Spivak's warning that one cannot simply 'listen' to the subaltern, since we perceive them through our own culture, discourse and desires, leaving misunderstandings and silences, as Santos-Febres notes (*Sobre* 61).

Baralt's *Esclavos rebeldes: Conspiraciones y sublevaciones de esclavos en Puerto Rico (1795–1873)* (1982), which Arroyo Pizarro references in *Afrohistoria*, exemplifies the thing-Zumbi paradigm (79). His study exemplifies the 'óptica patriarcal' ('patriarchal viewpoint'), which

Ramos Rosado argues that Arroyo Pizarro dispels in her introduction to *Negras* (17). Baralt's breakthrough is to show that, 'contrario a lo que siempre se había creído, los esclavos de la isla se rebelaron con frecuencia. El número de conspiraciones conocidas ... sobrepasa los cuarenta intentos' ('as opposed to what was always believed, slaves on the island often rebelled. The number of known conspiracies ... exceeds forty attempts') (*Esclavos* 11). Baralt is abandoning the myth of the peaceful hacienda where Afrodescendants accepted the paternalist care of the *pater familias*. He is also keeping in mind the particularities of Puerto Rico, which did not have large *palenques*, or fugitive families, due to geographical restrictions – captives would often attempt to flee to nearby islands like the Republic of Haiti in addition to forming small 'anti-Plantations' (158–9). According to Arroyo Pizarro, important exceptions were Santurce, Loíza and Río Grande, and her work should compel historians to delve deeper into their history (*Afrohistoria* 62).

Arroyo Pizarro's poem 'fugas y rebeliones' breaks with the 'great family's' colonial gaze and imagines how captive conspirators must have felt in 1821: 'la piel arrancada a latigazos / retoñará cicatrizada' ('the skin torn off by the whip / will sprout back in scars') (100). They plan to take Figueres's plantation, arm themselves and then 'liberarán esclavos de otras haciendas / atacarán a las mujeres blancas / a los niños blancos / a los amos poderosos' ('they shall free the slaves from other haciendas / they shall attack the white women / the white children / the powerful masters') (101). The repeated use of the future tense, which often has an epic tone in Spanish, adds excitement to the poem. It also highlights a future that never came to be, since betrayal undermined the attack (101). Arroyo Pizarro compares this betrayal to that of Africans that sold each other into slavery because of 'temer la destrucción española' ('fearing Spanish destruction') (101). While she likely means 'Portuguese destruction' on the continent, she is presenting Africa as a family that turned on one another in the face of colonial savagery. She notes that the enslaved are so enraged by this that they plan to eradicate everyone in the 'legitimate' plantation family, including women and children. While this may seem excessive, it is not different from what befell the so-called 'Slave Coast' of Africa.

The author's *marronage* subverts the paternalist literary canon. In the poem 'Arms', which depicts Tshanwe's rape, the narrator laments tragic mulattas like those Rivera Casellas analyses ('La poética' 101):

> everything smells like decomposition
> my putrefaction mulatta's name
> which is what I am now
> the bastard child of love
> my daughters will be some quadroons
> may say some Tapia y Rivera
> las hijas de la mulata (the mulatta's daughters)
> may mumble some Cayetano Coll y Toste
> these violators broke a path between the centuries
> they interfere the imaginary mulatto woman's universe
> parallel existence
> forever exclusions
> contradictions in my own experience. (51)

While she notes that the abolitionist Tapia and the folklorist Coll y Toste 'broke a path' that gave Afrodescendants a prominent role in literature, they are simultaneously 'violators' of both the Eurocentric canon and the voices of the enslaved women. The cognate in Spanish, *violador*, means rapist, so Arroyo Pizarro may be going so far as to compare the violation of their mediation of women's lives to the physical and emotional violation of rape, which Tshanwe experiences. While I find that she goes too far, given Tapia's efforts to end slavery through *La cuarterona*, she gives voice to understandable frustration with the depiction of Black, female characters without self-conscious Black writers, which amounts to the silencing of Black women throughout the period of enslavement. The poem also speaks of familial legitimacy, turning the notion on its head – instead of Tshanwe being merely part of the master's illegitimate lineage, the rape by white men that perpetuates this lineage is itself delegitimised.

Briefly, Arroyo Pizarro takes aim at the heteronormative depiction of the plantation that marks the 'great family' narrative. However, the only representation of lesbianism is rape, which confirms my position that, in *Saeta: The Poems* and *las Negras*, she is highlighting Blackness but not LGBTQ+ identity. Anyone can torture and humiliate regardless of their sexuality. Slave mistresses are decried for their abuses in 'no me castigues, ama' ('don't punish me, missus'), in which a captive begs her enslaver not to have her tortured for cavorting with maroons (87). The mistress in the previous poem, 'mi dueña me regala tres vestidos' ('my owner gives me three dresses'), combines torture with sex (83). The mistress burns the captive's dresses in a rage and tells her not to make any noise when the enslaver rapes her (83). Yet, when the two women are alone, the mistress makes her lift up her skirt and act out the rape while the mistress fingers her (84). She orders the captive to make sex noises for her in exchange for new clothes (84–5). Once again, this abuse points to the difficulty women from different strata of society have had in forming solidarity, since their positions of power have been the source of multiple forms of violence over the centuries.

'Matronas': Maternity and Marronage

'Matronas' ('Midwives') later appeared in Martín Sevillano's anthology *Puerto Rico indócil* (*Indocile Puerto Rico* 2015), which, as the title suggests, alludes to Marqués's figure of the docile Puerto Rican. Since 2000, however, Puerto Rican narrative has been marked by its focus on violence (Martín Sevillano 11). 'Los textos aquí seleccionados no solo cuestionan la idea de la docilidad, sino la misma idea de la nación y de la identidad a ella adscrita' ('the texts selected here question not only the idea of docility but also the idea of the nation and the identity that is ascribed to it') (11). Her statement indicates that the 'great Puerto Rican family' is being questioned not only by Afrodescendants like Arroyo Pizarro, but also by a variety of voices.

The story alters the Margaret Garner image to refashion violence as a tool of rebellion against the slave system. The Garner case occurred in Ohio in 1856 (Gunther Kodat 159). An Afrodescendant, she had escaped captivity in Kentucky for the North with her children. Yet slave catchers descended upon them, preparing to take them back, when she spared her two-year-old daughter from slavery by killing her. The obscure story was popularised by Morrison's *Beloved* (1987) (Gunther Kodat 159). 'Matronas' is also marked by marronage and liberating infanticide. An incarcerated midwife, Ndizi, recalls her escape from a Puerto Rican hacienda with Mandingos (67). They consider return to Africa but decide that death is the only escape (76). She begins to doubt God and decides to kill the children if she is caught (77). In prison, Petro, a friar, tells her she is not an animal, so she bonds with him, though not to convert (81). Ndizi and group of women conspire to breed an 'army' of women and dead children (83). While she is imprisoned, a guard rapes her; she bites off his scrotum, takes the keys and frees the Afrodescendant and indigenous inmates (86). She goes to work under the orders of the 'gran negra bruja de la plantación de la Catedral en Porta Coeli' ('great Black witch of the Porta Coeli Cathedral plantation') (87). While virtually any Black witch could be used as a symbol of women's resistance, this title ties her to a Puerto Rican tourist attraction and the Church (the museum of religious art in San Germán, a convent from 1531), signalling its hypocrisy. It also links her to Queen Nanny of the Maroons, a Jamaican revolutionary called 'Obea' ('Sorceress'), which the author renders as 'Bruja Mayor' (92). Thus, the maroon army of Puerto Rico is actually a battalion of a greater, pan-Caribbean revolutionary force. Colonial officials sentence Ndizi to the gallows for inciting a riot, so she confesses to Petro how she dispatched the children – but she shows no regret (94–5). The story dramatises Arroyo Pizarro's conviction, likely based more on how she would react under those circumstances than on historical evidence, that most enslaved African women, when their enslavers impregnated them, committed suicide or abortion as a form of *marronage* (*Afrohistoria* 91).

Ndizi, Arroyo Pizarro's version of a Garner-style slave rebel, alters the figure of the mother who kills her children to make death a means of collective resistance that turns deadly violence on both the enslaved and the enslavers. The English translation of the title, 'Midwives', only partially captures the maternal allusion of the original 'Matronas', rooted in the term *madre* ('mother') (trans. Álvarez Nieves 63). Just like Garner, she shows an extreme kind of love to enslaved children by sparing them a life of abuse. When Ndizi is a fugitive, she decides to opt not for suicide but infanticide: 'If I am ever caught again, the children shall pay' (79). In my reading, dispatching the master's children is different from euthanising the enslaved. The condemned killer meticulously confesses her crime to Fray Petro as she heads to the gallows, noting that many enslaved women want their children to be spared slavery through death and that the lost lives form a rebel army (934). A good Catholic, the priest has told her to confess and repent of her sins, but her confession shows not contrition but pride. She is celebrating the victories of a war. She is commemorating deliverance from servitude. Garner's infanticide has been interpreted as an act of deliverance (Brown, *Repeating* 24). At her trial, the abolitionist witness Lucy Stone defended Garner for killing the girl due in part to the sexual abuse she and other enslaved women suffered, which inevitably resulted in mixed-race children:

> The faded faces of the Negro children tell too plainly to what degradation the female slaves submit. Rather than give her daughter to that life, she killed it. If in her deep maternal love she felt the impulse to send her child back to God, to save it from coming woe, who shall say she had no right not to do so? (quoted in Brown, 'Margaret')

While her argument is Christian, Ndizi's point of view is a mixture of deep doubt in any divine entity due to the brutality of slavery and of African faiths she brought with her. The more dead they send to that astral army, the more spiritual energy they have to turn towards continued resistance to the slave system. Novelistic representations of this kind of army include the Haitian Revolution as portrayed in Alejo Carpentier's *El reino de este mundo* ('*The Kingdom of this World*', 1949) and Manuel Zapata Olivella's *Changó el gran putas* ('*Changó, The Biggest Baddass*', 1983). This spirit army of Black souls complements the living army that 'Matronas' imagines, run by a Black sorceress at the centre of Catholic power. On a secular level, each slave that never grows up is one worker fewer, as the masters who attend her execution note (93). They are casualties in a war, but they are loved very deeply, just like the Garner child.

More than mercy killing, she is out for vengeance. The story implies that Ndizi kills more than she confesses. Her initial goal is escape to Africa, which evolves into suicidal ideation. She then decides to make her plan into a series of murders that will likely lead to suicide. The idea forms as she escapes with an all-male group of fugitives that have disembarked the slaver undetected and met her on the coast. During their flight, the men rape her, so it is understandable that she mistrusts their plans and strikes out on her own path. 'Yo bostezo y hago juramento, por las deidades de los vientos de las que dudo ya, que si soy capturada nuevamente, me las habré de cobrar con los niños' ('I yawn and swear, by the wind deities I already doubt, that if I am captured again, I will have to take it out on the children') (77). She puts it bluntly to the priest:

'Os juro que quise morir, Fray Petro, a ser usada como animal. Os juro que luego quise matar a todos' ('I swear to you that I wanted to die, Friar Petro, rather than be used like an animal. I swear to you that at that moment I wanted to kill everyone') (83). More evidence that she is out for white blood is her process of gaining the family's trust, serving as an ideal domestic servant: 'Los he puesto a mamarme los senos hasta que sale leche, para convertirme en su nodriza' ('I have them suckle from my breasts until milk comes out, becoming their wet nurse') (87). Thus, the plantation image of the benevolent Mammy transforms into a menacing, subversive figure, breaking up the harmony of the hacienda. As in *Beloved* and Arroyo Pizarro's 'Los amamantados' ('The Suckled' 2016), lactation is abject violence. She uses the tools of the master to subtly wear away at the heart and stomach of the plantation: 'sé cocinar todo lo que me pongan en frente, y de todo exquisito. Puedo incluso confeccionar veneno de lenta interacción, aderezado con guarapo y canela' ('I know how to cook everything exquisitely that they put in front of me. I can even prepare slow-release poison, seasoned with sugar-cane juice and cinnamon') (74). Hence, the same act of killing, meted out on Black and white children, has opposite meanings. Killing children ends the cycle of oppressed and oppressor by removing the players from the beginning. It is an act of deliverance for the captives and a pre-emptive strike infused with vengeance against the oppressor. She shows sublime power over life and death, a liberating *techné* that goes beyond the traditional labours of enslaved women Ramos Rosado notes ('Mayra' 207). She shares with the voice of the poem 'Arrancada' ('Torn Away'), the desire not to have children in her great prison of the New World (Mendoza 1151).

Ndizi partially confesses her crimes to Friar Petro because he is a humanist who has taken up the cause of fighting the animalisation of the enslaved. He falls into the problematic human rights tradition of Antonio de Montesinos and Friar Bartolomé de las Casas, the famed 'Protector of the Indians' who advocated for them and achieved the New Laws that were designed to protect the indigenous (Kirschner et al. 3). Las Casas himself is a conflicted figure regarding the enslavement of Africans, since he was an advocate for it (4). Even though Ndizi has lost faith in the divine, she respects Petro for humanising her. Realising that she speaks Yoruba, he writes sentences on paper that assure her she is not a 'bestia' ('animal, idiot, monster'). She connects with him as an equal on some level, since he is learning one of her languages, even as she feigns being ignorant of Spanish. He brings her reports of the colours of the sunset – red, yellow and pink (91).

Arroyo Pizarro frequently uses chromatism as a device to link the three stories of *las Negras*. Yellow and red are the colour of war paint among the Namaqua, exemplified on the cover of the English edition. This secret message likely has the disguised meaning of rebellion to Ndizi, unbeknownst to the priest. His pink eyes are the last thing she sees as she dies, so humanism triumphs over religious and linguistic differences, giving her dignity in death and a fleeting reprieve from isolation (95). She stares the Church and humanity in the eye one last time as a *cimarrona*.

Ndizi is the anti-*ladina*. In Arroyo Pizarro's usage, *bozal* does not mean 'ignorant'; it means 'untamed'. It means that the individual has rejected the colonial system with every syllable of every utterance. Ndizi brags of speaking many languages but reveals very few. Colonial officials defined Ladinos as those who spoke 'Latin' or, in actuality, Spanish. The fact that Ndizi is controlling the language lesson for the priest inverts the colonial process. As in 'Saeta', language and violence complement one another. Ndizi's secrets and her gallows confession are a taking back of the symbolic violence that the colonial system universally meted out upon the enslaved. The fact that she is part of a group of midwives that are secretly dispatching hacienda babies means that her death is not only an escape for her but that it is only a brief interruption in the ongoing process of marronage in physical and symbolic violence that would continue from the days of the first *bozales* to the poetry and prose of Arroyo Pizarro.

Much of *Afrohistoria* (2018) reflects on the composition and reception of *las Negras*. Once again, this text clearly presents aspects of her queer identity as well as her search for her Black self and ancestry. Sometimes the 2018 text presents both aspects (queer and Afrodescendant) as oppressed identities, while at other times they are divorced.

In this chapter, I have shown that Arroyo Pizarro has assembled a family of choice as the first woman to marry a woman in Puerto Rico. Her identity and activism exemplify the fractal family. Her daughter, her wife and her grandmother are deep influences on the families she recreates in her work. She seeks Black heroes in the past as models for the future. Yet she seems to have works that are either only lesbian or only Black in their thematics. Like Santos-Febres, she uses Glissant's Caribbean discourse to break with the Insularism of the 1930s that still holds sway regarding race, gender and sexuality (197). *Saeta: The Poems* (2011) and *las Negras* (2012) show strong Black consciousness as part of the national family. They include female maroons, rélation, midwives and concubines. These families are often painfully formed. While African-American studies inspire her, she believes Puerto Rico has a unique history that deserves adaptation of paradigms to local concerns.

The settings of 'Wanwe' and the short story 'Saeta' extend to Africa, where African families are destroyed and rebuilt through the violent processes of colonisation, war and enslavement, shattering the harmonious plantation of the Insularists. She focuses on the female body and how it survives and rebels against rape, torture and captivity. The 'lions' of history are the 'Ancestras'. Arroyo Pizarro's innovation in Puerto Rican letters is to focus exclusively on Black women in her prose. She rejects religion as a decolonising atheist, but she keeps the figures of the Ancestors and the Orishas as an inspirational mythology for her work.

That said, like Gliassant, she rejects a single origin and national boundaries, filiation. The diaspora began with the Middle Passage, yes, but it began on the African continent with the destruction of its families, which included whole villages. The *bozal*, who cannot speak Spanish and remains unacculturated, is also used as a symbol of cultural preservation and rebellion, as opposed to the Ladino, who assimilated. The runaway slave community forms yet another element of a new kind of family. She dialogues with the 'thing-Zumbi' binomial, sometimes reaffirming marronage's masculinist violence and sometimes making it uniquely feminine, the work of a midwife holding a foetus. The writer engages with the Garner case. She creates a space that validates the rage and longing for vengeance that form part of the full range of human emotions and that were surely fostered in the enslaved by the brutality of the plantation 'family'. Arroyo Pizarro criticises the marginalisation of Black authors and characters in the island's literary canon. The author rejects national boundaries, creating solidarity with the African Diaspora in Jamaica and on the US mainland.

Conclusion

In conclusion, Arroyo Pizarro is writing against the colonial nationalist myths she inherited regarding the great Puerto Rican family. She mourns the African families that were lost due to enslavement. She places herself in a matrilineal family of *cimarronas* that resist with the weapons at hand – arrows, umbilical cords, words. Her Black poetry and short stories illuminate one another. In a way, as Rivera Lassén argues, to claim a Black identity in Puerto Rico is like coming out of the closet – affirming an identity that may lead to rejection by friends and family yet still seeking to form healthy relationships based on that identity ('Black' 70). While her queer identity is not central to these texts, as it is in her homoerotic work, she challenges heteronormativity when she brings up a mistress with lesbian desires in her poems. 'Carne negra' ('Black Flesh'), which debuted in *Palenque*, already ties the history of enslaved women to sexual diversity in the ludic verse 'toco toto toco toto vejigante come toto' ('I touch poon I touch poon bladder giant eats poon') (33). The poem ties her intersecting minority identities to the greater national identity through the *vejigantes*, the symbol of Carnival in Ponce and Loíza, making them *translocas* that challenge the Moor slayers (enslavers) of history (LaFountain-Stokes, *Translocas* 156). These glimpses aside, the period of *las Negras*, her TED Talk and *Saeta* present the *afropuertorriqueña* Arroyo Pizarro, almost in isolation, before the complete flourishing of the *afrolesbiana* persona that emerges in *Blancoides* and *Afrohistoria*. Falconí Trávez no doubt notes this when he divides his essay on *las Negras* into two halves: the Black half and the lesbian/queer theory half, which includes Blackness as a secondary element ('De cuerpos' 134). When *las Negras* debuted, the author says, she felt that when others accepted her as Black, they rejected her as a lesbian and vice versa ('La piel' 1). The collection stands in stark contrast to 'negro sabor', in which Black lesbians at a conference decide to taste their own vaginal secretions, to which the poetic voice reacts 'mi negro sabor es dulce' ('my Black flavour is sweet') (21). Her poetry now combines the intersecting struggles of Black people and LGBTQ+ people, which she now considers inseparable (*Blancoides* 79). Falconí Trávez sees this unified fight in *las Negras*, considering her heir to Black lesbian feminist Audre Lorde, but I do not, since no Black lesbians are depicted ('Puerto Rico' 85).

In some of her work, she has had to 'perform' as either lesbian or Black (Acevedo, interview 130). Nonetheless, in *Blancoides* and *Afrohistoria*, she does not choose – she is the *uno-múltiple* ('multiple-one'). Disappointingly, in the poetry of *Afrofeministamente* (2020), her only sign of solidarity with the LGBTQ+ community is a handful of gender-neutral pronouns (15, 54). I would like to see her devote the same historical depth to LGBTQ+ history in the future that she does now with Black history, since *sexodisidentes* have always been part of the Puerto Rican family. I do not expect her to represent both facets of identity (race/sexual orientation) in every work, but silence on an issue can be telling regarding the pressures rooted in colonialism that many authors experience.

Chapter 3
Yvonne Denis-Rosario: Fathers, Mothers, Fractals and Writing

This chapter analyses short stories about Black families in Yvonne Denis-Rosario's *Capá prieto* (2009). Hidalgo de Jesús considers her among the most important writers of this 'generation', comparing her to Arroyo Pizarro and Santos-Febres (*Mujeres* xxvi). Her thematic scope begins in slavery, like Arroyo Pizarro's *las Negras*, but a greater number of Denis-Rosario's stories are devoted to more recent historical events. Nonetheless, her work also devises an Afro-Puerto Rican nation and family that notes the abuses of the past as well as the Black heroes that have always been leaders, even when their options were limited. Her Afro-Boricua family extends to los Nueva Yores ('New York'), breaking with the Insularist tradition and showing the importance of Latinx and African diasporas to the Puerto Rican community.

Zapata-Calle, who has connected the work to *Fe*, sees the *capá prieto* tree as a metaphor for the Black roots of the author's identity and unearthing them as part of the nation's history (141, 143). I see her as fractal, and therefore rootless, meandering and reconnecting, so I prefer interpreting the title of the book as an allusion to the secret society that Afrodescendant Independentist Ramón Emeterio Betances founded in the nineteenth century (Arroyo, *Writing* 70; Ramos Rosado, 'Prólogo' 31). While Independentist, he can be seen as heir to the maroons of his time. 'Afro' and 'Puerto Rican' are not a contradiction in the book. Kirschner praises it for making visible the 'heterogeneous histories' of Afro-Atlantic people and challenging patriarchy (224). She includes more of the

Puerto Rican Black 'founding fathers' than Arroyo Pizarro does, but she portrays many influential women. I disagree with Miletti, who argues that Black identity is not a theme in the stories (191). An absence I note is that her textual family does not include LGBTQ+ people like Arroyo Pizarro's latest work. Her style is more sexually conservative in its representation of women, but it has an empowering goal:

> That thought about the other, that which is different, savage, all of that stuff continues in literature written by Afrodescendants and non-Afrodescendants ... It is a criticism I point out, and I give it to some of my colleagues that approach it from that angle, I criticise them. Because I don't need them to use the image of the Black woman to talk about her virtues. That image of the hot, passionate woman does not give women any benefit at all. Not only the Black woman, but the woman in general. That idea of constant, prevalent sex, I resist that as the main subject of a text. (personal interview)

On this topic, she is distant in her representation of women from Arroyo Pizarro and Santos-Febres. The *uno-múltiple* has room for this diversity. While she depicts less sex, she represents more death, and both are part of the rituals that form and maintain a family.

Gathering the Scattered Afro-Puerto Rican Family in 'Periódicos de ayer'

In the short story 'Periódicos de ayer' ('Newspapers from Yesterday'), Denis-Rosario uses the funeral of the female protagonist's father to provide insight into how Black males have influenced the family, the military, the academy and poetry. The funeral shows the family lineage of Black brothers that she develops in the novel *Bufé* (2012). The military contribution shows that Black people saved Puerto Rico from domination by the British. It gives a new perspective on Loíza that shows it is more than a centre of folklore and that its history is central to the nation. Family and history define much of the collection of short narratives. She represents the academic side of Black history via an acquaintance of Arturo Alfonso Schomburg who collects for Puerto Rico and a Río Piedras professor who steals back the stolen story of Loíza. The historical poetry declaimer Juan Boria becomes a hero of the people by ensuring punishment for a corrupt lawyer who sells Guayama real estate to a tourism developer. Afrodescendants had owned land there since at least 1836 (González García 161). On the other hand, she provides female-led parallels to all these achievements and foundations. The Black wet nurse is part of a matrilineal history of Afrodescendant women who haunt the white men who enslaved and later employed them. The fighters of Loíza are precursors to the woman killed upon eviction from her home there. In a less epic but still important story, she shows how negotiation with oppression can sometimes be as great a struggle as resisting through the quaint but inspiring story of Pura Belpré.[1] Her story and others in the collection show the translocal history of Puerto Rico, as Luz Angélica Kirschner notes (224).

In 'Periódicos', Denis-Rosario reinterprets *El velorio* ('*The Wake*' 1893) by Francisco Oller (1833–1917). It is almost impossible to depict a funeral in Puerto Rico without evoking the foundational work. The Iupi, where the author teaches, houses it. The painting is a symbol of autochthonous art. In it, people of different races and walks of life mourn a dead white child in a country home. The rural society depicted evokes the 'great family', even though it was finished twenty years after abolition: it includes Black characters, *jíbaros* ('peasants') and a priest in a cacophonous *baquiné* celebration to commemorate a white child's death. Torres Muñoz has joined the recent movement away from Eurocentric interpretations of the work and noted that Oller was an abolitionist ('Arte' 54). He painted a series of three canvasses depicting the enslaved in addition to *El velorio*, including *El negro flagelado, Hacienda Aurora (1888–90)* ('*The Flogged Black Man, Hacienda Aurora [1888–90]*') (Valdés, *Future* 54). Velázquez Collazo explains that Oller spoke out for the rights of Black people through his painting beginning with ten works at the 1867 Universal Exhibition in Paris that portrayed the suffering of Afrodescendants under slavery on the island, which Spain only abolished in 1873. Torres Muñoz claims that his anti-racist art is part of a hidden narrative of the nation that was an alternative to the whitening discourse of the 1930s generation (personal interview). Denis-Rosario makes mourning a dead Black man the cause of a wake, placing him at the centre of the national imaginary.

The protagonist's late father brings together a family that has been separated (750). He is identical to his brother Luis (750). The tone is sombre and reverent, unlike Oller's carnivalesque ceremony. The tale depicts a split, repeating – and thus fractal – family. There are two identical characters, one living, one dead, and they live divided between the island and the mainland. One branch gains success by owning laundrettes on the archipelago and moves to the continental United States (746). She is shocked when her aunt Mercedes – who appeared in previous stories in the collection and looks just like her – screams and shuts the door in her face when she comes to the island after twenty years of separation (516, 608, 746). The familial rejection expresses a common resentment of many people on the island. They cease to see the diaspora as 'true' Puerto Ricans. Zapata-Calle considers it an example of how the stories, which she calls a novel, look to the past but not the future (142). Studying history, as Santos-Febres argues, is a *sankofa* search in the past to address the future ('Caribe' 41:58).

Uncle Luis's house is an impoverished but Afro-Puerto Rican, decolonial general archive of the Indies that contains copious stacks of newspapers dating back to 1938 and numerous artefacts from the African diaspora (741). His niece must help him dispose of the house after her absence of decades, which can be seen as forgetting her past (741). He has developed a family of neighbours who deliver his post – these mail carriers think the house is haunted (790). This may be true – the ancestors are also part of the family (790). His 'craft' is collecting, and crafts are central to the collection, as Bolden observes (200). Zapata-Calle interprets these documents and those of other stories as tools to reconstruct a hidden Black past (143). Miletti praises the stories for showing that Afro-Boricuas can become professionals and archive their own history (192).

The fractal family of Uncle Luis has migrated to a development called Urbanización La Dignidad, since they have lost their land to gentrification (794). The theme of uprooting poor Black people is constant in Denis-Rosario's work, which Vilches considers a revisiting of González's 'En el fondo del caño'. This elderly equivalent of the Black boy also wants to see himself reflected and to preserve his identity beyond death as an inheritance. This is not filiation; it does not dominate. Nor is it a postmodernism in which Afro-Puerto Ricans sacrifice their right to the archipelago.

The uncle gives her a box of unique letters: his correspondence with Schomburg, which link and separate African-American and Afro-Puerto Rican history (832). The two men are Masons, and they meet at the Great Lodge in Puerto Rico (832). They share a love for collecting artefacts from the African diaspora, so they communicate via post (832). Schomburg asks him to warehouse artefacts from the Caribbean, which he obliges (849). One day in 1937, the uncle learns that Schomburg has sold his collection for $10,000 and that he is to mail the materials to the new owner (849). He sends them, but there are objects unique to Puerto Rico with which he cannot part (858). To these he adds his own collection, affirming Afro-Puerto Rican identity as local, not just a US import (858).

Denis Rosario's re-claiming of Schomburg's Puerto Rican heritage foreshadows Afro-Latinx scholars' 'rediscovery' of the Harlem Renaissance icon. Kirschner claims he is still largely unknown on the island (224). Schomburg was the great archivist of the movement whose project focused on dynamic and, in Kirschner's view (not mine), anti-essentialist representations of Black people (229). His personal collection became the largest assembly of Black artefacts in the United States and is housed by the New York Public Library (Kirschner 230). After the story's debut, Jiménez Román and Flores published *The Afro-Latin@ Reader* (2013), which shows the importance of Schomburg in forging an Afro-Latino identity (7). The collector was an activist with José Martí in Cuba and initially supported his philosophy that 'en Cuba no hay razas' ('there are no races in Cuba') (Fountain xiii). Later, in Manhattan, he broke with Martí on this matter and became active in the New Negro movement as a supporter of its artists. As Moreno Vega mentions, he was instrumental in Langston Hughes meeting Nicolás Guillén, for example ('Dr Marta' 8:20–47). Valdés, in *Diasporic Blackness* (2017), examines the historian's life as a foundational moment in the theorisation of the African diaspora, which included African-Americans, Afro-Latinxs and Africans. Arroyo argues that Freemasonry was formative to Schomburg and intellectuals of his ilk that were thinking through anti-colonial struggle and pan-Caribbean formations of nation and diaspora (*Writing* 32). Schomburg is a pivotal link between the island, African-Americans and the African and Boricua diasporas that overcomes the limitations of space and race that Insularism imposed.

While Uncle Luis supports the collector's promotion of Black culture, he believes there are some things that belong to the archipelago and that should not leave the family. This belief ties him to the opening story 'El Silenciamiento' ('Silencing') (110). Ironically, he gives his most treasured document to his niece who lives in the United States: an eighteenth-century document that lists the names of the Black soldiers who fought off the British at Boca de Cangrejos in 1797 (Denis-Rosario, *Capá* 881). It is likely that he thought she would preserve them, which she does not (872). The elder's legacy shows that Denis-Rosario is working to create a Black history with Black branches of the Puerto Rican family mangrove. His hope in creating a legacy is legitimised by a hand-written will and testament from Schomburg (877). It is sad but not surprising that they end up in New York, since the protagonist has forgotten her poor, Black family on the island (Hidalgo de Jesús, *Mujeres* 328). It also shows the need for a cultural and activist centre in Loíza such as the Casa Afro that Moreno Vega and Rivera Clemente lead in Piñones, represented by a portrait of Schomburg on its façade (Rivera Clemente).

While the uncle gives the document to his niece, his foil, a university professor whose race Denis-Rosario does not mention, is arrested for virtually the same 'theft'. Technically, the old man stole the parchment from Schomburg's trust, the private buyer, and the New York Public Library. Less technically, in 'Silenciamiento', Francisco Santaella smuggles a parchment about the same colonial battle in modern-day Loíza out of the General Archive of the Indies in Seville, Spain (817). This vital archive has similar documents, such as an image of a Black soldier in Puerto Rico from 1797 (Unidos 4). The researcher's crime is not a performance of family solidarity but of loyalty to a decolonial Puerto Rican identity. In a family of choice, he is at least an ally. He has stolen what he believes belongs to the island, since it was taken from the region that accomplished the feat, Loíza, by the United States in the twenty-first century and given to its previous coloniser, Spain (171). The documents were found hidden in the wall of El Morro, the nation's most famous colonial tourist site, like the family documents of 'Ama de leche' ('Wet Nurse') (488). Likewise, Kirschner has shown that he is rescuing the documents from banality and oblivion in the archive (228). The researcher likely wants to repatriate Afro-Puerto Rican historical documents to show that this marginalised, silenced minority has contributed significantly to the nation.

The Family of Loíza Saves the Island
Before its 1815 Whitening

Islanders often call Loíza 'La Capital de la Tradición' ('The Capital of Tradition') because it is a font of African-inspired folklore. While it is essentialised as the centre of Black culture, it is often depicted as having no history or only a folk history (Kirschner 232). Santiago-Díaz laments that its folklorisation has left it without an affirmative political dimension (23). Sixty-five per cent of residents identify as Black and almost half live in poverty (Kirschner 234). Historians have shown that parts of Loíza, Piñones and nearby San Mateo de Cangrejos were military outposts with an important legacy for the island. Some of the Black people of Cangrejos left to found Loíza (Franco, quoted in Viera-Calderón 168). They considered military service a craft, and they formed communities based on this *techné*, in this case, a community based on the island (González García 176). Today, Cangrejos/Santurce is often spurned due to racism and classism, when its history is in fact heroic (165). Furthermore, the events of 1797 highlight the importance of oral history, which Edison Viera-Colón uses to document the events, as Denis-Rosario does in her fiction (165). One of the founding families of Cangrejos is the Verdejos, a connection with Fe Verdejo (168). Others were Pizarro, like Arroyo Pizarro, and Llano, like Llanos-Figueroa, so there may be historical *cimarronas* in their bloodlines (Viera-Calderón 174)!

There is still much that is not known about the pre-1898 Black residents of Loíza, but since 2007, Denis Rosario has been familiar with the scholar-activist group Unidos Vencimos en 1797 ('United We Won in 1797'). Hidalgo de Jesús has noted the impact of oral history on the short stories in this collection (*Mujeres* 319). In 'Silenciamiento', the rogue scholar gives the parchment to them in 2007 (222). In an interesting parallel, the free Black captain of the Black Battalion is another Francisco, Francisco Lanzos (110). In the story, family is part of this repatriation, since one of the members is from the Lanzos line (225). Centring Lanzos sets history straight, since racist historiographers had credited the island's governor for his victory over the British (Kirschner 226). Kirschner ties their struggle to that of maroons dating back to 1514 who claimed sovereignty over their land (227). The parchment is family and national patrimony, and the story illustrates how Afro-Puerto Ricans are capable of preserving their heritage.

The Black Battalion's victory is an example of Afro-Boricuas' role in saving the Puerto Rican nation from Anglophone attackers. It indicts the Spanish for ignoring the heroes that saved them from invasion and loss of the Caribbean roughly a century earlier than it did in 1898. It is a milestone in Puerto Rican national history, since the conflict united the people in a common cause, though they seem not to have focused on serving the Spanish Crown so much as defending their homeland (1). Sadly, perhaps due to the US invasion, memory of the event began to fade after the 1897 centenary, a loss that Meléndez Muñoz lamented at the 150-year commemoration in 1947 (3). It seems academic silence on the battle has almost confined its memory to Loíza, and its commemoration is part of Black history, as its bicentenary celebration in 1997 with African-based bomba music and hip-hop indicate (3).

Afro-Puerto Rican history is national history in the events of 1797. The British, French and Spanish were fighting for control of the Caribbean and, in particular, of the rich sugar colony of Saint-Domingue. Most of San Juan at the time was of African descent: 37,711 free Black people and mulattoes, 6,537 African captives, 29,263 whites, so the Pardo (Mulatto) Regiment likely had family or community bonds with one another (53). The white soldiers in other battalions also cohabitated with Black or mixed-race women (59). The former were in Hispaniola fighting for the Spanish. The Black battalion stayed at home. Although colonial norms stipulated that Black soldiers could not attain advanced levels in the military hierarchy, service still gave them a sense of dignity (60). For some, it was a pathway to manumission (55). In all cases, their participation was subject to limitations and phobias on the part of authorities, since the Spanish feared that the Haitian Revolution might spread to Puerto Rico (69). All empires in the Caribbean wanted sugar money, so if Haiti fell, Cuba and Puerto Rico stood to gain (69).

Locally, the marginalised Puerto Ricans did not greet the British as liberators, but rather as colonisers who were more oppressive. Unidos Vencimos en 1797 likens the victory to the popular expression 'trabajar pa'l inglés' ('working for the English, being exploited') (2). The British invasion was part of the Age of Revolutions. In the Caribbean, many sailors and troops were in Santo Domingo attempting to wrest control of it from the French and the Haitians (Unidos 1). Britain had attacked Spanish Vieques in 1718, and they took Trinidad from Spain in 1797, just before the attempt on Puerto Rico (Denis-Rosario, 'Silence' 67). It sent the decorated military leaders Sir Henry Harvey and Ralph Abercromby to lead approximately 6,000 men in the assault (Denis-Rosario, 'Silenciamiento' 154; Unidos 4). According to Unidos, the British took Cangrejos after an initial defeat, and eventually invaded the region before ultimately being repelled (1). There were 125 free Black soldiers in Puerto Rico in what was called the Milicia de Pardos ('Mulatto Militia') (1). On 19 to 30 April, the soldiers of Cangrejos and Loíza fought in their own territory, and certainly all those of Loíza and most in Cangrejos were Afrodescendants (5). On 26 April, seventy troops from the Compañía de Negros (Black Company) attacked the British in canoes (6). The Afrodescendant Francisco Andino led a uerrilla assault with soldiers from Loíza in the mangroves of the Martín Peña Channel, and Black regiments arrested British spies (6). From 29 to 30 April, many Black and mulatto troops from Loíza and Cangrejos, likely attacking through Piñones, drove out the British. By 2 May, the invaders had fled (6). This episode is also part of French and British Black history, since approximately 5,000 of the invaders were Black people and mulattos from recently acquired Trinidad and Martinique (6). Afrodescendants were killing Afrodescendants in white empires' wars. On the other hand, they showed great valour and intelligence on both sides, virtues that the powerful rarely ascribed to Black people at the time. The *techné* of being soldiers gave them an important role in this community and ensured their 'subjugated freedom', however limited it may have been by today's standards (Arroyo, *Writing* 7). The Martín Peña Channel would become the slum where González sets 'En el fondo'. Both incarnations of Black history – poverty and heroism – are often invisible today yet recovered by literature.

 Yvonne Denis-Rosario's telling is an Afrodescendant counternarrative to the Catholic legend that Bishop Trespalacios prayed a *rogativa* ('litany') that distracted the British during the battle (Denis-Rosario, 'Silence' 65). Milagros Denis-Rosario shows how this legend helped to ease anxieties in the nineteenth century, since the tale portrays a Catholic priest and white Creole upperclass women as the diversion that led to the British defeat (65). The pillars of the 'great family' hid the Black side. On the other hand, in Yvonne Denis-Rosario's 'Silenciamiento', the ceremony is

Yoruba. Believers play the sacred batáa drums and spirit possession augured victory (123). She claims to be familiar with Regla de Ocha, since her maternal family practises it (personal interview). The ceremony unites prayers for success with prayers for those who are still enslaved (136). The drummers sing in praise of the battalion of 'la patria' ('the homeland'), not to Spain (141).

Let us compare the two versions of the event in *Capá prieto*. The battle fell hardest on Loíza and Cangrejos (Unidos 3). Unidos state that, in Loíza, there was an important corps of Black Milicias Urbanas ('Urban Militias') numbering around 135 (3). It is noteworthy that militias of this type were not always Black, but they did not have uniforms or modern weapons (6). They often fought with machetes, just as maroons and other rebels from the countryside did (6). The highly trained and uniformed Milicia Disciplinada of Cangrejos had a corps of Milicianos Morenos ('Black Militiamen'). The Milicianos Disciplinados of San Juan included Black infantry (6). These more prestigious groups included around 125 men (6).

Denis-Rosario preserves two re-tellings of the battle, one in an imaginary document owned by a Black man and the other in a document conserved by a man whose race is unmentioned. In the version from the General Archive of the Indies, Francisco Lanzos chronicles the events of the battle, noting that he is from the *milicia urbana* of Loíza (113). Lanzos claims that he and his men were highly trained (118). The fighter relates the Yoruba religious ceremony in detail (141). The tale describes the fury of the soldiers in combat as the British invade (159). Upon victory, they warn those of Martín Peña Bridge and on 20 April the legion leaves Puerto Rico (163).

In the other document of the battle, 'stolen' by Uncle Luis in Puerto Rico, the details are significantly different. The author is Juan Ramón de Castro, colonial governor of the island (880). It is a list of casualties (*heridos y muertos*, 'wounded and dead') from Boca de Cangrejos (880). Their names, ranks and service in battle (*méritos y servicios*) are listed (889). The British wounded Francisco Lanzos on 29 April 1797 (898). Victorio de los Reyes merely appears as 'tambor' ('drummer'), stripping him of his sacred Yoruba function (893). The Spanish reward Lanzos for stopping a grenade from destroying Spanish property alongside Mariano del Rosario (907). Whether or not events occurred in this specific manner, Denis-Rosario is writing her lineage into the foundations of Puerto

Rico (Rosario) along with her fellow Afrodescendants. Lanzos observes that *loiceños* apprehended spies that were serving the invaders (907). Nonetheless, the chronicle ends on a sour note when the governor relates their final services: 'fueron avanzando hacia las trincheras del enemigo, con ánimo de clavar algunas piezas de artillería si conseguían sorprenderlos. Fueron sentidos y recibieron una descarga de fusilería á que correspondieron los negros con un tiroteo, por no ser capaz esta clase de gente de obrar con la disciplina y arreglo necesario' ('they advanced towards the enemy trenches, wanting to direct a few artillery shots against the enemy, should they surprise them. They were overheard and they received a volley of enemy fire, which the Black people returned, since this class of people is not able to acquire the needed organisation and discipline') (trans. Marci Valdivieso 96). The highest authority on the island insults them and highlights their failures as if to disqualify their achievements. The Black thief and the non-Black thief – or, arguably, maroon intellectuals following Schomburg – collecting two different accounts of virtually the same events, are continuing the battle of Cangrejos, fighting to repatriate what was stolen from Puerto Rico. However, they are also struggling for Puerto Rico to change its reduction of Black people to fonts of folklore, as in the case of Loíza, to see them as heroes of the homeland and part of the national family as much as one appears to be Denis-Rosario's national family. As Milagros Denis-Rosario notes, doing so is to undo the whitening projects of the precursors of the 'great family' like Brau (66).

Adolfina Villanueva Osorio, Daughter of Oya, Warrior of Loíza, Afrodescendant

The fight for Black territory with the aid of university professors continues in 1980 with both the Church and state-sponsored murder of Adolfina Villanueva Osorio. The story ties together family legacies, continued oppression rooted in enslavement, and the role of the Catholic Church in supporting and complementing tyrannical regimes. It shows that the Black women of Loíza have also fought for their land, but in different contexts. Unidos claims that 'Más allá de las diferencias de raza y clase, en el 1797 luchamos y triunfamos. Los descendientes de los luchadores del 1797 siguen luchando por el derecho de sus comunidades a existir y a prosperar' ('Beyond differences in race and class, in 1797 we fought and triumphed. The descendants of fighters from 1797 continue struggling for the right of their community to live and prosper') (3). It is likely that poverty, racism and powerful outside interests are what the document means. Their land faced threat of invasion from tourism infrastructure in 2007, but they were able to fend off the invaders and celebrated by commemorating the 210th anniversary of the victory over the British (Denis-Rosario, 'Silence' 71). Sadly, there are more tales of intersectional struggle in the region.

These challenges are the topic of Denis-Rosario's version of the Adolfina Villanueva Osorio story, called 'Desahucio desde el palmar' ('Eviction from the Palms'). If the 'great family' held up the colonial homestead as a source of peace and stability, her story is matrifocal and fraught with change and violence. In effect, Adolfina is a single mother for extended periods (1310). Her husband leaves for months to harvest apples and potatoes in mainland United States (1310). He had only recently returned when police shot her (1310). His role shows, once again, that the story of the diaspora and the archipelago are inextricable.

The story opens with an epigraph of song lyrics by Tite Curete Alonso and Rubén Blades (1246). In 'Desahuicio' ('Eviction' 1995), the legends of salsa write a *bomba*, a traditional Afro-Puerto Rican drum-based song that memorialises Adolfina as the weakest point in a rope that snapped, one who paid the price for a corrupt, dehumanising system. The singers give her a place in heaven – since the rich own the land – and claim she will forgive her murderers there. Yet Denis-Rosario's tale is one of anger at injustice, not forgiveness. Unlike their class-based song about a 'pobre' ('poor woman') doing something 'ilegal' ('illegal'), Denis-Rosario's is about a marginalised Afrodescendant facing the legacy of colonialism. She is a *transloca* of Loíza fighting off the colonial forces of St James the Moor Slayer, but Denis-Rosario shows that there is method to her seeming 'madness' in clinging to her family's land (LaFountain-Stokes, *Translocas* 156). It is her home.

The narrative begins *in media res* with the police knocking on Adolfina's door to serve the notice. As in the best-known US shootings of unarmed Black civilians, the officer at the door, Víctor Estrella, feels threatened when a loud, stubborn and angry woman who will not leave the land she believes is hers answers him (1249).

The leitmotif of 'silencing' Black voices in history returns as the militarised, trigger-happy police eradicate a defenceless woman in order to 'detener la ráfaga de palabras' ('stop the gusts of words') (1249). This story and the events of 1797 indicate that Miletti is mistaken when he states that the author's characters are not excluded or limited by the government or business interests due to their race (189). He believes they murdered Adolfina due to her class, but he does not consider that she is an 'invasora' ('squatter') because her ancestors' enslaver, who gave them no title to the land, betrayed her family (191). As in *Daughters*, Black inheritance is constantly contested.

Adolfina's voice seems to return like the wind at the end of the story as a storm picks up. Denis-Rosario's understanding of Yoruba-based syncretic religions indicates Adolfina is a daughter of Oya, goddess of whirlwinds (Moreno Vega, *Altar* 107). The ancestors had given her a vision in her dreams to be alert and the specific image of her own death, just as she would be killed (1329). Oya is the goddess of death and rebirth, so this reaffirms her connection with Adolfina (107). The state warns her of her eviction, and she receives an initial bombardment of rocks from hoodlums whom an unknown patron sent. Yet she only capitulates in death. The state machine immediately moves in with a bulldozer that destroys all her possessions and only barely spares the lives of five children inside the home (1389). Denis-Rosario humanises Adolfina and shows her as a marginalised Black woman who is caring for her family.

Adolfina's family is a product of the society that eventually took her life. Her father, Victoriano Villanueva, was the descendant of manumitted enslaved Africans who worked for the Quiñones family alongside his relatives for sixty years (1280). The territory they occupied was the farm of Bienmundo Quiñones, who never indicated that he would remove them from it; they saw themselves as bound to the land (1280). Isabel Sophia Dieppa et al. claim that the family had resided there for a century before officials asked them to leave. When the landed patriarch died, the property went to his son Benedito, whom the Villanueva family had helped raise, protecting him from the sometimes-dangerous landscape (1289). Benedito betrays these neighbours and insists on expelling them to sell the land. Victoriano loses in court, though the governor allows him to move to coastal land where he and his family can fish for a living (1288). They all leave, except for Adolfina, who remains in place to raise her children.

In fact, the story shows both her generosity and her vulnerability through her craft of sewing. Adolfina is a respectful Catholic. When nuns want habits, she makes them gratis. When the Servants of Mary request that she restores the robes of the highest church authority on the island, Cardinal José Montes Benítez, she obliges (1307). She discovers that the robes belch cockroaches, another foreshadowing of how corrupt the Church proves to be (1316). He is the buyer who wants the land, and Quiñones grows impatient. Like the spies the militiamen discovered in Loíza, these nuns become informants for a powerful invading entity, represented by the insects that occupy her house and whom Denis-Rosario calls 'invasoras' ('invaders', 'squatters') (1321). In Denis-Rosario's version, Montes Benítez wants it to build a summer retreat – not unlike the tourist infrastructure that continues to threaten poor people's homes in Loíza (1339). Dieppa et al. report that the plan was to build a summer home for the Cardinal, recreating the colonial dynamic of the Church supporting Black dispossession.

In addition to being a generous and caring person, Adolfina is also a logical one. She taught her husband to read (1331). She has fought the Church and the elite in court, as her neighbour Chefín has battled against her purported landowner, and Chefín has won (1339). She has been in discussions with her lawyer for a considerable time before the incident and believes she has time to appeal the court's eviction ruling (1334). She is intelligent but vulnerable.

Perhaps her fight and her murder would have gone unnoticed without the value that her family affords to education. Her sister, Martha, is at the University of Puerto Rico when she learns of the murder, so she tells her professor Arturo Meléndez what has happened (1253). He encourages her to hold press conferences and make the murder known. It is partly due to his efforts that the four police officers are brought to justice. Meléndez associates the state killing of Adolfina to the silenced murder of Independentist activists from the Iupi (1253). He wants justice for both cases, and the mention of the two murders associates Afro-Puerto Rican rights with national independence. The Church has always been part of the hegemonic powers of Puerto Rico, just as it was in the slave system that left land to Benedito, the little boy who would grow up to replace his caregivers.

Kirschner argues that the case exemplifies the precariousness poor Puerto Ricans face – even before Hurricane Maria hit and devastated many lives – disproportionately Black ones (234). The Pulitzer Centre's 2019 post-Maria reflection on the events reveals a bleaker story with important details, as told by Augustín, her husband:

> 'They knocked down the gate and started firing from the beach to the inside of the house,' El Horizonte quotes him as saying. 'They locked us in. They started throwing smoke bombs, and when my wife threw herself on me, a police officer came and shot her.'
>
> The police claimed that Villanueva Osorio was brandishing a machete. According to Carrasquillo Pinet's account, those were false rumors and she was never holding a machete.
>
> No one was ever prosecuted for her murder.

Denis-Rosario's version presents the police account as stating he had gasoline in the house for making Molotov cocktails (1266). Why change from the symbol of slave and peasant uprising to the iconic weapon of leftist rioters and guerrillas? I believe it is to show that the state's lies exaggerate the threat of Black people, just as they did in the case of the Independentists murdered at Cerro Maravilla on 25 July 1978. In *Capá Prieto*, the police are suspended and imprisoned, which only accentuates the injustice of the real impunity they actually enjoyed. The inverted roles of Augustín jumping upon his bleeding wife who is riddled by bullets, only to be shot himself, makes her the centre of the action. Her voice like a storm is what this story intends to give to her and to other Afrodescendant women silenced by Puerto Rican history (1391). Its presence lets readers know that the land she occupied was not empty or up for grabs.

Dieppa et al.'s 2019 Pulitzer update to the story grants the poetic justice Denis-Rosario must fictionalise: once the Cardinal obtained Adolfina's land, construction began on the summer home. What the leader did not expect was that the *loiceños* would be so incensed at Adolfina's murder that someone would take down the construction every night. While nobody has proven this thirty-eight-year-old oral history to be true, eventually the Church appears to have submitted regarding the construction of a home on the land, which now lies fallow. It is an unintentional, empty monument to a life the state nearly erased.

The Pulitzer authors believe her case is indicative of the centuries-long struggle of *loiceños*:

> Under Spanish colonial rule in the 1600s, a crown decree from Spain instructed that captured runaway slaves be sent to the area that is now Loiza. Many of the current *loiceños* can trace their family history back to that colonial decree and earlier. And the unusual structure of Puerto Rican property rights as well goes back to when Puerto Rico was under Spanish rule and the fight for freedom from the Spanish crown.
>
> Land in Loiza has passed down from generation to generation. As Rivera Clemente explained to us, 'Let's say my sister and I own land and I have a house, I can tell my sister to build her house next to my house since it's our land'. There are many plots of land like this in Loiza. Siblings build multiple homes on the same inherited plot. What makes Puerto Rico, and by default Loiza, unique is that many people don't have formal titles to their land.

The legal system established to protect enslavers did nothing to protect the rights of the enslaved or their descendants. Inheritance, central to Glissant's filiation, was not designed to benefit Black families.

The issue that killed Adolfina is dividing Loíza families today. After Hurricane María, many residents needed US Federal aid. For this, they needed titles. Since these were absent, numerous families have suffered heated disputes over land. Reporters have described it as 'tearing the community apart', making it fractal. An alternative to these debates, the reporters propose, is the model of the Martín Peña Channel, which formed a collective land trust. Families own their homes, but the trust owns the land, protecting the community from being sold to a rich developer, be it speculators or the Catholic Church.

Today, global warming threatens Piñones and Loíza Aldea. The coastline is eroding and it is a flood zone. Both Denis-Rosario and Dieppa et al. show that the sea is 'angry' and is engulfing areas of the coastline that were spared in the past. One resident, called 'Chucho', says 'she' is angry – the sea, Mother Yemaya. The *loiceños* interviewed state that they will stay and fight for their land. Their struggle parallels *palenques* and *quilombos* throughout Latin America. Others must flee the island in search of relative freedom, fragmenting and reforming families. In many ways, they still struggle just as their maroon and military ancestors did against seemingly insurmountable forces of occupation and oppression.

The *Techné* of the Letter and the Family

Wordsmithing is a form of protecting Black communities and creating self-conscious Black literature in Denis-Rosario's short stories (Arroyo, *Writing* 9). 'Periódicos' and 'Silenciamiento' show how literature continues the fight for Afrodescendant families to have a place in the national family. 'In re: Federico Bruma' she connects Afro-Puerto Rican poetry to the struggle for land rights.

The story opens with 'The Pharaoh of Black Verse', the actor and poetry performer Juan Boria declaiming *negrista* and abolitionist poetry at the Instituto de Cultura Puertorriqueña ('Puerto Rican Culture Institute' (ICP)) (Denis-Rosario, *Capá* 989; Peña, 'Boria'). Boria recorded the poems as *Majestad negra* ('*Black Majesty*', 1978), and they exemplify the strong bonds of Black poetry to music as well as writing. He recites poems from the Hispanic Caribbean, including the Dominican Republic and Cuba (989), and demonstrates that poetry is more than art for art's sake – it is politically powerful. As Moreno shows, the ICP, which complemented Operation Bootstrap, was a promotor of whitening ideology (39). Boria brought Black visibility to the ICP, but generally the non-Black *jíbaro* was the national symbol and whitening was the norm due to hispanophilia (Kirschner 224). Miletti notes that Denis-Rosario breaks with the focus on the *jíbaro* (198). The poem '¿Y tu agüela aónde ejtá?' ('What about Your Grandmother, Where is She?'), included in *Majestad*, is an indictment of mixed-race but light-skinned Puerto Ricans who view themselves as superior to those with more visible African heritage. It is so popular with the new wave of Afro-Puerto Rican novelists that it became the title of Arroyo Pizarro's TED talk. In both cases, preserving a poetic tradition that includes Boria and Fortunato Vizcarrondo is a step towards raising Black consciousness.

Boria's talent for preserving literature makes him a hero that saves the land of the poor, helping to avoid another tragedy like that of Adolfina (1016). He is contracted to bind legal documents for the lawyer Federico Bruma (1030). His secretary hired him but did not communicate with Bruma, who mistakes the Afro-Boricua artist for a thief (1092). It turns out that the lawyer not only has racial prejudice in common with an enslaver, but that he is also abusing the law to cheat poor people out of their land in the town of Guayama. His ultimate goal is to sell the parcels, which had been people's homes for over fifty years, to investors for a multi-million-dollar tourism complex (1137). While the graft and abuse are contemporary – occurring from 1990 to 1994 – the roots are in the same dehumanisation of marginalised communities that Boria felt in the flesh when the lawyer thought that he, a great performer and poet, was a thief. Unlike the Catholic Church in Loíza, Bruma is not powerful enough to avoid arrest for his own thievery. Poetic justice is served. The homage contributes to Afro-Puerto Rican collective memory, as Hidalgo de Jesús observes (*Mujeres* 329).

A gentler but better-known figure of Afro-Puerto Rican history is Pura Belpré (1899–1982). She is the welcoming librarian and educator that gives voice and representation to working-class Puerto Ricans, particularly Afro-Puerto Ricans, in El Barrio. She is a beloved maternal figure. Denis-Rosario takes much poetic licence, though. The story 'La cucaracha y el ratón en la biblioteca' ('The Roach and the Rat at the Library') shows that the struggles Afro-Boricuas face on the island are also present in Manhattan, linking the two communities (916). This *liberadora* ('liberator'), as Ramos Rosado calls her, was the first Puerto Rican librarian at the New York Public Library ('Mayra' 207). In the story, her superiors associate her with filth (938). When she arrives for her job interview, the head librarian, Lindsay Adams, mistakes her for a maintenance worker, a common job for Black women in the segregated United States (939). Ramos Rosado considers the awkward interview an act of racial othering ('Mayra' 205). After hiring her, he discovers, to his disgust, that she is entertaining the children with puppets of a cockroach and a rat (916). It seems that he is revolted by the 'invasion' of poor, Black and 'foreign' people into his library. He views Belpré's puppets, and by extension her and the children she teaches, as 'invasoras' like those that claimed Adolfina's shack (1321). The roles are reversed: the 'invaders' are not violent or powerful like the Cardinal, but innocent children coming to learn. The inclusion of her job interview and her challenges as a young professional in *Capá prieto* shows that negotiation with oppressive systems creates as many heroines as the valiant deeds of the maroons in direct conflict with them, such as the valiant death of Adolfina.

Despite what the story says, the library was already racially integrated, and the person who hired her was the white woman Ernestine Rose, who sought to make the library staff reflect the community they served, as Núñez shows (139). Rose founded, alongside Black leaders, the Division of Negro Literature, History and Prints, in 1924, so Núñez considers her a powerful ally, not an oppressor to Belpré (139). Rose also led efforts to purchase the Schomburg collection (142). Belpré was the first Latina librarian in the city, but she had allies (Oliver Velez).

Belpré's life is more complex than that of a Black Puerto Rican woman who overcame segregation, as Núñez shows, arguing that Black migrants had diverse experiences (143). In the 1920s, she came to New York among the Boricua pioneers who settled in central Harlem. She worked at the 135th Street branch with Schomburg while he was curating his famous collection, interacting with the writers of the Harlem Renaissance (135, 140). In this, she is like Uncle Luis and Schomburg himself in connecting the movement to the island. She also worked at the 115th Street branch, serving more Puerto Ricans, so she was a link between US Black people and Afro-Boricuas (140). Nonetheless, she never discussed her racial identity explicitly (136). Núñez notes that she grew up in Santurce (Cangrejos), an area with many Black role models, some of whom were middle class like her, and they fostered her through her year of study at Río Piedras (136). She married an African-American New Yorker, Clarence Cameron White (137). Today she is honoured during Black History Month (Oliver Velez). More than a children's librarian, Belpré published eight books, was a folklorist, and taught many Puerto Ricans to read (135). Like Arroyo Pizarro, she created representations of racial and ethnic diversity in her children's books (Oliver Velez). Belpré was honoured posthumously with an award in her name for children's fiction in 1996 (Oliver Velez). She went to the South Bronx as part of the war on poverty in the 1960s (Núñez 136). Her migration and hard work to empower herself and others make her a leader of the Afro-Puerto Rican fractal family who moulded their youth, a mother in a fractal family that included her *barrio* ('neighbourhood').

Black Mothers Remembered

Belpré's achievements with children also highlight the role of Black women as caretakers and mothers in Puerto Rico and its diaspora. The final two stories of this analysis deal with the colonial roots of Black women's caregiving for their own families and for the families of others. 'El turbante del maestro' ('The Teacher's Turban') and 'Ama de leche' ('Wet Nurse') are a diptych that portrays a matrilineal family of Black women tasked with providing cleaning services and childcare for white families.

'El turbante' depicts a ninety-eight-year-old woman's reminiscences of her struggles to learn how to read. She shows the role of gender in the shortcomings and achievements of a national hero, Rafael Cordero y Molina (1790–1868), the Black teacher known as the 'father of public education' on the island. Cordero ran a school for boys that educated both Black and white people. The white Gorrión family in Old San Juan have a son, José, who studies at the school (527). Like Manzano, Cuban author of Spanish America's only official slave narrative, the Black narrator Fela spies on her little enslaver's lessons (523). Her mother Josefa Osorio Villarán, known to her children and those of her enslaver as 'Maíta' ('Mammy'), determines that she will get her daughter into Cordero's school (545). Despite having to run errands while her daughter is in class, despite being rejected twice and despite having to rent her daughter's labour out to Cordero's sister Celestina, she gets an education for her daughter in secret (580). Hidalgo de Jesús points out the importance of including this trailblazing Black woman, a foremother in the nation's history, who has remained largely unknown (*Mujeres* 327). She continues at the Academia del Sagrado Corazón ('Sacred Heart Academy') with help from her captor (460).

Maíta and Fela's lineage continues with Maria Antonia, who demonstrates the same fortitude as her forbears. She goes to high school and learns English, which is the new code that grants prestige and opportunities in the twentieth century (496). Sadly, many of the challenges remain the same for this family of urban domestics. María Antonia cleans houses in San Juan like her predecessors. She faces violence as they do, only with more opportunities. She threatens her abusive husband with a knife and eventually divorces him for his mistreatment (500). This lineage is important because it shows the continued obstacles to progress for *afropuertorriqueñas* after enslavement, but it also humanises them and attempts to imagine their points of view, delivering them from their roles as sex objects or a flat characterisation of a Mammy. Through struggle, they form families of choice.

'Ama' provides further nuance to the story of Maíta by examining the love and the debt of the white children she raised for their families (364). Maíta is more than a wet nurse for the Gorrións. Their mother dies after giving José Dolores four children (363). After abolition, Maíta leaves the family for a short period, but she returns until José Dolores remarries and has children with his new wife (399). For them, she exemplifies the 'Mammy' trope since she is viewed as limited to the role of caretaker for whites and they call her only by that name (Wallace-Sanders 6). It is clear there is an affective bond with the orphans, but she is anything but the 'jolly' Mammy stereotype (Wallace-Sanders 6). Their bond continues in the form of vivid dreams that seem to suffocate the men of the family for generations, all the way to the new millennium. They dream of a Black woman's breast that is so huge it blocks her face from their view, repeating the image of corporeal excess associated with the Mammy (6). Jones has argued that the Mammy figure, not limited to the US plantation, has reappeared throughout Atlantic slave-based societies as a stereotype of both animality and brutish voicelessness (326). However, 'Ama' is both tender and disturbing. The boys suckle and suffer in silence, awakening during the night only to return to the same dream. The vision reaffirms the Mammy's perceived timelessness or 'static Mamminess', something they cannot move beyond because they cannot fully acknowledge her humanity (Jones 332). Agamboue Azizet considers the nightmare a haunting, which she links to *Fe* (263). The facelessness of Maíta, perhaps a result of the men recalling their childhood looking up at her, is a stand-in for all the unnamed wet nurses of Puerto Rico.

In the new millennium, Richard, the heir to this maternal debt, also receives a great fortune. The story mentions that his family has been bankers for the 'Banco del Pueblo' since before the 1873 death of the first white biological mother (460). When she passes, José Dolores – whose name means 'suffering Joseph' – becomes 'absorto entre números y dolor' ('absorbed amidst numbers and pain') (350). While it was common in Iberian societies for white women not to suckle their children and to have wet nurses, the norm in San Juan was for white women to feed their babies with their own bodies (364). When the 'banco de leche' ('milk bank') of the mother runs dry, she must 'borrow' from the woman she 'owns' as an enslaver (364). This custom continues the Iberian practice of using African *nodrizas* ('wet nurses') (Jones 323). The children's first and most lasting bond was a secret shrouded in shame. Despite being 'owned' (enslaved), Maíta is, as the title suggests, owner of something vital, an 'ama de leche' (literally, 'owner of the milk, in contrast to *ama de esclava*, 'owner of a slave') (337). The debt to this unpaid 'seller' is owed by the people ('pueblo'), not just by the banks, like the historical Banco Popular of the island.

One cannot think of Puerto Rican finance without considering the extreme debt into which Puerto Rico began to fall in 2012, the culmination of a process that had been developing for nine years when the book was published (Sullivan). Denis-Rosario revisits the classic Mammy-sex slave binary of the colonial home in the context of the struggle for Afrodescendant rights and Puerto Rican solvency. Zapata-Calle considers the story a call to redress the debt owed to these women through historical research and recognising their labour (143, 236). Ramos Rosado argues that one way is to note their impact on writers such as Palés, who depicted Black people and mulattas under the influence of these relationships (*La mujer* 127).

The kind of debt the story depicts is highly Freudian. Benigno Trigo is among Puerto Rico's leading psychoanalytic cultural critics. If the obsession with infant eroticism, mother-child relationships, dream analysis and oral fixations were not justification enough for this theoretical approach, the image that decodes the dreams of the bankers and the nature of their 'deuda que nunca se pagó' ('debt that was never paid') is discovered in the patriarch's bedroom (488). Richard works through his trauma by returning to the primal scene. In the master bedroom of his family's home in Old San Juan, the Spanish colony and the capital, he finds, hidden in the wall, a letter from his ancestor José Dolores Gorrión, Hijo ('Junior, Son') (488). In it, he relates the haunting dream, his filial love for Maíta, his erotic love for his *hermana de leche* ('milk sister') Fela, his pain for never visiting her, and his paternalist self-congratulations for buying the flowers and camera that captures his 'mother' (478–83). For generations, the men in his family have never repaid what she did, leaving Richard to inherit the image of a woman without a face, as the opening sentence states, while José

Dolores, Hijo is at least able to call to mind the sight of the lips that sang him to sleep as a child (478). Jones, following Hill Collins, argues that the Mammy, the Black woman in the white home, is always the 'outsider within', but that she also forms part of the Uncanny 'Other within' of these men (338). She is repressed, but she returns.

Trigo argues that Puerto Ricans owe a debt to maternal bodies, and he adopts a Kristevan approach to the topic. He notes that Kristeva studies culture using the concepts of sublimation, apoptosis and necrosis. Sublimation is the ability to elevate unconscious drives (sexual and violent) into socially acceptable forms (Felluga). Richard certainly feels an inability to sublimate his unconscious drives, screaming at the engineer who discovers the photos and calls him, cancelling all his appointments, isolating himself, and psychologically absorbing every possible detail of the dark, moist and frightening house that seems like an abject maternal body (434–51). Apoptosis and necrosis are updated concepts based on Freud's *Eros* and *Thanatos* (life and death drives). Kristeva sees something unique when she examines how we discuss DNA research (15). She sees a programming in the cells of human embryos to self-destruct (15). This chemical drive is to either collapse or to die in a pattern, which is to say, to form body parts and whole organ systems out of the living cells, which are programmed to carry out a task before they die. In apoptosis, the cell dies but does not destroy others, which is the nature of necrosis (15–16).

Trigo argues that Puerto Rico must approach its 'unpayable' debt, announced as such on 28 June 2015 by Governor Alejandro García Padilla, by keeping in mind 'apoptotic' acceptance and solutions (20). He argues that Puerto Rico should repeat and sustain its 'cycles of sublimation' (21). By avoiding 'necrosis', he means 'tone down the apocalyptic and militant rhetoric provoked by these emergency proclamations [of cataclysmic debt]' (22). He justifies continued government investment in the arts in order to sublimate 'our phantasms, nightmares, and illusions' (22). As a professor at the University of Puerto Rico at Río Piedras, already projected to have its budget cut by 56 per cent at the time and continuing to face apocalyptic austerity, Denis-Rosario would agree (21).

She would no doubt concur with Trigo that 'purity (racial and otherwise)' is a form of necrosis, since it had already led to murder and hate speech under Trump, not least at Charlottesville in 2017 (20). While Trigo avoids mentioning Trump's voracious intensification of racism and xenophobia, he is concerned that US discourse of 'racial purity' will only contribute to continued violence, symbolic and otherwise, towards Puerto Ricans leaving the island, whom he calls 'exiles', not only 'immigrants' (21). The implications of the article, then, are to continue to fund the humanities, to reduce xenophobia and to accept the financial (self) destruction and reshaping of Puerto Rico.

Denis-Rosario is concerned with 'a debt never paid', and she is clearly opposed to notions of racial purity like those that have led the Garrións to hide the milk that has kept their children alive (364). Where they differ is in their assessment of finances. It is tempting to consider what reparations for slavery from Spain (the second-to-last empire to abolish the institution in the Americas) might look like and the difference that it would make for the impoverished archipelago and its descendants. Repaying the debt to Black families, or members of the national family, would radically alter the situation of Puerto Rico, but that is unlikely. What other means are there to repay Black women? She shares with Trigo a trust in the arts as a form of therapy. She works to give a face and a psyche to the women perceived by these men as bodies only. In so doing, like the unexpected photograph from Maíta's funeral, she is giving some answers, some peace, and a sense of family reunion to all the children that Afrodescendant women have raised since 1493.

In *Capá prieto*, Denis-Rosario devises an Afro-Puerto Rican nation and family that acknowledges the traumas of the past as well as the forgotten Black leaders. Her Afro-Boricua family extends to Manhattan, breaking with the Insularist tradition and showing the importance of overlapping diasporas of the Puerto Rican community. I see her fiction as fractal, and therefore rootless, meandering and reconnecting with the outside, yet Independentist in acknowledging the importance of the freedom movement that Betances founded in the nineteenth century (Ramos Rosado, 'Prólogo' 27). He can be seen as heir to the maroons of his time, a kind of Afro-Boricua family. The short-story collection includes Black forefathers and foremothers, though it remains sexually conservative and cis-heteronormative. She intentionally avoids the 'sensual mulatta' stereotype, choosing more death in the families she imagines.

In 'Periódicos de ayer' ('Newspapers from Yesterday'), Denis-Rosario uses the funeral of the female protagonist's father to provide insight into how Black people influenced the family, the military, the academy and poetry. Denis-Rosario reinterprets *El velorio*. The fractal family of Uncle Luis has migrated from the Martín Peña Channel to a development called Urbanización La Dignidad, since they have lost their land to gentrification (794). His 'craft' is collecting, like his friend Schomburg, and artifacts are central to the collection.

The stories show how Afrodescendants demonstrated the *techné* of military formation at Boca de Cangrejos in 1797, when they expelled the British like maroons fought off enslavers. It gives a new perspective on Loíza and Afro-Boricuas in general that shows they are more than a font of folklore and that their history is central to the nation. It subverts the *rogativa* ('litany') legend, in which a bishop distracts the British with a procession to save the city. While the story itself is a counter-narrative to previous notions of nation, its preservation by a Black Boricua and a non-Black ally represents a modern-day struggle for cultural preservation.

The murder of Adolfina Villanueva Osorio unites family legacies, continued oppression rooted in slavery, and the role of the Catholic Church in supporting colonialism. It shows that the Black women of Loíza have also fought for their land and continue to do so. If the 'great family' held up the patriarchal hacienda as a source of peace and stability, her story is matrifocal and fraught with instability and violence. While Adolfina lives like a single mother, her husband works with his hands in the United States, so their family spans the Caribbean. She is a *transloca* of Loíza fighting off the colonisers. The family had resided there for a century before officials asked them to leave. Their struggle parallels *palenques* and *quilombos* throughout Latin America. Others must flee the island in search of relative freedom, fragmenting and reforming families.

In a comparatively lighter story, Juan Boria becomes an Afro-Puerto Rican hero by ensuring punishment for a corrupt lawyer who attempts to illegally sell historically Black Guayama's land. Its light tone parallels that of Ancestra Pura Belpré, who served as a maternal figure to generations of children of colour in New York.

Hidden documents in a colonial home, like those that documented the Battle of Cangrejos, tell a fuller family story in 'Ama de leche' ('Wet Nurse') (488). The Black milk nurse is part of a matrilineal history of Afrodescendant women who haunt the white men who enslaved and later employed them. More than a Mammy, the protagonist serves as a surrogate mother for the family, amassing an in some ways unpayable debt. Yet, like Trigo states, the arts and humanities are central to repaying a kind of debt to the past in a constructive manner, and the continuation and growth of Afro-Puerto Rican literature and cultural studies is one form of symbolic, if partial, repayment.

The Black-raised children of Borinquén inhabit the continent as well as the archipelago. Let us now consider Dahlma Llanos-Figueroa, the first of two Latina writers that clearly show that Afro-Boricua literature and cultural studies must consider both sides of the *charco* ('pond'). Her novel begins on the plantation but spreads outward to Nigeria and New York. Her English and Spanglish text, which re-evaluates and affirms Blackness on the island, shows that linguistic purity is no reason to exclude Afro-Boricua authors. Like the three island authors I have discussed, Llanos-Figueroa is revising the history of Afro-Borinquén and imagining a new model of communities – racial, familial and national.

Chapter 4
Oshun and the *Palenque*-Plantation in *Daughters of the Stone*

Daughters of the Stone (2009) is the most explicit and complete revision of the 'great Puerto Rican family' of the corpus that this book studies. It imagines Afrodescendants' fight for agency and justice on the Puerto Rican colonial plantation. The captives and free people of colour achieve this empowerment on a level that, at times, is historically highly improbable but that expresses desire to belong both to the foundational community of Puerto Rico and to the African Diaspora. The matrilineal family reaches this goal with the help of the goddess Oshun, to whom all five generations of the novel give their devotion and whose characteristics they display. In important ways, Oshun is the matriarch of the *Daughters* family because she governs the earthly matriarchs. Her sacred number is five (González-Wippler 105). La Caridad, a Black-owned plantation that she inspires the women of the novel to found, represents an empowered Afro-Puerto Rican community. It is the fleeting utopia that the family creates as they triumph over slavery and the lost ideal to which they fight to return, even in the twentieth century. According to Yomaira Figueroa, it is through La Caridad that the novel 'reimagines lives under the heel of oppression as well as possibilities beyond it' (5).

The following chapter is structured by a critical overview of the deity and the novel; a description of how *Daughters* deconstructs the slave plantation and the runaway community; the traumatic, Morrison-esque journey of the family to La Caridad; and how Llanos-Figueroa Africanises the common trope of the will and testament in Puerto Rican letters. The storm that destroys the hacienda supplants key moments in national history like abolition and the War of 1898, keeping the focus on Afrodescendant communities. Once La Caridad is lost, its matriarch's descendants seek to recreate it by imagining a new Afro-Puerto Rican community through love and solidarity. Now, let us turn to the mother goddess of the family, Oshun.

Lady Oshun, *Daughters* and Literary Criticism

The goddess's role in *Daughters* deserves greater depth of analysis, though she has been referred to in previous studies. Feracho mentions the deity in her essay, which argues that she is part of Llanos-Figueroa's contribution to a boom of Afro-Hispanic transnational resistance narratives (127, 144). Feracho notes, following Quiñones Rivera, that Llanos-Figueroa writes against the 'great Puerto Rican family', defined as the achievement of racial equality through miscegenation (Feracho, 139; Quiñones Rivera 163).

Herrera considers Oshun part of remembering African heritage and matrilineal family legacy or 'maternal herstory' (34, 56). However, she does not present her as a source of the Black feminism that her article promotes (37). She sees Africa as the work's 'original maternal home space', while I will show that home is an idealised Puerto Rico where Afrodescendants are free (34). While Herrera claims that, for the characters, the 'new village' of Black people in Puerto Rico cannot replace the original village family in Africa, I argue that the characters create a new community based on the archipelago (56).

Hurtado and Lam show that the novel reinterprets Black bodies to undo whitening myths that dark-skinned Puerto Ricans descend (only) from Taíno Amerindians (Hurtado, 'Resilience' 1; Lam 3). Hurtado reads the novel as a decolonial approach to the island's historiography regarding those she calls 'Latinegras' ('Resilience' 2). She theorises Llanos-Figueroa as a decolonial 'artist-as-curandera' (1), by which she means that the novelist heals the traumas of slavery and colonialism and subverts the stereotypes that those systems created (1, 7). She works to decolonise theory by drawing on indigenous scholars seeking empowering storytelling as well as Moreno Vega's arguments for maintaining an African consciousness and Spiritism in the face of imposed Christianity and colonial narratives (*Altar* 2, 6, 8–9). Hurtado sees psychological, physical and spiritual healing in the novel, as does Lam (Hurtado, 'Resilience' 7; Lam 3). However, I disagree with Hurtado's position that the novelist rejects cultural nationalism ('Resilience' 10). She rejects a Eurocentric nationalism, but she clearly argues for the Puerto Rican nation as her protagonists' homeland and imagined community – even the emigrant (leaving) and remigrant (returning) generations (Flores 33). Lam argues, as do I, that Llanos-Figueroa subverts a 'racially exclusive narrative of Puerto Rican nationhood' (2). Hurtado, Lam and I agree that Afro-Puerto Rican women should be protagonists in that nation and be aware of their family history on the African continent.

Hurtado analyses the novel through decolonial and trauma studies (*Decolonial* 713). She views storytellers, like the narrator Carisa, as 'transmitters of trauma', beginning with the rape of her ancestor Fela (860). Hidalgo de Jesús shows that women were the primary storytellers in many African groups, so the feminine voice in this tradition is the polar opposite of Pedreira's paternalism ('Mujer' 1). Hurtado's fascinating approach to Llanos-Figueroa's intergenerational oral archive focuses on inheriting trauma at the cellular level, since scientists believe that survivors leave a genetic mark on their offspring (*Decolonial* 2426). They curate the past and pass down pain.

A shortcoming of Hurtado's study, however, is that she ignores internal racism on the island, considering its problems to be reduced to Spanish and 'Anglo-US supremacist constructs' (2395, 2465, 2562). Racism on the island existed before, during and after 1898, as the novel shows, and it cannot be attributed solely to US notions of race, as demonstrated in Lloréns's study ('Identity' 29). Hurtado notices Oshun as part of 'decolonising memory' and seeing a space beyond coloniality, but she does not analyse how the goddess affects symbols of the work beyond her role as character (2529, 2786).

Surprisingly, *Daughters* does not figure in Valdés's masterful discussion in *Oshun's Daughters* of the deity's role in crafting female subjectivity through an empowering non-Western epistemology based in Yoruba thought (*Daughters* 2). For the Yoruba, she is the goddess of all women (10). Valdés sees Regla de Ocha as a 'transgressive tool' to reimagine womanhood in Latin America (*Daughters*

1). She notes that the religion has no notion of 'sin' and that the deities have human qualities, such as the aforementioned vengefulness (5). She sees in the goddess the hope of redemption on Earth, a contrast to Christianity's future 'Kingdom Come', which is often used to justify oppression in the present (6). She notes the goddess's bond with the spirits of the 'ancestors', a commonality shared with Morrison's writing (7).[1] The deity's role as seductress influences Valdés's contention that sexual intimacy is a form of liberation (*Daughters* 17). There is a vast anthropological body of work on Oshun and the other Orishas, including Lydia Cabrera's classic *El Monte* (1954) and Robert Farris Thompson's *Flash of the Spirit* (1983). Valdés's interpretation of Oshun as a source of feminine empowerment relates to my revision of the 'great Puerto Rican family' as exemplified in the narrative of Llanos-Figueroa, since she is the mother of mothers who helps women claim their own bodies and own their land.

While the five-generation scope of the novel denotes linearity, it is not 'filiation' in the sense that Glissant uses the term or the sense that Santos-Febres rejects in her 'fractal Caribbean' (*Caribbean* 73; 'Caribe' 19:04). Plantation-rooted societies, for these theorists, create linear notions of logic and time to ensure the perpetuation of inequalities for the benefit of the Westernised elite: fathers beget sons who inherit their property, for example (*Caribbean* 73). While Oshun is a spiritual matriarch, she is mother to all generations, transcending chronology. The narrative is circular: the prologue and postscript reveal that the youngest generation, Carisa (Cari), is 'creating' the older ones for the reader by narrating their stories (1325). Conversely, the stories create and sustain her carrying her like a 'primeval wave', giving her strength, guidance and harmony throughout her life (1). The family structures themselves are fractal and more complex than the triad of father, mother, child, so dear to Pedreira (Gelpí 2212). The matriarch Fela is torn from her partner in Africa, raped by an enslaver and 'seduced' by another. She has a child, but her strongest adult bond in Puerto Rico is with women. A natural disaster, migration to New York and a tyrannical mother-in-law tear future generations apart. Men come and go, often alienated by racial dynamics and societal changes beyond their control. Ultimately, Cari forms families of choice with elders of diverse backgrounds, a professor and a lesbian photographer with whom she shares a special bond. Her family spreads far away from the confines of the island, reaching back to Nigeria. Yet, in some ways, the maroons of the archipelago had already formed a unique kind of family, that of the *palenques*.

The Runaway Village, the Plantation and Mati's New Home

Benítez Rojo has argued, focusing on Puerto Rico in a Caribbean context, that the *palenque* (synonyms *quilombo*, *manigua*) is the anti-plantation that the empire sought to destroy (42, 252). The 'great Puerto Rican family' myth presented a harmonious plantation in which a white patriarch ensured the harmony of a hierarchical community. Black women writers have shown that this society was violent, unjust, racist and sexist. Benítez Rojo, like many of the authors in this book, is looking for a Black utopia and a claim to the land upon which he can build an argument for a postcolonial understanding of the Caribbean. Likewise, Llanos-Figueroa imagines a *manigua* that is, itself, a just plantation or collective that Oshun governs.

In his essay *O Quilombismo* (1980), Nascimento explains what *quilombos*, runaway slave communities, mean to him. Palmares, led by the rebel Zumbi, was the largest, longest-running and most famous independent Black kingdom in Brazil. Under King Zumbi, Palmares remained sovereign until his recorded death on 20 November 1695, now a public holiday recognised by the Brazilian government as Black History Awareness Day. For Nascimento, Zumbi was the epitome of a just outlaw who rejected colonialism. Zumbi relentlessly continued African practices and a struggle for freedom. The king was a model for a unified Black consciousness in opposition to the capitalist and neo-colonial realities of Nascimento's day. In the *quilombo*, Marxism, anti-colonialism, Afro-centrism, feminism and nationalism find their utopia for Nascimento. One of his goals was to revise Western history, that of Brazil in particular, to overcome Eurocentric bias (*Quilombismo* 256). He works to reveal the horrors of slavery and the nobility of the struggle against it, which transcends the colonial context and Brazilian borders to include the entire African Diaspora (256). Nascimento dreamed of establishing a new Palmares where there would be no private property, African diaspora religions would be treated as equal to all others, labour would be based on civic duty, leadership would be

Black but all would be welcome and half the jobs would be reserved for women (280). Like Palmares, the afro-agrarian collective Llanos-Figueroa imagines empowers all these marginalised groups, even if it does so in a much more limited manner. They work the land and trade with nearby farmers and merchants. Mati is exceedingly altruistic towards her former fellow prisoners.

The renaming of the *hacienda* from Las Mercedes to La Caridad is the foundation of an ideal home for Afro-Puerto Rican women – and Black Boricuas in general before abolition and before the island changed hands to become a US territory (119). It is a foundational fiction that is a way around hispanophilia and the justification or romanticising of slavery. Herrera, like Lam, notes the renaming of the property as a symbol of empowerment, but she does not see the centrality of Regla de Ocha religion to it (Herrera 62; Lam 8). While both titles refer to Spanish saints, in Ocha, Nuestra Señora de las Mercedes ('Our Lady of Mercy') corresponds to the Orisha spirit Obatalá and La Virgen de la Santa Caridad de El Cobre ('The Virgin of Holy Charity, who reportedly appeared to Afrodescendants in the Cuban town of El Cobre') masks Oshun (González-Wippler 102). Obatalá is the owner of all things white, and he plays a central role as one of the creator gods, but his mystic colour seems to be Llanos-Figueroa's concern (González-Wippler 77). This name resignifies the colour white as a creation of African gods, not as a myth of racial superiority.

Las Mercedes is a mostly traditional sugar plantation in the 1850s, but La Caridad is a virtually impossible hacienda owned by a manumitted mulatta before abolition. Colonial authorities would not have allowed it to last. First, the enslaver Don Tomás cedes the plantation home and the nearby sewing cabin, called Las Agujas ('Needles'), and gives the slave barracks to the daughter of Oshun Mati along with the manumission of all of those who are still under bondage (94). Not wanting to exploit her workers like her white father, Tomás, she divides her inherited riches among the collective:

> [Freedwoman] Rosalba's humble windows were now hung with lace and silk curtains. Embroidered napkins now served as diapers for brown babies who had always gone bare-bottomed. People who hardly had enough to eat before now ate their beans and rice and pig's feet from fine china plates and sipped their mondongo from silver soupspoons (119).

The sullying of the *hacendados*' finery is in some ways a vengeful fantasy – enslaved women wore callouses on their hands for generations making these napkins and now their children can shit on their former masters in effigy. Santos-Febres likely would call this the end of the plantation hierarchy. However, the redistribution of wealth, the realm of Oshun, does not mean a lack of sophistication on the part of the enslaved – Mati decorates her home with beautiful tapestries representing her noble female Afrodescendant bloodline and a tryptic of the goddess that represents her as young, mature and elderly (120). One represents Mati's male partner, Cheo (120). They have an African-inspired wedding ceremony in an African language with the eldest among the *libertos* 'freed Blacks' ignoring the priest who had lied to and cheated both of them (126). Most freed men and women form a collective, practise subsistence farming, pool their crops and crafts and sell to local townspeople (117). These fragments of the land support fractal families. Others work in the house for a salary, transforming it from a 'genteel [white] lady' into a 'big, handsome woman of a house' that reflects many of the bodies belonging to its new, Afrodescendant owner and staff (118). The corporeal terms recall Santos-Febres's focus on the body and González's Black-affirming Marxist vision of the nation as a house (*Cuatro pisos* 1). The harmonious *palenque* has been transformed into a radically new plantation, but it has no substantial lands on which to grow massive crops like Don Tomás's family did for generations. This is because, like historical *palenques*, in the eyes of colonisers, it should never have existed. Hence, like the military, police and religious assaults on virtually all known *palenques* in history, legal attacks begin on La Caridad before it is even inherited. To recover the acres of canebrakes to which she is entitled, Mati will have to make a deal with Oshun that will ultimately lead to the destruction of La Caridad.

Mati's largesse is, to a large degree, a fantasy that displays Llanos-Figueroa's desire to incorporate Afro-Boricuas into the national imaginary without objectifying them. She has to admit that many captives sought to rise in the hierarchy of the system that surrounded them, like Chica da Silva. According to the novel, in Puerto Rico, 'unbelievably and shamefully, there were rich *negros* who sometimes had slaves of their own' (84). She transfers her own shock into the mouth of her character (84). The author (and, likely, the reader) projects twenty-first century democratic thought onto a reality that is over a century old. González García shows that *moreno* ('Black') Michael Godreau was a powerful planter whose family influenced politics in Salinas throughout the twentieth century, yet she mentions no manumissions (190). Slavery was traumatising but not shocking to the enslaved born on the archipelago – no more than the violence of neoliberalism is overwhelming today. While there were definitely maroons that freed themselves from bondage and freed others as well, those who rose in the colonial hierarchy seldom had the option of subverting the system that began to provide freed Black people and mulattos relative, if unjust, benefits.

Llanos-Figueroa personifies these benefits in the conflicted foreman Romero, the cruel and neurotic mulatto who seems to be attempting to beat the Blackness out of himself as much as the captives that he 'breaks' and manages. He, too, inherits his own home from Don Tomás, but he serves as a foil for Mati's constructive solutions. The villain attempts to burn down La Caridad, but Mati stops him and joins the freed Black people in incinerating his house (Llanos-Figueroa, *Daughters* 96). Filled with the spirit of Oshun, her foremothers and Romero's own mother, she disarms him and drives him into the river, where he is never seen again, despite his curse of a long life of shame (Llanos-Figueroa, *Daughters* 98). He can only utilise physical violence, not the law, to harm the enslaved, and it backfires in another great moment of vengeance like Arroyo Pizarro's story 'Saeta' (130). He is clearly not part of the Black family of La Caridad, but he repeatedly chooses not to be and instead aligns himself with the hierarchy.

Foundational Rape and the Journey to La Caridad

The mothers that opened the path for La Caridad make up the first section of the novel. Fela, Mati's mother, is a Yoruba born in what is now Nigeria. She made a deal with Oshun to overcome her shame of being childless (Llanos-Figueroa, *Daughters* 11). The goddess grants her wish and gives her a blessed stone as a talisman, but she simultaneously gives her the task of notifying her village elders that slavehunters will sack and capture them (22). Oshun, like all Yoruba deities, is transactional and her favour is not unconditional. In a fleeting moment of self-centredness, Fela and her partner Imo make love in a romantic scene by the river (22). Fela falls asleep in his arms and forgets to alert the village, so she awakes to the nightmare of the assault and, soon after, to her captivity.

As in Santos-Febres's novel, there are doubles here. Fela has two enslavers who serve as foils for one another. Don Tomás, who leaves the land to Mati, is the white father who unwittingly helps the girl to repay her mother's deep debt to Oshun when he 'romances' her (Llanos-Figueroa, *Daughters* 50). He purchases Fela because of her sewing skills, a gift from Oshun that spares her the horrors of fieldwork and protects her from sexual assault due to the watchful eye of Doña Filomena, who profits directly from the finery that the women produce and to whom the fruits of their labour contribute a reputation of refinement (Llanos-Figueroa, *Daughters* 15). They bring her income and therefore the goddess of money, Oshun, protects the captives through the white enslaver (15). Their *techné* provides 'subjugated freedom' as others do in Arroyo's work (7). Nonetheless, Don Tomás is so filled with romantic desire that he courts her 'like a white woman' (45). He sends her gifts and spies on her as she bathes (45). Eventually, he is too much overcome with passion in the deity's moonlight and, on the banks of the river, he takes Fela, in a gentler version of her previous master's more animalistic assault (48). Herrera, however, correctly notes that this act is still rape ('Women' 58). She calls the scene 'problematic' and claims that 'the novel presents this act as Fela's choice', but she does not consider its importance to Fela as a follower of Oshun, the goddess who allows her release from her obligation and escape from the plantation through the act (58). It is not Fela's choice; it is her fate. Hurtado calls it 'an act of the gods', not victim-blaming (2599). Like the benefits of captivity in Las Agujas, Fela's agency is relative, but the goddess gives her escape: she feels nothing and expresses no false joy during the act (49). Don Tomás realises 'there were many ways of not having another person' (50). Her silence and withdrawal are a protection of her secret inner self, much like what silence represents in Morrison's *Beloved* (182). As Hurtado notes, the Orishas give the rape survivor 'sentience in the face of dehumanisation' ('Resilience' 6). Fela dies giving birth to Mati by the same river (55–7). The volatile Oshun frees her of her debt, but she has also made her daughter a New World Creole. Beyond her future legal entitlement to the land, culturally and psychologically, she is Puerto Rican, though that identity was not codified as such and certainly did not include full citizenship for non-whites.

Oshun helps Mati subvert Don Tomás's paternity. In the nineteenth century, the father granted his name to his legitimate children and his captives, but the novel typically avoids last names, creating a matrilineal focus. The centrality of mother-daughter relationships is another commonality with *Beloved*. Don Tomás does not control how Fela reacts to her insemination, and likewise he has no power over Mati's sense of self throughout most of her life. She sees him only as her mother's assailant. She prefers her 'soul father', Imo, to the *pater familias*, the colonial standard of naming and inheritance, so her paternity is 'fractured' and divided by the Atlantic (95). Don Tomás fancies himself a uniquely enlightened master whose punishments are only those necessary for his hacienda to function. Romero's sadistic behaviour as foreman – whipping a slave's back until he exhausts himself, forcing a woman to cut sugar cane moments after giving birth – proves that this plantation is no more benevolent than any other (15, 24). Nonetheless, Don Tomás's relative laxity has gained him a reputation for creating maroons, and his peers are reticent to buy his captives (94). This mistrust explains why there was never a legal challenge to Mati receiving the house as inheritance – the 'spoiled' slaves were thought better off in what amounts to a manicured *manigua*, as opposed to wreaking havoc on other estates. Rebellions in neighbouring islands had enslavers on high alert (94). Harmony and unity are under siege. This is why, in all likelihood, the Spanish would have 'pacified' Las Mercedes with armed forces and managed the sale of the fields and the captives. An extended tract of land that does not recognise slave laws would have been a draw for runaway slaves across the island – she would likely have been treated like an accomplice to theft. It was not legal at the time for a woman, Mati, to inherit land, much less to do with it what she does – turn it into a refuge for Afrodescendants. Llanos-Figueroa is likely aware of all this, so she uses Oshun to explain a way around the historical reality.

Nevertheless, Don Tomás's paternalism deludes him to the end. Doña Filomena passes without having a legitimate heir (81). The lack of filiation is a planter crisis. Death without producing a nuclear family was a common nineteenth-century trope regarding the unviability of a political system. Alejandro Tapia y Rivera's *La cuarterona* ('*Juliet of the Tropics*', 1867) and Cuban author Cirilo Villaverde's *Cecilia Valdés* (1882) are works in this vein. Llanos-Figueroa builds on the abolitionist tradition with a Yoruba epistemology. Doña Filomena dies holding a baby rattle (81). Children's toys represent the child-like, mischievous deity who opens and closes destinies like doors, Elegua (Moreno Vega, *Altar* 270). Don Tomás's fantasy of benevolence is hollow given the fact that he has run out of options for legitimacy, likely due to Oshun's intervention. As that door closes, another opens when he devises his 'enlightened' plan to free the captives in his will and recognise his eldest, if, until then, illegitimate and disregarded daughter. His three witnesses, who personify late Spanish colonial hierarchy, are the priest, a lawyer and a medical doctor (Llanos-Figueroa, *Daughters* 89). They dismiss the will as delusory and hatch a plan (89).

Don Tomás calls his captive daughter to his deathbed, but she has only open spite for him, channelling the goddess's pride (87). Yet it is the deity and her mother's spirit that convince her to take the parchment from her silenced progenitor (87). As expected, the men carve up the land and leave her only with the house and adjacent small plots for the *libertos* ('freed Black people') to inhabit (92).

Oshun brings the collective of La Caridad into existence, but she also destroys it, leading to subsequent fractals. Over two years, Mati uses the family *techné*, special powers that she has cultivated as a *curandera* ('healer') to make her usurpers ill (Llanos-Figueroa, *Daughters* 11). Oshun is the goddess of herbal medicine, but she is also the patron of poison, as in *La amante* (Valdés, *Daughters* 10). Once the enslavers are ill, after exhausting all other remedies, they call Mati for relief (Llanos-Figueroa, *Daughters* 116). This pattern is described in detail when she visits Don Próspero Herrera y Torres, the first of her victim-patients (91). Given his refusal to relinquish the land, she telepathically tortures him by contorting his organs (114). His reply is to call her – 'a daughter of a thousand *diablos* from the bowels of hell. *Bruja mala*' (Evil witch) (114), a designation that can be seen as a leitmotif of the novel. Hence, he evokes the 'great family's' Catholic identity and the Church's history of oppressing non-Christian practices (Herrera 65; Hurtado, 'Resilience' 8). As in the other stories analysed in this book, *brujas* are both healers and rebels. Mati uses her magic violence to regain all the land described in her will. Since the sorceress uses her gift for harm, she accrues a debt to Oshun. The medium will only settle it with the destruction of La Caridad.

One of the challengers to her father's will and testament, slaveocrat Don Próspero, is born of monsters. Torturing him is vengeance for one of the most savage scenes in the novel that rocks the foundations of the harmonious hacienda myth. Carisa has chosen not to name Don Próspero's father (47). His anonymity reverses the removal or replacing of slaves' names and focuses on the captive's point of view. As Don Tomás attempts to seduce Mati, she has traumatic flashbacks to her first enslaver in the New World (47). While Don Tomás is patient, debonair, attractive and generous (46–7), the father of Don Próspero is beastly. He rapes her in a barn (47). Ever tenacious, Fela bites a bleeding gash in his neck, for which he punches out some of her teeth (47). The penetration on the floor is described as 'searing hot pain that had torn apart her groin' made only worse by 'his rancid breath on her face' (47). He abandons her as 'he would an animal that had performed her task' (47).

An enslaver raping a captive in a barn evokes one of the most traumatising scenes in *Beloved*. Llanos-Figueroa admits her deep debt to Morrison, and I see in *Daughters* echoes of the African-American's masterpiece (The Latino Author). Barnett considers the latter to be 'haunted by the history and memory of rape specifically' (418). It unveils not only the Black woman Sethe's suffering, but also Paul D's sexual trauma (425). Sethe recalls the rape in a barn in which young enslavers steal her milk while her husband watches, hidden and afraid (70). Halle, her husband, was attempting to escape the torment of the plantation in the barn, but his hope for relief was certainly dashed by this trauma that he could only stop with the certain death of attacking the master and his boys. The pain is so great for Sethe that it eventually drives her to kill her favourite child rather than allow her to be newly enslaved and suffer the same fate (250).

If *Beloved* notes the limit that Sethe reaches in order to bring some form of justice for sexual assault (sparing her child) and the pathos of witnessing rape, *Daughters* indicts the men who sexually assault Black women and the white women who enable it. Hurtado sees the assault as the slave system's narrative of her as 'naturally available for such exploitation' (2579). She is silenced, but her body remembers it like Fe Verdejo's (2599). Fela is a *bozal*, so she can barely speak Spanish. She hopes another woman will show solidarity or take pity on her. She goes to Don Próspero's mother, called simply la *patrona* (literally, the 'female patriarch', but usually translated as 'boss') (48). She is playing cards with the other ladies. She is more concerned with her honour than with the humanity of her captive, keeping with the norms Suárez Findlay describes (53). She calmly finishes the card game before ordering an overseer to cut out the rape survivor's tongue (47). If Morrison shows the emotional reactions of Black characters nearly broken by sexual violence, Llanos-Figueroa shows the total numbness of the planter class to human suffering. Fela discovers the dangers of revealing their cruelty, breaking up their violent harmony and unity, reaffirming why minority communities are reticent to trust readers and listeners with details about their suffering. A veterinarian is called to stop the bleeding of the animalised captive (48). The *patrón* ('enslaver') does not deny his crime, so after the glossectomy, he sells Fela to keep up appearances (48). This foundational rape symbolises not only the very real patriarchal savagery of the plantation but also the central divide that Black and white women found in forming feminist movements. Rivera Lassén, for example, has worked to ameliorate this divide since 1976 ('Black' 70).

Fela's silence is a metaphor for the recurring theme in these novels – the exclusion of Black women as speaking subjects in history and literature (Hurtado, 'Resilience' 5). Herrera sees the land as Mati's only means of reconnecting with her lost mother, but the critic overlooks the spirits (62). Oshun allows Mati and the subsequent generations to heal the matriarch's torn anatomy, psyche and culture. The establishment of La Caridad sets right some part of the amputation and her silencing, which the glossectomy symbolises. When the enslavers steal Mati's inherited land and divide it between them, Mati compares it to carving up and distributing her mother's body, which she reassembles piece by piece as something new (92). Notably, this maternal body is not Mother Africa but instead Borinquén. Mati sees herself as an Afro-Puerto Rican before the concept has a name.

The Will and the Land in Zeno Gandía, Ferré and Llanos-Figueroa

Willing La Caridad to Mati has parallels with Manuel Zeno Gandía's classic novel *Garduña* (1896). Llanos-Figueroa's intertextuality with the author reaffirms that she is working to create a new imagined community in Puerto Rico. Aníbal González considers Zeno Gandía one of the founders of Puerto Rican literature and an architect of national culture through his five-part novel series *Crónica de un mundo enfermo* ('*Chronicles of an Infirm World*'), of which *Garduña* forms a part as the sequel of his greatest success, *La charca* ('*The Pond*', 1894) (67). Binder shows how the series attempts to reform the 'backward' nation by 'curing' its social ills, represented by its unwashed peasantry, the *jíbaros* ('peasants') (62). He never considers them white (62). Binder traces this racist ideology from Gandía to Pedreira's 'great family' as a cultural whitening project in the name of progress (62). Nouzeilles analyses race in the series, noting that the non-white masses of the *jíbaros* represented for Zeno Gandía a 'pond' (putrid, non-moving, amorphous mass) that could not advance due to its barbarism and atavistic racial traits (100). The liquid metaphor, along with the archipelago's peasant women – who copulate with all races – give the reader argumentation that the island must reform to progress in the nineteenth-century eugenic terms so loved by naturalists such as Zeno Gandía (100). As it does for Pedreira, the hacienda, a 'benevolent' panopticon, represents the nation-state since it argues for the control and norms of the planter class (Nouzeilles 99). Despite Zeno Gandía's fascination with secular, positivist and scientific-medicinal progress, he supports Catholicism as the morals through which to control the 'barbaric' races and classes (Nouzeilles 98).

Like Zeno Gandía's problematic classic *Garduña*, Mati receives a 'true' will that cannot be ratified (29). She also has her land taken away by a duplicitous lawyer and his two henchmen, the doctor and the priest (9). Yet she breaks with the nineteenth-century naturalist by providing more agency and nuance to Black and mulatto subjects. In Zeno Gandía, just like the anonymous mulatto who raped the *triqueña* ('dark mulatta') Úrsula, the mulatto Honorino has no honour, demonstrating a Don Juan hyper-sexuality (13, 18). The *bozal* woman who serves Tirso Mina is docile and loves her former master in spite of his physical abuse, unlike *Daughters*'s first two generations (45). Llanos-Figueroa also breaks with naturalist pessimism by proposing a Yoruba-based solution: Mati uses her powers to enact justice, get her land back and share it with her people. Hence, La Caridad prospers during her lifetime. This Afrocentric alternative to the dead patriarch's *hacienda*, Mina de Oro, encapsulates a desire for a Boricua 'family of choice' without the oppression that defined historical plantation life along the axes of race, gender and status.

The unexpected will and testament is also an important trope in Rosario Ferré's novella 'Maldito Amor' (1986). Moreno analyses the text as an anti-racist allegory of the nation (59). She notes that Ferré's *pater familias* Don Ubaldino, like Zeno Gandía's patriarch, dies of syphilis, the product of his philandering (68; Zeno Gandía 12). However, in the end, the matriarch Doña Laura is the one on her deathbed. She confesses the family secrets – that the distinguished family member Don Julio hides his African ancestry, that her husband was physically abusive and that her lover Gloria is to become heir to the Central Justicia ('Justice Mills') along with her future husband Nicolás (70). While 'Maldito Amor' occurs during the time of the early US occupation, little has changed since abolition. Gloria is the sensual mulatta that the men of the family frequently abused, and so the reader shares her catharsis when she burns her newly inherited plantation with her abusers inside the house (71, 82). As Moreno notes, the fall of the patriarch, his biographer and the family home ensure an end to the legacy of racial oppression and a radical subversion of the great family myth (71). She highlights the allusions to slavery, like the whip, human backs and sugar cane during descriptions of the fire, which parallel those of Romero (Moreno 71; Llanos-Figueroa 99).

Ferré's depictions of Black characters in 'Maldito' and 'Cuando' is a subject of debate. Along with Ana Lydia Vega, she is the culmination of the 1970s generation's dismantling of the 'great family' by non-Black authors focused on challenging heteropatriarchy and racism (Gelpí 2259). Gelpí notes the constant presence in her work of marginal characters that do not belong to the 'great family', including Black people and lesbians (2268). In the story 'Cuando las mujeres quieren a los hombres', the white, landed Isabel Luberza meets Isabel La Negra (Isabel Luberza Oppenheimer), who would later be the focus of Santos-Febres's *Nuestra Señora* (2283). The patriarch dies, leaving half his property to La Negra, and a battle is expected. However, the two women choose one another and become lovers, which for Gelpí 'completes' the mulatto national project Palés began (2336). 'Maldito Amor' marks the destruction of the paternalist canon for him (2439). Ramos Rosado praises the work for demanding the destruction of plantation myths and replacing them with a new, democratic nation (*Destellos* 121). Branche reduces the interest of Ferré's generation in Afro-Puerto Ricans to a 'fad' and calls her representation in 'Cuando' 'colonial' and 'negative' (154). He accuses the 'legitimate' Isabel of complicity in the abuse of the 'illegitimate' one, but Fela's first mistress is a far better example than Ferré's privileged woman who chooses change (156). He does not see the similarity of the bordello the women found together with La Caridad – an appropriation of the patriarchal family home of the rich – to create a 'family' of sex workers who do their craft with relative freedom and dignity (156).

Llanos-Figueroa shares with Ferré's 'Maldito Amor' a spectacular fire that sets the colonial order right. Gloria tells the Afrodescendant servants Néstor and Titina that the whites never would have given them the small plots of land on which they live (Ferré 26–7). In Llanos-Figueroa's case, land and liberty come to the enslaved only partly because of Don Tomás, and his power is weak in comparison to Oshun, Fela and Mati's, who use magic to control the actions and the destiny of the privileged. The implicit message is that Black women must look to their spiritual ancestors for the greatest power, not just the institutions born of slavery – the university and 'enlightened' elites and their justice.

Splitting: Oshun Exiles Her Daughters

Mati achieves justice, vengeance, power and recollection when she inherits La Caridad, but they come at a price. Implicitly, Oshun takes in return her partner, her life and the destinies of her progeny (116). Mati's relationship with Cheo, the man who gave her a daughter, Concha, unravels (147). The two had been in love since Concha was born, and arguably before it, since he is the young carpenter who carved her first cradle. While Oshun is the metaphysical cause of Mati's suffering, her secular problems are rooted in her identity as a Black woman. She is manumitted by her biological father, inadvertently taking away the freedman Cheo's pride at being able to free his wife. He does not trust her magic at any point, least of all when she uses it to break his leg and leave him with a limp for life (72). He feels emasculated by the woman he fears as a *bruja* ('witch') (74). Eventually, Mati becomes so engrossed in her practice as a herbal healer that he calls her *nueva patrona* ('new woman boss', literally 'woman patriarch') and leaves the family, much to the chagrin of his beloved daughter Concha (147).

However, the reader should not place the blame solely on either partner – Cheo surely feels an overwhelming impotence due to his being born enslaved. The radical changes of instant manumission and challenges to his Catholic upbringing are understandable, given that captivity was normal for him. The things he expects to be able to change are already changed, and he cannot cope with that. One can compare his reaction to Paul D's in *Beloved*. When he and Sethe attempt to reconcile the present with the traumatic past of her rape on Sweet Home and the infanticide she commits in Ohio, he feels that her love for her daughters is 'too thick' (164). In addition to how he sees her affection, he feels himself too broken by slavery to love her as she loves him:

> Listening to the doves in Alfred, Georgia, and having neither the right nor the permission to enjoy it because in that place mist, doves, sunlight, copper dirt, moon – everything belonged to the men who had the guns ... So you protected yourself and loved small ... Anything bigger wouldn't do. A woman, a child, a brother – a big love like that would split you wide open in Alfred, Georgia. He knew exactly what she meant: to get to a place where you could love anything you chose – not to need permission for desire – well now, that was freedom. (162)

Cheo's patriarchal attitude of not feeling needed on the plantation is part of their separation. However, his emotional state is like Paul D's – he cannot make the psychological leap to love this powerful woman who may want him but who does not need him. Like Paul D, he cannot give his wife a home and the type of love she needs, and so he must leave her (103). Ultimately, Paul D learns to love Sethe and returns, listening to her as he rubs her feet, but Cheo cannot open himself to love on the hacienda-*palenque*.

Mati is saddened by losing the man who was to rule La Caridad alongside her, but soon she faces an even greater blow. She and her family are devastated by Hurricane San Cristobal, Oshun's final punishment upon her disobedient daughter. While the goddess is not associated with storms, they are the realm of her sister Oya, her fellow riverine goddess (Valdés, *Daughters* 10).

Mati's daughter, Concha, cannot cope with losing her mother. The daughter has already begun to leave the safety of La Caridad before the storm hits. Cheo's faith in the West has led her to go to school and forget her devotion to Oshun, mentally trapping the deity's implements in a chest and forgetting them (175). If this psychological break with her mother is not bad enough, she has learned to ignore her own *techné* of a spiritual connection to nature. Herrera notes that school teaches her anti-Blackness (64). Santos-Febres probably would mourn her capitulation to colonial, linear thought.

While Concha's gift came from the African goddess of rivers, the author has chosen a Morrison-esque form of this gift: she connects to plants by sensing them through her feet, a trait Herrera notices but does not connect to the African-American author (64). Hurtado sees this trait as a unique, corporeal way of knowing, since the feet are full of nerve endings with which to sense one's environment (2663). While it is tempting to reduce these powers to a foot fetish – as is evident when she makes love to Toño – it is also another connection to *Beloved* (*Daughters* 131–56). In Morrison's masterpiece, Baby Suggs ministers to the enslaved as they cross the Mason-Dixon Line (88). Her gospel is a kind of love that the enslaved have not known in the United States before meeting her in the Clearing, the area where she preaches: 'In this here place, we flesh; flesh that weeps, laughs; flesh that dances on bare feet in grass. Love it. Love it hard. Yonder they do not love your flesh. They despise it' (88). Lam, in her interpretation of *Daughters*, argues that recognising the bodies of the enslaved – which have been brutally disciplined by the slave system – creates a 'restored sense of self and community' (3). The critic says Llanos-Figueroa is 'foregrounding the body as a way of knowing', which she shares with Santos-Febres (6). Those bare feet are the joy of a self-loving and family-loving Black childhood that Concha loses as school teaches her to leave her country life on La Caridad.

The trauma of the hurricane and Mati's death leave Concha catatonic. The loss of the relatively ideal living conditions – humble, but stable and equitable, with a sense of belonging – is the turning point of the novel. Concha's illness leaves her daughter, Elena, feeling abandoned and severed from her family's traditions. This sense of amnesia is compounded by her moving to a New York tenant building, likely in El Barrio (East Harlem), and then to the Bronx (144). Her daughter, Cari, reverses this course as a 'remigrant' who returns to the island to study at the University of Puerto Rico at Río Piedras before proceeding to Nigeria in search of her family's roots (Flores 34). Her journey back to the source parallels Moreno Vega's, and it is the US Civil Rights and Black Power movements that push her back to the island, where she discovers that the official institutions – universities, government – support whitening (291–2).

The abyss between Concha and Elena also evokes a variant of *Beloved*'s 'big love' among Black families in an Afro-Puerto Rican context. When Concha comes out of her catatonic state – one of many metaphors for unspoken trauma and lack of empowering historical and literary representation in *Daughters* – she has difficulty relating to her daughter Elena. Toño, Concha's husband, chastises her for being too harsh on her daughter:

> For five years she put everything in her life second and you first. Just as you did with Mati. Isn't that what your [mental] illness was all about, putting Mati before all the rest of us? Elena learned from you. Her silence and her anger are no different than yours. All you women feel too much. Everything is too big with you. You love too big and fear too big and have too much anger and too few words ... Be careful. Your love burns the rest of us. (192)

The family's collective love and pain come from generations of surviving trauma – first the Middle Passage, then plantation slavery and now natural disaster and poverty. Llanos-Figueroa makes these themes, which Morrison explored so profoundly, more Puerto Rican by making them all daughters of Oshun, a beloved deity of the island's marginalised, syncretic religions. Oshun is a deeply loving goddess of maternity and fertility, but she also has a deep rage and can start conflict between headstrong mothers and daughters (Valdés, *Daughters* 10).

A Family, Not a Filiation, of Borinquén

The hurricane is a literary device used to tie Oshun's magic to the history of the rights of Afro-Puerto Ricans, which often shows more continued limitations than progress. It is difficult to conceive a history of slavery without abolition, and it is hard to imagine the history of Puerto Rico without the War of 1898, yet the novel mentions neither. As Herman Bennett argues, there is much to be learned by considering the history of the African diaspora without a notion of linear progress culminating in English-led abolition, which resolves the problems Afrodescendants face due to the institution and its ramifications (57). In Cuba, Luis notes a similar lack of change or progress with the abolition of slavery in 1886 for Miguel Barnet's informant Esteban Montejo in *Cimarrón* (1966) ('Politics' 477). For Mati's progeny, the same silence is striking. In order for Don Tomás's will to manumit the enslaved of Las Mercedes and for trade to be affected by the 'strange' farm of free Black people, it would have had to occur at least two years from 1873, when Spain abolished slavery. That is the amount of time that it takes Mati to recuperate all her land. La Caridad emerges in 1871 or before.

The novel uses flashback and focus on interpersonal conflicts to avoid chronological time, thus skirting abolition and the 1898 invasion. Llanos-Figueroa claims that the lack of dates in the book comes from her focus on plot development, since she is not a historian, and to universalise the character's trials ('Interview'). The *palenque*'s relative isolation contributes to this psychological, but not exactly historical passage of time. Mati receives Las Mercedes, approximately, when she is twenty-three (104). The novel claims that she is twenty-five when she finishes assembling La Caridad, so that would mean she was born, at the latest, in 1848 (104). The hurricane is called San Cristobal, and the novel seems to imply that it happened in 1938 (279). A hurricane by that name only occurred in 2014 (Associated Press). Llanos-Figueroa bases her hurricane on San Felipe from 1876 but claims that the date does not matter ('Interview'). Fractal Caribbean time does not proceed like chronological time (Santos-Febres, 'Caribe' 19:04). The shock from the storm leaves Concha institutionalised for five years, Oshun's sacred number (González-Wippler 2015). Once she returns to live with her family, her daughter almost immediately wants to go to nursing school in San Juan. For Elena to study nursing in San Juan, she would have to do so at the School of Tropical Medicine (which was founded in 1931) like Micaela Thorné (193). She is graduating high school, so she is roughly eighteen (193), meaning that she was born in 1913. Unlike the previous two generations, there is no mention of when Concha was conceived or born. Hence, she may have originated when the couple married in around 1873 (at the latest), since no mention of Concha is made before. That would make her at least forty when Concha came into the world. Thus, Concha, despite having access to formal schooling, does not mention that the island changed hands in 1898. Concha should have learned of the US invasion through the press. Llanos-Figueroa leaves this out, presumably because it apparently made no difference to the residents of La Caridad. They have achieved independence, even if they remain isolated. They have achieved a *palenque*-plantation, a space for the 'great Puerto Rican family' in which Black people are loved and respected. They are not obsessed with 1898, the point of origin for hispanophile Insularist thought (Ríos Ávila, *Raza* 124). Another national family has emerged.

In the novel, characters merely adjust to the modernisation projects of the island. The hurricane abruptly forces Elena into the world of US science. However, in the 1920s and 1930s, psychotropic medicines and formal mental health professionals are US imports. While this approach to Concha's suffering is ineffective, it is only part of the collective forgetting of life before San Cristobal. Elena, her daughter, struggles to bring her back to society through oral storytelling and the stone that Oshun has blessed (184-5). This experience likely inspires Elena's career trajectory. While she may not know it, Elena is continuing the family tradition of herbal healing in a westernised setting like Santos-Febres's Micaela.

Elena's path back to a plenitude like that of La Caridad takes her on the classic journey from Puerto Rico to New York in the 1950s (201). She takes her young son and daughter there to escape her dysfunctional husband and mother-in-law (204). She has taken back the house where the couple had planned to begin again, ending the potential for a new La Caridad (202). Elena's life of repeated exile sends her to El Barrio, part of Santos-Febres's fractal family (Llanos-Figueroa, *Daughters* 212; Santos-Febres, 'Fractal' 34:41). The superintendent is so miserly that he refuses to turn on the heat during an unexpected cold front, so her son Danilo dies of hypothermia (229–31). She and her husband Pedro, who follows her to New York but continues to be absent in her life, live with a 'ghost' sleeping between them at night, the absence of their lost son (234). She has 'twins' of grief and guilt in her heart, evoking Oshun's twins, the Ibeyi (Llanos-Figueroa, *Daughters* 231; Valdés,

Daughters 10). If the ghost Beloved is the Garner baby come back to life (among other possible interpretations) after her mother intentionally kills her, Danilo is a 'guilt-ridden and ghost-bearing silence' that seems to blame Elena for leaving her island (231). The expectation that the Puerto Rican government and Marqués had that Puerto Ricans who leave the island would and should leave the 'great family' and assimilate to US culture turns out to be wrong (Moreno 41). The child's death is at the heart of the alienation Elena and her husband feel while in New York.

Carisa's Queer(?) Return to La Caridad

Elena's daughter Carisa 'remigrates' to Puerto Rico, a homeland that she has never known first-hand (Flores 33). It is tempting to note biographical elements of the novel, since Llanos-Figueroa is Nuyorican, but she claims her life is generally a 'mould' for her ('Interview'). It is important to note that Llanos-Figueroa was raised visiting Carolina, Puerto Rico, so her perspective is as heavily influenced by the archipelago as the mainland ('The World'). The author says that she associates her time on the island with family and community, the central themes of this study ('Q and A'). Like Carisa, she sees women's oral storytelling as a preservation of family history that one can find in neither history books nor digital media, which I consider a fractal font of knowledge ('Q and A').

Carisa seeks to reassemble the pieces the storm has shattered, which is impossible, so she forms another fractal. Her return as a 'remigrant' stands in stark contrast to Luis's contention that Nuyoricans of the second and future generations begin to identify more closely with the US mainland as minorities than with the island as a longed-for homeland (Luis, 'Latino' xxii). Carisa makes it to college, a long way from the previous generations who faced race, gender and class barriers to formal education, but her Black alienation continues as professors discourage her from writing about her family's past and their syncretic traditions, leaving her depressed (*Daughters* 273). Her spiritual mother Oshun is the goddess of artistic creativity, but they do not know this or see it manifested in the Nuyorican's work due to their Eurocentrism (González-Wippler 104). Like Morrison's characters, she is rightly suspicious of white schoolteachers well after slavery is abolished, since they continue the violence of slavery by suppressing Afrodescendants' culture and history (Elia 4–5).

This characterisation of Afro-Latinx New York is limiting and unwittingly paternalist. Instead of noting female and queer trailblazers, Llanos-Figueroa limits her 1970s generation narrator-protagonist to the influence of Piri Thomas and a search for Blackness in the all-white Iupi. For many, he was a foundational figure, including post-1980s Nuyorican and Afro-Puerto Rican poets (Richardson 97). Luis perceives his influence on Llanos-Figueroa and Marta Moreno Vega in their negotiation of Afro-Nuyorican identities (Luis, 'Afro-Latino/a' 39). Likewise, Llanos-Figueroa treats Thomas as a solitary founding father on the mainland and ignores Black pioneers on the archipelago. One wonders where the *palenque*-plantation is in El Barro (East Harlem) and the repeating barrios of the US mainland, which themselves bear the scars of the abusive plantation family. The Young Lords and the Nuyorican poets emerged in the 1960s, yet they are absent (Luis, *Looking* xxii, 295). Gelpí warns against forming generations around a single, heroic figure like Pedreira, since it recreates the paternalist structure of the plantation in the canon (157). In fact, Cruz-Malavé considers Thomas the author of an 'anti-foundational foundational fiction' – one that does not create what Glissant calls 'filiation' but one that unveils a colonial corporeal history that haunts the nation (i.e., Blackness) (4). The critic problematises the search for an affirmatively Black father in his work, and yet he is treated as a literary progenitor (7). He sees that Thomas's family, like the 'great family', represses not only Blackness but homosexual desires as well, yet they both haunt his tenement (13). His masculinist work was incomplete and needed feminist writers of the 1970s such as Angela Jorge to give voice to Afrodescendant women (Jiménez Roman and Flores 9). Arguably, creating verisimilitude based on gender roles of the time is a valid reason to leave out other 'founding fathers' of Afro-Puerto Rican literature – Llanos-Figueroa's protagonist is kept at home to protect her, so smoking in bohemian poets' cafés and burning garbage in the streets with activists in berets would likely have been off limits to her. Homophobia and transphobia were also barriers, since many Nuyorican poets were LGBQT+ (Jaime 1). But to treat Thomas as a patriarch ignores Moreno Vega's development of the Museo del Barrio in 1973 and Nicholasa Mohr's fictionalised memoir of the

Bronx from a young woman's point of view in *Nilda* (1973) (Moreno Vega, *Altar* 57). Conversely, she did not cross paths on the island with Zenón or Rodríguez Torres, whose *Veinte siglos después del homicidio* ('*Twenty Centuries after the Homicide*') debuted in 1972 (Santiago-Díaz 266). While the reader loses the context of other Afro-Boricua writers through Llanos-Figueroa's choice to exclude them, she is making a valid point: Afro-Latinx writers had, and have, to look outside the white-dominant academy in order to decolonise their identities and tell their stories, and only since 2007 have role-model writers become plentiful.

Carisa moves to Puerto Rico to live with her grandmother, who replaces her anti-depressants with herbal remedies and a community of elderly mother figures who reaffirm her sense of self (275). It is no coincidence that her name is usually abbreviated to 'Cari', indicating that her issues of identity apply to the Caribbean ('*Caribe*' in Spanish) as a whole. She works to do that on the archipelago, but her studies at Río Piedras prove to be a disappointment (291–2). At this time (1942–71), the direct heir of Pedreira's Insularism, Jaime Benítez, was university president (Santiago-Díaz 123). The curriculum all but ignores the history of African people and slavery on the island (291–2). Carisa's US background taught her that having an Afro hairstyle was normal and even liberating, but she finds herself surrounded by the white and whitened elite at the Iupi (291–2). When she finds herself caught in the brutal police suppression of Independentist protesters, she discovers a way out of the alienating, Eurocentric prisons in which he has found herself (293).

The photographer María Luisa rescues Carisa from the police and drags her from the Río Piedras campus to her nearby photography studio (294). She introduces a new kind of family to the daughters of Oshun in search of La Caridad. María Luisa is an Afro-Puerto Rican photographer who goes around the island documenting its popular history (306). Her work is very important for cultural memory, since many of the people are illiterate and since the government – local and federal – under the auspices of Operation Bootstrap, is modernising or 'sanitising' the island's present and past of oppression at the time (306). One can see the metaphorical ghost of Hacienda Las Mercedes in the decrepit coffee estate they photograph (304). That land and the carcass of its manor house are full of suffering. The photographers mourn it, but in a way they reclaim it. They give it presence in a time when the academy and the arts are marked by its idealisation or absence. Hurtado argues that these experiences develop 'intuitive consciousness mechanisms' to fight coloniality, the political and epistemological system that she has been taught to accept as normal but which has constructed her oppression due to Insularism (2743). As María Luisa makes these stories visible, Carisa gives them voice by writing tales that fill in the silences of people's memories (309). The book they write together is a precursor to the book the reader is consuming, since Carisa is the fictional author of the novel (325). While the secrets of the book are never revealed, one knows there is more to the story.

María Luisa and Carisa's relationship is, like the text that they write, complimentary and greater than the sum of its parts. Llanos-Figueroa could be accused of being coy in presenting a lesbian relationship and bending to the virulent homophobia on the island (Ríos Ávila, 'Queer' 1129). Perhaps she intended for the book to be consumed in high schools where homophobia is often endemic to school culture (Russell 125). If María Luisa and Carisa are lesbians or bisexual, the clues that hint at their love stand in stark contrast to the work of Arroyo Pizarro, which at times has unapologetic representation of queer subjects through explicit eroticism and the open confrontation of homophobia, as in *Violeta* (2013). Llanos-Figueroa has expressed solidarity with LGBTQ+ activism in an interview, so she is an ally (Lassauze). There is a beautiful subtlety to María Luisa and Carisa's relationship. Lesbian sex, which is never mentioned, is not the first queer sex act in the novel, as Mati's foot fetish shows, so the reader should not rule out a queer interpretation.

In fact, the text never states that the Nuyorican and the islander have a relationship beyond employer/mentor and apprentice. It is never said that they do not, but there are hints. After their time together, María Luisa gets another assistant, and Carisa happens to see them on the corner:

> I was about to run across the street to help with the cameras when I noticed a middle-aged woman in men's overalls lifting the last of the equipment before walking over to María Luisa. They embraced and kissed for a long moment before María Luisa released the woman, who walked back into the studio and closed the door. (316)

The woman could just be a friend and co-worker, but there are other instances of innuendo, all of which involve Carisa. When the young woman presents her mentor with the book that they wrote together, they embrace one last time, and María Luisa says: 'Better be careful. You know how evil tongues wag' (317). It is hard to believe Carisa, in this stage of discovering herself in the late 1960s or 1970s, otherwise single, and travelling the archipelago alongside this woman that she admires deeply, had only a professional relationship with her (307). María Luisa alludes to her 'closest companion', likely Carisa, when she shows the young woman her photos of Afro-Puerto Ricans and *jíbaros* (307). They help bring the history of slavery and oppression 'out of the closet' like Rivera Lassén says, but it seems they remain in it as lovers ('Black' 70). One day, Carisa meets a young professor of anthropology at the Iupi. She is doing fieldwork on marginalised Puerto Ricans, and he helps her get a research assistantship at the university as part of the 1970s new historiography that focuses on the marginalised, as Herrera notes ('Women' 42). Carisa reflects on their likely closeted bond: 'I dreaded telling María Luisa. Ours was more than a simple working relationship' (311). The phrasing creates plausible deniability. However, innuendo creeps into the dialogue that dramatises the bittersweet separation of the partners:

> [The photographer] put her hand up, as though shielding herself.
> 'Is it the work or is it the boy?'
> 'Wha ...?'
> 'You know damn well what I'm asking, Storyteller. Don't treat me like I'm an idiot. So I ask you again, is it the work or the boy?'
> I thought about it a moment.
> 'It's both, but more the work, really'.
> 'Then you must go'.
> 'But I –'
> '*Mira*, Storyteller. Nothing lasts forever. When the music stops, you find a different fiddler'. (312)

The violins connote a personal, amorous relationship more than a professional one. However a character or the reader defines their relationship, it is deeply meaningful to the couple. They spend five years – the number of Oshun – together discovering the island, themselves and each other (González-Wippler 105). They exemplify the goddess's creativity and vivacity, but I think that they also represent her eroticism, just in a way that is different from the other characters (104).

At the very least, this family of choice is a message of tolerance and empathy. Like the Black community of La Caridad, there is more than shared suffering in queer families, there is also a deep and unique love like that of the street queens LaFountain-Stokes analyses (*Translocas* 77). This kind of family would have remained an even more closely kept secret during the time of La Caridad. The subtlety with which Llanos-Figueroa treats this tender relationship makes the reader want the music to last as a new La Caridad is imagined for the fractal future of Afro-Puerto Rico.

The photographer and the young griot create a sort of aesthetic homeland on the soil that holds so much African blood. Carisa's separation from her and her male lover is a new beginning (315). La Caridad represents home on the island. While Las Mercedes is a place where love is taken away or silenced at every turn – making Black love a form of rebellion – for Carisa, love is much more of a choice: love for herself and her community (Lam 4). Carisa, with the mobility and knowledge of the twentieth century West, goes beyond the island, beyond healing its wounded memory to the place she hopes to find a semblance of the African village European-incited genocide and her ancestor's metaphysical misstep destroyed – and a new beginning (323). Alongside a quest for Fela's village, Carisa is seeking to counter the stereotypes of Africans as primitive that even her loving Afro-Puerto Rican grandmother holds due to representations in the media (320). She wants to find some part of the ancestral spirits, but she also wants to begin anew. Herrera calls Nigeria the family's 'home place', but I see it as one part of their foundation of Afro-Puerto Rico on the archipelago ('Women' 73). Like her great-grandfather Cheo, she wants to possess a double consciousness with 'two ways of knowing', one Western, based on letters and one African, based on oral traditions (137). Like Morrison, she wants to give visibility and value to America's 'alternative knowledge' of African-derived spiritual and medicinal traditions (Wisker 72). She wants to build a new community that is anything but insular through her writing, and the justice that La Caridad represents is an ideal that she, and the reader, can spend a lifetime seeking. She goes 'sin permiso' – without permission from anybody, a freedom her ancestors never had (313). She is breaking with the patriarchal norms that travel from the

Oshun and the Palenque-Plantation

plantation to El Barrio that control women's movement (313). Her new partner, Adrián, like the reader, can seek that journey and that community with her or abandon it – she is an independent, evolving fractal (317). The novel invites the audience to make that journey of eternal return with the characters to build a more just (Afro-)Puerto Rican nation.

This chapter has shown the creation of La Caridad, the journey to it, and the work to return once it is lost. This free land is governed by Mother Oshun, the matriarch of five generations of women. La Caridad deconstructs the *quilombo/*plantation binary in that it is a utopian 'family of choice' for Afro-Puerto Ricans in the space that was once their prison. La Caridad is inherited, but it is also hard-earned through magic, the family craft, and suffering. Harrowing rape and torture to silence Fela evoke the imagery of Morrison's *Beloved*. This savagery dismantles the notion of enslavers romancing their captives, which a white Creole later attempts. The veneer of the 'great family' plantation is stripped. The captor's shame leads him to bequeath the hacienda to his 'illegitimate' daughter. Even the inheritance requires struggle and the imagined process dialogues with Zeno Gandía and Ferré on this theme, adding new Afrodescendant agency and centrality of the Orishas. Mother Oshun's rage takes the plantation-*palenque* away from the family. Their trials make abolition and the Spanish-American War seem far off and irrelevant to their lives. Subsequent generations metaphorically seek a way back to La Caridad. The search for land and community leads them to New York, where Morrison-esque trauma awaits, further fragmenting the family. Carisa, the young griot of the family, returns from New York to the island. Llanos-Figueroa seems to ignore texts and spaces beyond Afro-Latinx patriarch Thomas's writing (Santos-Febres, 'Fractal' 34:41). On the archipelago, she discovers a new family bond, that of two women. Her journey, like others discussed in this book, takes her far beyond an insular notion of Puerto Rico to its diaspora and even Nigeria, another territory far beyond the boundaries of the plantation.

Conclusion
Afro-Borinquén Today and Tomorrow

This book has endeavoured to show that Afro-Borinquén is a fractal family. Our approach to it should not be a homogeneous, hierarchical, linear continuation of colonial, racist, patriarchal and heteronormative structures. One should look at the situation prior to Africans' arrival at the plantation, as in Yolanda Arroyo Pizarro's 'Wanwe' and 'Saeta'. The reader should look to resistance and 'illegitimate' sexual relationships on the plantation, as in Mayra Santos-Febres's and Dahlma Llanos-Figueroa's work. We should look at maternal – and anti-maternal (*Fe, La amante*, 'Matronas') – figures like those of all the writers depicted. We cannot forget the racial identity of the author, keeping in mind Santos-Febres's desire to be both Black and Puerto Rican. Race is not in conflict with the concept of nation, though it stands opposed to the racist myths of the past, like those of the 1930s and 1950s generations, led by Pedreira and Marqués. Independentism is not in conflict with African and Puerto Rican diaspora identities, since these are fractals that extend from New York to Lagos, down to Buenos Aires and north to Chicago. Despite being scattered across the globe, Black writers and characters in these works have a right to the archipelago that once excluded them through slavery, discrimination and silence. Lest we wax romantic, we must not forget that this family is fractal because of the traumas of colonialism, racism, sexism and cis-heteronormativity. There is a lot of pain in this beautiful formation, a lot of tearing things apart. Much of that rending began as part of the 'great family' itself, and now Afrodescendants must form a family of choice to find freedom. There is no incentive to seek a homogeneous Afro-Puerto Rican identity, since it is constantly repeating and changing like the shapes of coastlines at the edge of the sea that connects Puerto Rico to the rest of the Caribbean.

I have placed Mayra Santos-Febres at the centre of this book, but I caution the reader not to treat her as a second Pedreira. Gelpí is reticent to speak of literary 'generations' like that of the 1930s, since they create hierarchies with a single figure at the centre (161). Likewise, Celis and Rivera consider Santos-Febres a departure from the culture of the celebrity novelist (17). She has achieved unprecedented international success for an Afro-Puerto Rican female writer, but she admits she did not do it alone. Oquendo-Villar has shown that she should not be seen as a 'mother' of a generation but part of a workshop of collaborators (47). The UPR programme had precursors in the informal reading and creative writing group that Arroyo Pizarro led, which she describes in the interviews that follow. The bachelor degrees in Afrodiasporic and raciality studies would not exist without the three international Afrodescent conferences in Puerto Rico that Torres Muñoz and Quiñones Hernández led in 2015, 2018 and 2021. Ramos Rosado, who taught the first seminar on Afro-Puerto Rican writers, gathered allies to hold previous conferences. They are all part of a legacy of representing Black women that we are only now beginning to see in formation, like the testimonies of captive Africans in *Fe*. As the interviews at the end of this book show, the other writers are trailblazers and activists beyond their literary works.

In 2021, following a severe financial crisis, two major hurricanes, incompetent and sadistic leadership by the US Republican Party, repeated local political scandals, the largest mass-shooting of Latinxs in US history (the Pulse Massacre), exodus, widespread closing of schools, brutal defunding of higher education, earthquake swarms, a state of emergency caused by femicides and a global pandemic, mean that it is difficult to be hopeful. Yet, like their *cimarrona* ancestors, these authors and thinkers are building institutions that were once thought impossible. Under Marta Moreno Vega and Maricruz Rivera Clemente, Casa Afro is making Loíza no longer a foreign space excluded from the nation, as it was in previous generations, but a centre of knowledge (Rivera Clemente; Moreno Vega, 'Co-Founder's Perspective'). Trailblazers like Ramos Rosado, Torres Muñoz, Quiñones Hernández, Moreno Vega, Rivera Clemente and Arroyo Pizarro are seeing their efforts make palpable change in the University of Puerto Rico Río Piedras Afrodiasporic and raciality undergraduate degree. These institutions are the fractal family in its scholarly, academic and activist forms. Black people and allies can come to the Iupi to be welcomed and enlightened by Black professors, many of them female. It will be led by Santos-Febres, who, along with Torres-Muñoz, has earned a Mellon grant to fund positions for other faculty members in Afrodiasporic and raciality studies (Universidad de Puerto Rico). Like the fractal, it is not confined to a linear canon of patriarchs, so it is inherently interdisciplinary and housed not in Hispanic studies but general studies. The Casa Afro, the Corredor Afro, and Afrodiasporic and raciality studies, in addition to a long list of organisations that Reinat-Pumarejo mentions, will continue the legacy of the fractal family – not through filiation but through a scattering and growing over time (68). In her speech 'The Fractal Caribbean', Santos-Febres notes the importance of family, re-defined as a multiracial network of trusted friends, religious communities, elders and ancestors, in recuperating after disasters (16:00). I will now revisit the main arguments of my previous chapters, adding suggestions for future research on this rich body of work from four gifted authors and their precursors.

An implied element of this study on the 'fractal family', which has discussed enslavement, marronage, US-imposed racial segregation, migration, sterilisation campaigns, ghettoisation, the lack of land rights and the collective forgetting that many Afro-Puerto Ricans have suffered are but a few examples of the *sankofa*, another element of the 'fractal Caribbean' (Santos-Febres 'Caribe' 40:00). This word, meaning 'recuperating the forgotten past' among the Akan people of Ghana, is symbolised by a bird looking backwards while its feet face forwards (Reinat-Pumarejo 72). Reinat-Pumarejo considers it a form of therapy for the collective traumas of Afrodescendants (72). The image is visible in the front matter of Arroyo Pizarro's *Las caras lindas* ('*Beautiful Faces*' 2016), for example. Evoking Glissant, Santos-Febres calls it a 'prophetic vision of the past' in which one uses new knowledge from history to form a vision for the future, bearing African traditions in mind (Santos-Febres, 'Caribe' 40:00; Glissant, *Caribbean* 64). It is the symbol of the Cátedra de Mujeres Negras Ancestrales 'Ancestral Black Women's Study Group', of which Santos-Febres and Denis-Rosario are members and which Arroyo Pizarro directs. Let us now look to the past to imagine a better future, more informed by history, literature and culture and more democratic in our representation of Black women as authors and scholars of Puerto Rico.

Families of the Future

Fractal Familes is about Afro-Puerto Rican literary prose writers who, since 2007, have been rewriting the origins and history of the archipelago and its diaspora. Santos-Febres, Arroyo Pizarro, Denis-Rosario and Llanos-Figueroa are imagining a counter-narrative to the 'great Puerto Rican family' that includes increased Black, female empowerment. They return to the hacienda to recreate enslaved women's point of view, and they relate it to today's concerns of continued racial prejudice and sexism.

They imagine the archipelago as a transnational '*uno-múltiple*'. Santos-Febres proposes a family of choice based on performative, fluid identities with optional relationships. The Afro-Puerto Rican nation-family allegory is not structured in the same manner as the 'great Puerto Rican family'. It is matrifocal, marked by Black rebellion, and includes rights to the land. While my focus has been on land inheritance, ecocriticism will surely find new insights into this relationship. In 'Fractal', Santos-Febres notes that nature, the realm of the Orishas, resists binaries, just like her understanding of the Caribbean chaos that Benítez Rojo previously theorised (22:40).

The fractal family's *techné*, healing, midwifery, traditional medicine and dialogue with the Orishas and other African spirits, are a source of creativity, sense of community and tradition. These can be seen as alternatives to the colonially imposed notions of purity and whitening that justified so much oppression in the name of family. These writers are reforming institutions that promote nationalism and are making the island less hierarchical. This community is a repeating, irregular, unpredictable shape, or fractal, that somehow belongs together amidst the fragmented, super-syncretic Caribbean.

These Black feminists have overcome racism among feminists and sexism among Black activists and elsewhere. They are continuing a legacy of intersectionality that spans the Atlantic from enslavement to today. Intersectionality, along with performativity, has created theories like those of *transloca* LaFountain-Stokes, who has Caribbeanised the notions of identity performance. The concubine and the sex worker also form part of an Afro-Boricua notion of family, which is the basis of the new national allegory of the fractal family, alongside rebel families or *palenques* presented as the precursors of today's Black solidarity.

Gender and sexuality have informed Black womanhood among African-Americans. In Latin America, since 2000, Afrodescent as a political identity has increased Black consciousness, but it must be nuanced with other aspects of identity. Race intersects with national identity, and the fractal family these authors imagine is one that, while postmodern in the tradition of Glissant and Benítez Rojo, remains Independentist, granting Black ownership to the island. LGBTQ+ networks, Afro-Boricua families and the overlap between the two need interpretive innovation as one reimagines the translocal nation.

These authors are not the first to criticise Pedreira, the Insularists or, later, Marqués's allegories of the national family. Gelpí and other scholars have shown that the 'great family' was oppressive and exclusionary since at least Pedreira and Marqués's iterations of it in the context of the 1930s and 1950s generations. That imagined community was a racist, sexist, conformist, colonial cultural nationalism that justified the hegemony of the island to the benefit of the white upper class. Pioneers challenged elements of the model, which, after Pedreira, included a whitening myth of cultural and racial miscegenation. Afro-Puerto Ricans Schomburg, Thomas, the Young Lords, the poets of the Nuyorican Poets Café and Moreno Vega formed affirmative Black identities, which, sometimes, intersect with femininity and queerness. Vizcarrondo, Rodríguez Torres, Rivera Lassén, Zenón and Ramos Rosado display Black identities in their writing. They form part of the *uno-múltiple* of the transnational Puerto Rican family of choice.

My approach to Santos-Febres's 'fractal Caribbean' is limited to her Black feminist approach to Glissant and Benítez Rojo. She has also recognised the thought of Achille Mbembe's *Necropolitics* (2019) and *Critique of Black Reason* (2017) in her conception of Blackness and the Caribbean ('Fractal' 46:08). Future research might investigate her development of his work in the context of the Hispanic Caribbean and in the light of the concerns of Black women and their families. More recently, she expressed admiration for Pedro Lebrón Ortiz's *Filosofía del cimarronaje* (*'Marronage*

Philosophy', 2020) (¿Qué es la literature afro?). Her endorsement of his work calls for an examination of the role and limits of the maroon figure as a symbol of Black resistance. The twenty-first century theorisation of marronage should be compared to the actual statements and documented actions of historical maroons throughout the centuries in different spaces that are now the republics (and Free Associated State) of the Americas. In this way, we can increase dialogue with some of the most marginalised subjects of history, African captives, while developing the most sophisticated answers to life's most probing questions of liberty, justice, agency, truth and beauty.

I have shown how Santos-Febres imagines lovers of unequal positionalities as they research the history of Latin America's enslaved Africans in *Fe en disfraz*. They create a new kind of connection and self-discovery. Through sexual kink, they explore traumas rooted in foundational rape. Venezuela and Puerto Rico, personified by the protagonists, are ambivalent communities scattered by US interventions, often leading to immigration to the mainland United States. Martín, the white (yet, he learns, not-so white) Creole male, ceases to represent the objective voice of authority, succumbing to Fe and the abject elements of the Insularist 'great family'. Fe revisits her traumas as she wears the metal underpinning of Xica (Chica) da Silva's 'cursed' dress. Mirror imagery allows them new performances of self-discovery. Erotic in the tradition of Bataille, balancing pleasure and pain, their relationship is not focused on reproduction of bodies, property or oppression. Often, rediscovering Afro-Puerto Rican history involves tracing families that are mostly or all women and noting their limits, which continue today as the relative lack of 'slave narratives' in Latin America pushes scholars to seek evidence in other archives.

The novel reveals a fractal family, one of choice, one with Afrodescent, one with Orishas and ancestors, one that is *transloca* in its queer kink and transnational setting, but it deserves scrutiny. Santos-Febres overlooks the fact that Xica was an enslaver and presents fictional captives, not those documented in archives. She does not present a model for collective action to undo racist and sexist structures permanently in her fiction.

La amante de Gardel, like *Fe*, is a family allegory of Borinquén without direction for the future. Thorné's family includes the Orishas and powerful ancestors. I have traced the crafts of healing and destruction to Oshun and Yemaya, each of which personify loose equivalents to Derrida's philosophical *pharmakon*: medicine and poison (63). The family is matrilineal and translocal. Sex work is another family craft that links her to the former gigolo Carlos Gardel. Oshun could also be punishing her for betraying her secrets to the West in exchange for money. The colours of the novel, gold and blue, represent the interplay of the two mothers who govern the plot, proud Oshun and sad Yemaya. The novel deconstructs Afro-Puerto Rico and 'European' Argentina.

Micaela feels shame for her Afro-Latina origins and, to an extent, escapes them through education. By revealing the family secret, the *corazón de viento* ('wind heart'), she ceases to make its inheritance filial and linear. Instead, she makes it fractal and scattered as it changes form and is known and used by others on and off the island. She and Gardel become one, changing into one another like Fe and Martín do. Also, the novel reunites the tango singer Gardel with his oft-overlooked Black 'brother' el Negro Ricardo and the Tano who is likely not *napolitano* but probably an Afrodescendant in denial. The Black women of the novel make Puerto Rico not a 'sick' country, as Zeno Gandía would have it, but a place of healing through affirmative Blackness. Likewise, *La amante* adds nuance and realism to Palés's island-mulattas. Santos-Febres creates combinations of Western and non-Western ways of thinking family and identity. The transatlantic journeys of the novel deconstruct the intersecting histories of Afrodescendants, musicians from the Southern Cone and European explorers.

La amante broaches the topic of reproduction choices, which are fundamental to family formation, by depicting women's lives in the 1930s. That is the decade mass sterilisation began on the island, which would continue for almost fifty years. Santos-Febres hows how women used birth control to gain agency, but it is clear that this government project was taking control away from women. Yet, would so many women have chosen sterilisation had they had access to *corazón de viento*? Also, when is it empowering and despoiling to reveal a marginalised group's secrets, violating their right to opacity?

Santos-Febres continues to produce high-quality literary and cultural texts. Her work will likely continue to grow and deserve further analysis. Although *Fe* has resulted in a substantial body of work, I would like to see more on *Nuestra Señora de la Noche*, her first novel to focus on Blackness, although I hope that scholarship does not divide between the queer focus in *Sirena Selena vestida de pena* and that on on Black history in the trilogy of *Nuestra Señora, Fe* and *La amante*. The latter are new but highly complex texts that, with time, will surely generate more exciting scholarship that relates the Black past to contemporary concerns such as Hurricane Maria, the continuing economic crisis and Puerto Rico's relationship with the United States and Latin America.[2] Further comparative work between Santos-Febres, Fátima Patterson and other Afro-Caribbean, African American and Afro-Latina women will help scholars better understand the still-developing generation, even an acephalous and translocal one, as Santos-Febres would have it, of Black women writing their history, religion and lived experiences. Patterson's Afro-Cuban identity exemplifies the shared history of the Hispanic Antilles and the need to look beyond Insularism.

I have focused on aspects of allegory in Santos-Febres's work, but her aesthetics are more varied than just that trope. A formalist approach could shed more light on her aesthetics. I read her as a Black writer, but that is not the only valid approach – in fact, the more foci critics use, the richer the dialogue will be and the less she and other Black writers will be treated as 'specimens' like Sarah Baartman, the image she was afraid of creating by embracing her Afro-Puerto Rican identity as a writer ('Confesiones' 43). Affect, love and the inchoate field of 'porn studies' are still other approaches to be developed in the work of an author who focuses on these issues (Jones and Leahy 1).

Transgressive love has been an important aspect of Arroyo Pizarro's life. She formed a family of choice as part of the first lesbian marriage in Puerto Rico. Her Black lesbian identities and activist network exemplify the fractal family. The women in her family as well as African-Americans inspire the families she imagines in her work. She seeks *cimarronas* in history as models for contemporary resistance. Arroyo Pizarro has works that discuss only lesbian or only Black themes. *Saeta: The Poems* and *las Negras* show strong Black consciousness as part of the national family. They include midwives, concubines and sexual assault survivors. These families are often painfully formed. Focused on the island, she believes Puerto Rico has a unique history that deserves adaptation of US Black paradigms to local concerns.

Like Santos-Febres and Glissant, she rejects a single origin and fixed national boundaries. The diaspora began with the Middle Passage, but it also took place on the African continent. The *bozal*, who cannot speak Spanish and remains unacculturated, is also used as a symbol of cultural preservation and rebellion. The *palenque* is a new kind of family, an African village in the Americas. She dialogues with the 'thing-Zumbi' binomial, sometimes reaffirming its masculinist violence and sometimes making it feminine, the work of a woman with children, as in the Garner case. She validates the rage fostered in the enslaved by the savagery of the white Creole 'family'. Arroyo Pizarro criticises the marginalisation of Black people in the national literary canon.

Arroyo Pizarro's work, like Santos-Febres's, shows that queer theory cannot and should not neatly be separated from Black studies. If Afro-Boricuas are reimagining the transnational history of the archipelago as a democratic family without rigid hierarchies, they cannot ignore the rights and needs of LGBTQ+ people or overlook the scholars that these groups have inspired to challenge the naturalisation of cis-heteronormativity.

Arroyo Pizarro's 'Wanwe' and 'Saeta' include Africa, where families are destroyed and rebuilt through colonisation and enslavement, shattering the harmonious plantation of the Insularists. Her protagonists are Black women, and readers learn how they survive and rebel against imprisonment, insult, rape, beatings and torture. Arroyo Pizarro is among the first to focus exclusively on Black women in her prose. She espouses a decolonising atheism, but she uses deified ancestors and the Orishas as an inspirational mythology for her writing.

Arroyo Pizarro's atheism begs another difficult question, though: is it a case of cultural appropriation when one uses the Orishas as an aesthetic or interpretive tool and yet does not believe in their divinity? Is it anachronistic to believe that enslaved Africans, who often processed the world through myth, doubted the veracity of their religions? Some *santeros* feel their religion has become commercialised and exploited (García, 'Magic'). What are the ethics of using a mythology that has suffered marginalisation to degrees that have reached extremes, such as the tortures of the Inquisition, and which is still often misunderstood and reviled by groups ranging from traditional Catholics and enlightened atheists to fervent evangelical Christians? My initial answer is that, in order for me to appreciate the form, content and even criticism of these writers, I have to have a basic understanding of their cultural and religious backgrounds. I have worked to present them in a respectful, if critical, manner. As Black studies grows in its interpretation of religions, we must find a balance between exploiting the beliefs of the oppressed on one hand and censoring ourselves into ignorance by saying only the initiated can read and write literature on Regla de Ocha and similar syncretic faiths. A key example of great work is Robert Farris Thompson, whose study of the faith, *Flash of the Spirit* (1984), is an inspiration to Santos-Febres ('Fractal' 28:38), Moreno Vega ('Dr. Marta' 12:30-40) and other devout *santero* thinkers. Regardless of religious differences, Arroyo Pizarro has expressed solidarity with Moreno Vega's fight for Black and *santero* rights ('Río Piedras' 113).

There is so much more to learn about Arroyo Pizarro. Her poems, plays, short stories and novels are scattered across more than 100 publications. She cultivates lesbian erotica (*Cachaperismos 'Dike Stuff'*, 2012; *Violeta*, 2016), historical fiction ('Los amantados' ['The Suckled'], 2014), crime fiction ('Las cosas que se cuentan al caer' ['Things Told While Falling'], 2016) and children's fiction. Some examples of the latter are her biographies of role models *Marie Calabó: De niña curiosa a mujer líder* (*'Marie Calabó: From Curious Little Girl to a Woman Leader'*, 2017) on Marie Ramos Rosado, one of several Black-affirming stories, the Independentist *Oscarita: La niña que quiere ser como Oscar López Rivera* (*'Oscarita: The Little Girl Who Wants to Be Like Oscar López Rivera'*, 2017) and the LGBTQ+-affirming *Mis dos mamás me miman* (*'My Two Moms Spoil Me'*). She has adapted the testimony of an enslaved Afro-Puerto Rican for children in third grade and beyond as a play called 'La medalla mágica de Juana Agripina' ('Juana Agripina's Magic Medal', 2016). Her *Afrofeministamente* (2020) poems and *Las caras lindas* (*'Beautiful Faces'*, 2016) short narrative and drama explore Black themes. Space limitations kept me from analysing 'Los amamantados' here, and in it are told the traumas of rape that Afro-Puerto Rican women suffered under enslavement. 'Las cosas' depicts the violence they suffer today, in particular those who are seen on the island as particularly Black, Afrodescendants of the Anglophone Indies (121). Critics are only just beginning to appreciate her large, diverse oeuvre.

Arroyo Pizarro's creation of community is most evident in her organisation of writing groups and publishing projects. The Cátedra de Mujeres Negras Ancestrales ('Ancestral Black Women's Study Group') has yielded self-published fiction by Raquel Brailowsky Cabrera, E. J. Nieves, Lala García, and Miranda Merced based on archival research. They use historical documents as inspiration to tell the lost stories of enslaved Black women in honour of the United Nations Decade for People of African Descent. Other writers associated with the group are Tania Cruz, Zulma Oliveras Vega, Rosario Méndez Panedas, Yolanda López López, Paxie Córdova Escalera and Eloísa Pagán Sánchez, and they are waiting to be discovered.

Denis-Rosario, alongside Roberto Ramos-Perea, is disseminating information on Black history to young and old alike as a screenwriter of cultural modules on Juan Boria, Arturo Alfonso Schomburg, Pura Belpré, Ruth Fernández, Celestina Cordero, Rafael Cordero, Julia de Burgos and Ismael Rivera, among others (Peña). I do question the claim of the series title and theme song, sung by the famous performer Lucecita, that Afrodescendants are from a 'raza pura' ('pure race'). I think the notion of racial 'purity' is anathema to democracy, though the continuation of the verse, 'pura rebelde' ('nothing but rebellious') definitely engages with the marronage throughout the centuries that continues to inspire Black consciousness. I appreciate its importance in recognising Black pioneers and heroes on the island, building a fractal family history, and believe that it can yield further innovative scholarship.

Denis-Rosario's module on Rivera shows a particularly telling limitation of *Fractal Families*: there is very little music discussed in it. One of the benefits of my approach is to avoid the continued folkorisation of Black people (Santos-Febres, *Sobre* 76). They do more than sing, dance and party. On the other hand, Barbara Abadía-Rexach has shown that music has been central throughout the twentieth and twenty-first century in affirming Black Boricua identity in *Musicalizando la raza* ('*Musicalising Race*', 2012). Denis-Rosario affirms this in her story 'Calle Felipe Rosario Goyco' (*Capá* 588–684). Singer Ruth Fernández is the protagonist of 'Las nietas' ('The Grandchildren') in *Las caras lindas*, which is named for an Rivera song (37–8). These musicians' lives and work merit more study. This knowledge will illuminate these texts as well as the classic *El entierro de Cortijo* ('*Cortijo's Wake*', 1983) by Edgardo Rodíguez Juliá, which shares with Denis-Rosario a focus on Black death.

In *Capá prieto*, Denis-Rosario devises an Afro-Puerto Rican nation and family that acknowledges the nation's Black forebears. Her Afro-Boricua family extends to Manhattan, breaking with the Insularist tradition and showing the importance of overlapping diasporas (Afro and Latinx). I see her fiction as fractal, and therefore errant and reconnecting with the outside, yet Independentist in honouring the mulatto Betances. He can be seen as heir to the *cimarrones* ('rebels') of his time, a kind of Afro-Boricua family.

The short stories are socially conservative and cis-heteronormative, and they intentionally skirt the 'sensual mulatta' stereotype, opting for more death than sex in its families. In 'Periódicos de ayer' ('Newspapers from Yesterday'), Denis-Rosario uses the funeral of the female protagonist's father in intertextual dialogue with Oller's *El velorio*. The fractal family of Uncle Luis have lost their land to gentrification (794). His *techné* is collecting, like his friend Schomburg, from whom he keeps artefacts that he believes belong to the archipelago.

The stories show how Afro-Puerto Ricans displayed protonational consciousness and war craft at Boca de Cangrejos in 1797, when they fought off the British like their maroon ancestors. The battle gives a new perspective on Loíza and shows they are more than a font of folklore. It subverts the *rogativa* ('litany') legend, in which a bishop distracts the British with a procession to save the city. The preservation of historical documents on these events by a Black Boricua and a non-Black ally represent a modern-day struggle for cultural preservation.

The police murder of Adolfina Villanueva Osorio unites family legacies, continued oppression rooted in slavery, and oppressive acts carried out by the Catholic Church. It shows that the Black women of Loíza have also fought for their land. If the 'great family' held up the patriarchal hacienda as a source of peace and stability, Villanueva's story is matrifocal and fraught with precariousness. Adolfina lives like a single mother. She is a *transloca* of Loíza fighting off the neo-colonial state and the police that enforce its laws. The family had resided there for a century before officials evicted them. Their struggle parallels that of maroons throughout Latin America. Poverty and injustice like that she faced force others to flee the island, fragmenting and reforming families and identities. In a comparatively lighter story, Juan Boria turns in a corrupt lawyer who attempts to sell historically Black land in Guayama illegally. Its humour parallels that of the story on Belpré, who was a mother figure to the children of New York and beyond.

Hidden documents also tell a fuller family story in 'Ama de leche' ('Wet Nurse') (488). More than a Mammy, the milk nurse serves as a surrogate mother for the family, amassing a debt of gratitude. Like Trigo states, the arts and humanities are a means of repayment. I have contributed by analysing *Capá Prieto*, which is thematically most related to the other works here, given the focus on enslavement and family. Yet her novel *Bufé* (2014) also depicts a contemporary Afro-Puerto Rican woman on the island and in New York. She and Ramos-Perea have adapted it for the stage and had it performed, which calls for analysis of the two versions (personal interview). Her *Sepultados* ('*Entombed*', 2018), published after Hurricane Maria, continues the meditation on death explored here. It deserves comparison to other works that the disaster inspired, such as Santos-Febres's *Huracanada* (2018) and *Antes que llegue la luz* ('*Before the Lights Come On*', 2021), as well as Arroyo Pizarro's poetry in *Huracana* (2018). All the authors from the island that I study here are also poets, which compels us to look beyond narrative, as I did with *Saeta: The Poems*, in the creation of the fractal Afro-Puerto Rican family. Denis-Rosario's *Delirio entrelazado* ('*Intertwined Delirium*', 2015) deserves a closer look at its verses.

Mother Oshun's spiritual progeny create, lose and work to reclaim the plantation-*palenque* of La Caridad in Dahlma Llanos-Figueroa's novel *Daughters of the Stone*. The oppressive plantation becomes a liberating family of choice when Mati inherits the land where she was held captive with her mother. The latter, Fela, made the first of many deals with the deity to find love and survive the horrors of enslavement and racism on the archipelago. Family trauma in the novel recalls its depiction in Morrison's family saga *Beloved*. Inheritance, a theme shared with Zeno Gandía and Ferré, brings to light the struggle for land and the craft of healing and poisoning with magic. Unlike the Insularists, 1898 is not foundational; it is not mentioned. The classic journey to New York is undertaken by a Black Puerto Rican family, where a matrifocal family unit struggles to survive and rise through education. At the turn of the 1970s, Carisa, the griot of the family, returns from New

York to the island in search of an affirmative identity after finding no support in higher education. The author seems to ignore texts and spaces beyond the work of Thomas. On the archipelago, she discovers a familial bond with a lesbian photographer. She travels beyond insular notions of Puerto Rico.

Readings of *Daughters of the Stone* will no doubt change with the exciting publication of *A Woman of Endurance* (2022). It tells of a dark-skinned *bozal* woman who faces the challenges of enslavement in Puerto Rico while following the goddess Yemaya, a prequel to *Daughters* that focuses on a single protagonist. My discussions of family, enslavement, plantation, nation and overcoming racism will contribute to continued comparisons between her texts and others on these topics.

Llanos-Figueroa, the sole mainland author in the study, shows the importance of Latina writers to the fractal family. Moreno Vega, only mentioned here, deserves continued deep analysis of her memoirs, documentary, speeches and activism. The Young Lords is a group where women became Black leaders but also faced sexism in the 1960s and 1970s. The Nuyorican Poet's Café was a space for awakening Black and queer consciousnesses, and they deserve future study, keeping in mind the emerging notion of families of choice.

In conclusion, I wish to thank these authors for their contribution to understanding Puerto Rico, its diaspora and the history of the Americas. Their works are sophisticated, complex, compelling and diverse. Consciously or otherwise, they have taken on the patriarchs of the 1930s and 1950s, Pedreira and Marqués, the people who created superficially harmonious notions of the nation as a family rooted in the plantation. These novelists pull up those roots. They form a family that reaches back to 1493 and reaches forward to a more diverse, more just Puerto Rican community. The family stretches from Nigeria and Namibia to Argentina, Colombia, Venezuela and the United States.

I have worked collegially not only with the Afro-Latinas who write these exciting works of prose fiction but also with Afro-Latina and Afro-Latinx scholars from a diverse array of backgrounds. I congratulate LaFountain-Stokes on his *translocas* concept, which is closer to home for more Puerto Ricans than Butler's performance while maintaining many of its benefits, namely denaturalising gender identity. I invite readers to consider 'The Statement', a declaration in the scholarly manifesto tradition, of the Black Latinas Know Collective that calls for more consideration of this population's scholarship. They have been marginalised historically in academia, as all the authors of this work have shown in different ways. There one will see Yomaira Figueroa, Jiménez Román, Abadía-Rexach, Lloréns and Quiñones Rivera, names mentioned in *Fractal Families* as creators of knowledge. I want to be an ally in their efforts to change how literature is read, as all readers of Black and Caribbean litearature should. I hope to have shown that a generation of Afro-Latina writers have written their own and their ancestors' histories and, in so doing, have conceived of Puerto Rico as a more democratic space. Likewise, a generation of Afro-Latina scholars both on and away from the archipelago are working to make universities just as diverse, dynamic and expansive. They are forming the '*uno-múltiple*' of the ever-growing fractal family.

Appendix
Author Interviews

One of the joys of being a critic of contemporary literature is the chance to speak with the writers that I love and the faces of a quickly developing group of Black Boricua authors and the critics and intellectuals who promote their work. I am impressed by how resilient and creative they are in the face of constant emergencies. The following interviews occurred between 2016 and 2020.

Mayra Santos-Febres
18 June 2016
JTMIV: You and I met at the First Afrodescent Congress last year at UPR Río Piedras. Why did you decide to attend?

MSF: I was very honoured to accept the invitation to participate. So it was not a decision. However, I have been waiting for an invitation like this for a very long time. I was invited to act as keynote speaker. Besides, the existence of an Afrodescendant Studies Programme has been a dream project that I have shared and worked for with many academics and graduate students at UPR.

JTMIV: What explains the rise of a Black cultural movement in Puerto Rico?

MSF: Since the 1980s, there have been associations in Puerto Rico to fight against racism and racial inequality. Martha Moreno Vega did previous conferences. However, the UN's declaration of 2014–25 as the Decade for People of African Descent has a lot to do with the matter, not only in Puerto Rico but in Colombia, Paraguay, Chile and the rest of Latin America. Of course, this important step in the acknowledgement of our presence in Latin America is the result of many decades of continuous struggle. But the time has finally come. There are censuses everywhere, taking count of an

Afrodescendant population that was never counted before. Governments are issuing laws and public policies that revise education, services, civil rights and policies. History is being rewritten. It's a great moment to study and to be Afrodescendant in the history of Latin America.

JTMIV: Why do you believe slavery has become a central theme in Puerto Rican historical fiction over the past ten years?

MSF: I do not think slavery is an important topic in Puerto Rico nowadays. I think that race and the institutionalised politics of racism are. Since the 1980s, there have been important historical and cultural revisions of slavery. What happened was that those books operated under the radar because there was not a visible discussion about race in the cultural and public scene. If you notice, Edgardo Rodríguez Juliá's book is from the 1980s–90s. My novel *Fe en disfraz* is from 2009. *Bathika* – a historical novel written by Colón Santana, Esquire – is from 2016. Yvonne Denis's short stories as well as Yolanda Arroyo's are from the early 2000s. So, the fact that slavery is being discussed now is because of the previous work that Fernando Picó, José Curet Vega, Guillermo Baralt, Martha Moreno Vega and many historians did before, during the 1980s and 1990s. Our history as people of African descent did not start with slavery and has not ended with its abolition. Therefore, writers, poets, moviemakers and other artists, activists and intellectuals are producing more and more texts that examine racism and its cultural, political and social structure in the Americas.

JTMIV: Why did you write *Fe en disfraz*?

MSF: I needed to write it, I guess. My intentions remain somewhat obscure to me. I often do not know for sure why I feel compelled to write what I write. It is not part of a plan. However, I must confess that I felt very strongly about writing the novel. To take a look at such a difficult and silenced theme as slavery felt like a must to me. I hope I can write a longer novel about the topic one day.

JTMIV: What did you read to prepare to write the novel? Historiography? Literature? What works or studies?

MSF: I have been studying slave narratives all my life. First as a doctoral student at Cornell, under the tutelage of Henry Louis Gates. Then, out of curiosity. It felt strange to me that the only 'slave narratives' known in Latin America where Juan Manzano's [poem] 'Treinta Años', *Autobiografía de un esclavo* and [Esteban Montejo's] *Biografía de un cimarrón* from Cuba. So I have been on the lookout for the publication of bits and pieces of scholarly publications that sometimes give accounts of primary documents that can be read as 'slave narratives'. The same happened with literature. I have studied Afro-Hispanic, Afro-Latino and Caribbean Literature all my life. It a central part of my academic and scholarly formation. So without a direct purpose I had all the preparation I needed to write *Fe en disfraz*.

JTMIV: Postmodernity rejects truth claims. On the other hand, you are unearthing lost truths about a vulnerable, enslaved population. How do you manage the balance of historical truth and creative freedom in your work?

MSF: I have to be creative because I am doing a kind of 'archeology of knowledge' by unearthing lost or partially erased knowledges due to racism and marginalisation. I have to trust personal memories, family stories, intuition and plain 'faith' that I somehow have access to what has been historically denied to me and my people. Postmodernity is all about the *desmontaje* or deconstruction of an idea of the Self, of an idea of 'identity' that comes from Western Civilisation, and also an idea of 'objectivity' that comes from the same tradition. I am an heir to that tradition, but a marginal, 'unaccepted' heir. Therefore, I do not feel uncomfortable at all by not paying that much attention to postmodern concepts such as 'fragmentation' or 'construction' of identities. History (slavery, racism, patriarchy) has created centred selves and uncentred, marginal, sick 'selves'. From the margins of such a discourse I am claiming the existence of another tradition of defining and talking about identity that is in part 'true', in part 'unearthed' and in part 'imagined'. Can there be any other way? I follow Édouard's Glissant's idea of 'prophetic vision of the past' as a tool to talk about our identities.

JTMIV: Do you identify with Fe? Why?

MSF: I identify with all my protagonists. If not, it is impossible to write their stories. With Fe I share the academic formation, the fact that both of us are scholars and that both feel in but outside Academia, not because of up-front marginalisation (and there is) but because the structure is organised by Eurocentric laws and methodologies that [only] value other types of knowledge as 'minor' knowledges. Other practices of producing *saberes* ('knowledges') and discourses are frowned upon. The body, ancestral memories and personal (not 'intellectual') curiosities are still frowned upon in Academia. So Fe and I are colleagues in this way, being intellectual Afrodescendants in the twenty-first century.

JTMIV: What do you feel the roles of rape, sex, sadomasochism, cosplay and eroticism are in the novel?

MSF: I must admit that rape, sex and sadomasochism, role-play and eroticism are very central in the novel, as they were very central in the history of slavery, especially as it was lived by women. Black women were raped, lashed, bound, displayed and over-eroticised constantly during slavery. It is impossible to write a novel that does not touch on the topic. It has not been possible to do so. If one reads Gayle Naylor's *Corregidora*, or *The Colour Purple* by Alice Walker or *Beloved* by Toni Morrison, the 'eroticism' is there. The fact of the matter is that this is a political novel. Women have been exploited as sexual objects for centuries. How can anyone write as a woman and evade the topic?

JTMIV: Why did you choose Halloween/Samhain as the topic of the novel? Do you feel this holiday represents Puerto Rico? Why? Is the work an allegory?

MSF: This is a tough question. Halloween is a way to bring in the topic of ritual time versus chronological time. The 'magic' versus the 'secular'. European 'paganism' and other types of spirituality. That was all. Halloween is celebrated everywhere in the West. I wonder why? Maybe because 'Reason' cannot explain or steer every aspect of life, can it?

JTMIV: Do you see your novel as an attempt to heal a collective or individual trauma? Or is it less healing for readers and more an affront to myths of a harmonious plantation past on the island?

MSF: To heal, you might make people a little uncomfortable. It is part of the process.

JTMIV: Your work is cosmopolitan, alluding to enslaved women in Venezuela, Brazil and Puerto Rico. Why did you choose this diasporic approach? Why *Xica da Silva* in particular?

MSF: Slavery was diasporic. If one consults the historical documents, there is always a slave moved from one country to another, one plantation to another, either because they were sold, their owners moved or were forced to move, et cetera. To escape racial inequality and racism you also have to be very diasporic. 'Keep this nigger boy running', as Richard Wright said. Afrodescendant identity is diasporic as well. So Xica da Silva is as much my ancestor as is [Afro-Colombian] La Negra Casilda or [South African] Saartje Bartman, or [Afro-Uruguayan] Virginia Brindis de Salas, or Julia de Burgos or Georgina Herrera. We are all part of a continuum.

JTMIV: The humanities, and especially literature, are considered to be in 'crisis', and Puerto Rico's recent economic crisis only exacerbates the situation. Why read literature – especially literature on divisive issues like race, sexuality and gender – when technology provides other forms of entertainment and when other areas of study are more lucrative?

MSF: I cannot say that my way of life is in crisis. My country is in crisis. I, on the other hand, am witness to the increasing need for stories and presence of a different kind of intellectual and artist. Maybe what is happening is that certain kinds of organisation, be they political, academic or social, are experiencing a decrease in their centrality in controlling people's lives.

21 August 2020

JTMIV: In the introduction to the *Afro-Hispanic Review* issue you wrote with Zaira Rivera Casellas, you state 'María quitó el manto verde que cubría con su voluptuosidad boquetes de la pobreza más abyecta en nuestros pueblos y costas' ('Maria removed the green mantle that covered the potholes of the most abject poverty in our towns and coasts with its voluptuosity') (Rivera Casellas and Santos-Febres 10) and that the face of marginalisation in on the island is 'mujer y negro' ('female and Black') (11). How does an academic focus on Afrodescent in Puerto Rico help readers and students to understand better the unique position Afro-Puerto Ricans occupy in these ongoing times of crisis?

MSF: Since George Floyd's murder, Afro-Ricans have moved in unprecedented ways to fight racism and ask for the decolonisation of institutions. I believe University of Puerto Rico's Afrodiasporic Studies Programme is a response to these historical times. AfroRicans hold very tight connections to other Afro-Latinxs and African American communities. We are also a social bridge between Afro-US communities, Afro-Latin American and Caribbean communities.

JTMIV: In an interview from 2012 on the Festival de la Palabra, you state that Caribbean cultures tend to be matriarchal. The hacienda is, inherently, a patriarchal and racialised space centred on a New World variant of the *pater familias*. Could you discuss how Puerto Rico's culture can be simultaneously matriarchal and patriarchal, or matriarchal within a patriarchal space? How families – whether they are individual families or the 'great Puerto Rican family' of the romanticised plantation – can be both matriarchal and patriarchal and what results from the tension between these two forms of power?

MSF: If you throw 'race' into the mixture, you would see clearly why white *hacendado* identity, family and discourses would privilege a patriarchal society, while Afrodescendant and racialised communities tend to be matriarchal. We have no choice. Most of our males are either in jail, sick, unemployed or dead. I myself am a single mother of two. Therefore, because of racial and colonial history, Puerto Rico, as well as many impoverished, racialised countries in the world, tend to be more matriarchal.

JTMIV: I notice that your work, whether as a novelist or as a public speaker, is highly diasporic and globalised on one hand, yet very nationalist on the other. Something that stands out about the Afrodiasporic and Racialisation Studies programme, as well as the Afrodescent Puerto Rico Congresses before it, is that they present a unique kind of nationalism. Despite being highly aware of occupying a place within global networks, you have often remained tied to a specific Spanish-speaking land, a nation with a unique culture, despite its political status as a colony.

MSF: I don't believe in nations, I believe, however in provenance, in connections to a land and a culture as a point of departure to forge relations with the world. That is why you see several aspects (race, gender and Puerto Ricanness) intertwined. Maybe it would be easier to understand what all of my public humanities projects work is about if we think in terms of organic fractalities and reticular thought and Rationality, which is an Afrocentric rationality, instead of the old Eurocentric rationality that insists in binary oppositions, supremacy, hierarchy and rejection of all 'contradictions' as irrational or erratic. The Monotheism of Reason as the only organizational principle cannot account for multidimensional, global, diasporic, reticular knowledge production.

Dahlma Llanos-Figueroa
25 February 2017
JTMIV: Why did you write *Daughters of the Stone*?

DLF: I wrote my first novel because I felt that there was no accurate representation of my life and my community in the dominant dialogue of our country. I felt that silence or erasure is the quickest way of killing a culture and I refused to let that happen. The United States invaded Puerto Rico just before the turn of the century and made it a colony, as it remains today. Since then we have fought wars, worked in factories, cane fields and garment districts of the United States. We have joined unions, paid taxes, contributed to the sports, science, music, art and language of the United States. It's time to recognise that in weaving the literary tapestry of the nation.

JTMIV: Is there any historical basis for an enslaved woman in Puerto Rico ever becoming owner of a plantation? Or is this a product of wish-fulfilment?

DLF: I don't know of any enslaved woman becoming the owner of a plantation in colonial Puerto Rico. However, Don Salvador Vives, owner of Hacienda Buena Vista outside Ponce, did give one of his enslaved women, Isidora, her freedom for exceptional services. He also left her one-third the value of his assets (3,000 pesos) upon his death at the rate of 15 pesos a month for the rest of her life. Unfortunately, his son, Carlos María Vives, the sole heir, did not comply with his father's wishes and Isidora had no way of fighting him in court. Doña Isabel Díaz, the widow, refused to sign off on even the modest one-lump sum proposed by her son (Baralt, *Buena Vista* 64–5). I have no specific knowledge of the relationship between Don Salvador and Isidora, but thought this situation deserved exploration in fictional narrative form.

JTMIV: What do you feel the role of sex and eroticism is in the novel?

DLF: These are the great humanising elements. Enslaved women experienced their bondage differently from men because their sexuality was often used against them in very gender-specific ways. Also, though there have been studies on the male enslaved experience, the women's experience, until recently, hasn't had anywhere near as much attention. In terms of eroticism, I wanted to show the range of female eroticism. It lends a level of humanity that has been lacking. I try very hard to write sensual scenes rather than sexual encounters. That is a fine line that isn't always respected when writing about Black women and sexuality. While Fela honours her religious beliefs, her very human need to have a baby overrides other considerations. Concha may be taciturn and rigid in many ways but behind closed doors, she is also a loving and sensual woman.

JTMIV: Why did you have the stories of African-Americans, US Jews and Afro-Puerto Ricans told side-by-side at the end of the novel?

DLF: Although this novel is firmly rooted in the experiences and social conditions of plantation society Afro-Puerto Rican women, I wanted to show the universality in the struggle of, apparently powerless, working-class women, regardless of culture. They were the keepers of the family, culture and oral traditions that sustained them during the worst of times. This can also be said of rural women in Appalachia, China, Jews in the shtetls, the Gypsies throughout Europe –hundreds of other subcultures that have been excluded from their countries' dominant narratives. These women shared tenacity and monumental endurance under the harshest of conditions.

JTMIV: Could you comment on the role of the Orishas in the novel?

DLF: Some people refer to this aspect of my work as religion, some magic realism, some mysticism. It doesn't matter what it's called. These African deities are central to my narratives because they are central to the characters and to the culture. I wanted to bring them into the light because these images have so often been appropriated and abused by people who have no understanding of their roles in our societies. That is one reason why the word *bruja* ('witch') is such a trigger in the novel. Too often in the history of many cultures, women's ways of knowing are, at best, ridiculed and, at worst, demonised and ultimately criminalised ... I wanted to show these female deities as they are seen within their cultures—as sustaining forces that help the characters endure the unendurable reality of their lives. Oshun/Ochun appears in *Daughters of the Stone*, Yemaya is central in my second novel, *A Woman of Endurance* and I plan for the Orishas to continue playing a major role in each of the novels in this series.

JTMIV: Why do you think the maroon is such a captivating figure in your work and in general?

DLF: There was nothing benevolent or sustaining about slavery to the people who experienced it. The enslaved, like every human being, sought to self-actualise, yearned for the ability to direct their own lives and the lives of their children. This drive is intrinsic to one's humanity. I tried to show that even under the best of circumstances, the only way to maintain such a system was to brutalise people in order to break their spirit. In the end, it couldn't be maintained because, sooner or later, spirit wins.

JTMIV: Your work is cosmopolitan. Were you intending to break with a perceived Insularism in Puerto Rican fiction? Or has Puerto Rico always represented geographical and cultural fluidity for you?

DLF: As a colony, Puerto Rico has had to insist on its insular/native culture as a matter of *survival*. The more a foreign entity has tried to eradicate that, the more we have insisted on maintaining it. So there were literary movements to reflect this focus on the insular/native, which developed, in part, as resistance to outside influences and valuing the indigenous. That said, I think the great Puerto Rican writers, artists and thinkers have always gone beyond the boundaries of the island to explore life on a larger scale and to see themselves within a global reality ... The mere fact of the island being a colony of Spain and then the United States attests to the fact that those influences have left a very strong imprint in our native culture. From my perspective, the Puerto Rican experience is absolutely fluid, as it is for people of any diaspora. In my work, I focus on the fluidity between the West Africa, the United States and the island. I grew up and live in NYC, so I consider myself an Afro-Newyorican in the best sense of the word. That is, I am bilingual and multicultural. I am nourished by West African, Puerto

Rican and American cultures. I constantly travel back and forth to Puerto Rico in my need to sustain all sides of my nature. I also have travelled all over the world and studied many other cultures. A more encompassing vision is crucial, especially in this time in history when we are told that there is only one way to be American. I, an individual Puerto Rican in the diaspora, am a microcosm of our fluidity.

JTMIV: Do you see your novel as an attempt to heal a collective or individual trauma?

DLF: I see my work as giving voice to stories that have been silenced and a face to a culture that has been ignored, or worse, stereotyped in the national and insular narrative. I write about the story not told, the people not recognised. The plantation myths would be laughable if they weren't so pervasive. We need to throw open the windows and doors and take a good honest look at ourselves. We need to reject the self-racism within the colonised Black communities and the selective memory and myth of a colour-blind society that has marked Puerto Rican culture both in island and US communities. Until we recognise and embrace our differences, we won't move forward, not really. I hope that my work is an invitation to a dialogue that is long overdue, both on the island and in the United States. Perhaps we can start with discussing the characters in a fictional work and go from there.

JTMIV: Do you see yourself as part of a literary generation or movement in New York or in Puerto Rico? If so, with whom? Why?

DLF: I absolutely see myself as an elder in the African diaspora in the United States, which is where I make my home. And while I don't live on the island, I also see myself as part of the movement there. I am Puerto Rican wherever my body resides. I love watching more and more young artists, both in New York and Puerto Rico, insisting on their Africanness, their *afrodescendencia*, within the context of their native Latin American countries as well as within the United States. The Afro-Latino movement has much in common with the African-American demand for equality and recognition. We have much more in common than we have differences. The international African diasporic movement is in its nascent stage and there is yet much to be fully explored. I hope I am around to see it flourish. I am so happy to see younger voices join the chorus.

JTMIV: You and I met at the First Afrodescendant Congress at UPR Río Piedras. Why did you decide to attend? Do you see a greater political movement emerging around Afrodescent in Puerto Rico?

DLF: When I found out about the Afrodescendant Congress, I was surprised but so happy that this issue was finally on the front burner. I absolutely see the growth of this movement in the arts – literature, fine arts, craftsmanship. But also in the growth of the artisanal agricultural movement, young people reclaiming the land, opening new businesses that celebrate our patrimony, demanding to be heard and included. People are starting to look at old concerns and search for better answers. They are going within and re-examining where they have come from and where they want to go. The political landscape is a whole other matter. When so much of what happens in PR is dependent on what happens in Washington, and with so much of what is happening in Washington is so unpredictable and alien, I have no idea where either one is going.

28 September 2020

JTMIV: I see important parallels between your work and Toni Morrison, particularly regarding the themes of love, sexual violence and intergenerational trauma. Could you speak more about her, particularly about the impact *Beloved* had on you?

DLF: Toni Morrison was absolutely a major influence in my development as a writer. Universal themes are expertly treated in her work (family, community, religion, leadership, trust, vulnerability, love, jealousy, frustration, rebellion, colourism, sexism, classism, etc.) and examined through the lens of systematic racism. In her world, a mother may champion the sale of a treasured daughter in hopes of securing a more benevolent master for her child, as in *A Mercy*, or, as in *Beloved*, a loving mother resorts to infanticide rather than condemn a child to a lifetime of brutality. I wanted to see how these themes could be explored within the world of nineteenth-century Puerto Rican society.

JTMIV: You have been a teacher of literature and creative writing as well as a young adult librarian. Today, you teach creative writing to a variety of groups and ages around New York. How do you believe your role as an Afro-Latina altered the institutions of the classroom and the library? Did you often find yourself in the role of 'first' (woman, Black person, Latina) and the pressures and challenges that come with it?

DLF: When I began teaching, almost fifty years ago, there were precious few books I could share with my students that mirrored their experience. I struggled to teach concepts without the bridge that literature could provide between the known and the unknown. My students were at a definite disadvantage. They devoured the Nicholasa Mohr books and appreciated that I was trying to make their educational experience more relevant to their lives. As a librarian I did the same. By that time, there were more books available. But regardless of the times or my role within them, I felt a need to bring my students into the world of story and to encourage them to add to those stories on whatever level they could master the language. When I taught creative writing workshops, I brought my mantra with me: *what you have to say is more important than how you say it*. I made a deal with them, I could teach you how to say it, but they had to dig in deep and tell me a story. The hardest part was convincing them, from teenagers, to adults, to seniors, that they had something valuable to add to the human story. It might never get published but it merited respect and reflection. I hope that being an Afro-Latina in front of the room transmitted its own message. I think it did. I look forward to the day when we stop noting being the first. I hope my journey becomes routine. I don't really think about it other than to hope that the younger generation lays claim to what is theirs. And every culture needs the next generation, whichever one that is, to tell their story their way.

JTMIV: Many natural disasters have befallen Puerto Rico, including Hurricane Maria, an earthquake swarm and now a pandemic. The list of natural disasters goes on, but could you comment more on what these disasters have revealed about the struggles of Afro-Puerto Ricans on the island and in the mainland diaspora? The aftermath of Maria reminds me in some ways of 'San Cristobal's' destruction of La Caridad in *Daughters*.

DLF: A year after Hurricane Maria, my husband, photographer Jonathan Lessuck, and I went down to the island to talk to artists and find out about their experiences after the hurricane and how that experience had impacted on their art. The one message that kept coming through was that the hurricane cleared away the prevailing notion of a quaint island. The winds literally blew away so much foliage that anyone could see the class and racial differences left behind. With the greenery gone, you got to see that luxury condos were built right next door to the ramshackle homes of the very poor. Like Hurricane Katrina, it exposed a world people would have preferred not to see. The reality of the disparity was too obvious to ignore. Unfortunately, I don't know if that message came through to the United States in general. And yes, it was a very similar hurricane to the one in *Daughters*.

Yvonne Denis-Rosario
(Original interview in Spanish; my translation)

18 May 2016
JTMIV: I perceive a new generation of Afro-Puerto Rican women writers on the island and the diaspora. That includes Mayra Santos-Febres, Marta Moreno Vega, Dahlma Llanos-Figueroa and you. All of you are dealing with the subject of slavery in particular, but generally with the history of Afrodescendants in Puerto Rico. I would like to start the conversation by asking you if you perceive a new generation of women writers, if you write in dialogue with other people or if you see yourself as apart from the group. Can we talk about a 'generation' yet?

YDR: In the past few years, there has emerged a generation of female writers – and I agree with your hypothesis – that are talking about Afrodescent through gender. And also we are approaching more often the hidden history of slavery that literature, specifically Puerto Rican literature, tried to avoid. It was more of an historical character, an anecdotal character. There were other cultural situations, and I have to make the connection with racism. The writers broached the idea of racism in our country. They wrote on slavery but with a focus on racism. An example is Carmelo Rodríguez ... a Black author from Vieques who started to delve into his situation, his condition as a Black man ... And now I think there has emerged, perhaps rooted in the Decade for People of African Descent, a fairer perspective towards Black people. Women writers, especially Afrodescendants, are working more on the topic. There is more of an attempt to empower ourselves and our history through fiction. Yes, there is a new generation. I think it is really interesting. It is taking approaches against discrimination, for Black justice. Especially for women.

JTMIV: Who is part of that generation, in addition to the names I mentioned?

YDR: I should point out Isabelo Zenón [Cruz], who was a man, Carmen [Colón] Pellot, who was a poet, Julia de Burgos, Ángela María Dávila. All those women who worked in poetry have left us a legacy and a pathway for us to pick up the topic of Afrodescent. They worked on it from their own experiences and I think that we – the ones you just mentioned – Mayra Santos [Febres], Marie Ramos Rosado, who is a professor at the University of Puerto Rico who has also worked on the topic, Marielba [María Elba] Torres [Muñoz], who has also worked on the topic through art by Afrodescendants. That entire cluster of information that revolves around the topic of Blackness has allowed all of us, through fiction, to cull these stories.

JTMIV: You mentioned the impact of Julia de Burgos on *Capá Prieto*. How is it different to write on Blackness through narrative rather than poetry?

YDR: I think in *Capá Prieto* there is a mix of many things that I worked on ... I think that to an extent I have a peculiarity – I do not want to sound vain – that is different – but it is – the treatment I have in fiction for Afrodescent – is very close to the lived experience of Black people. I wanted to transpose in that book the reality of an Afro-Puerto Rican. For example, in the first story in which I talk about a historical aspect that has to do with what Black people did in 1797 and how they defended a specific area in Puerto Rico. History forgot them and they are not even remembered. Specifically at that point I wanted to show, even when I was using history to create a short story, history had forgotten those Black people. It is a way that I tried to work on and design through narrative. In another story, 'Last Rites in the Palms', which alludes to Adolfina Villanueva [Osorio], has to do with prejudice, discrimination, gender through a real story that Puerto Ricans lived through and that once again I approached reality through fiction. And the story of Pedro Albizu Campos *vis-à-vis* structures, power, empire. How does one locate a reader in that historical background and at the same time highlight that important Puerto Rican nationalist? I mix fiction with aspects of reality, aspects from poetry ... I think that was the most correct thing that your book of criticism is doing that that is different from many others that are working on Afrodescent. Afrodescent has always been part of my criticism and, in fact, in my doctoral dissertation I talk about how the subject of Afrodescent has been worked on in Puerto Rico very pathetically. It is always the servile Black woman, the prostitute, the hot woman, the hypersexualised man who has no mental faculties. People with no knowledge, incapable people. I wanted to turn it around. And that was the main purpose of my book: to show the Afro-Boricua Black person from the internal perspective of his/her/their experience.

JTMIV: Do you think being a woman plays a role in this writing? Or not? It is something more universal?

YDR: I think it is universal. What I wrote, a man could have written. What happens is, without getting into who is more sensitive than the other, what I think happens is analysing that aspect through Mother Africa. For Afrodescendants, women play a very important role. I believe that approach, that levelling has a lot to do with the image of the great African woman, who is also Africa, Mother Africa … In the institution of slavery, the woman was the most valuable [captive], the most desired because she reproduced. She produced other Black slaves for the planter. So he had his stronghold … She played it and continues playing it in Afrodescent. This book is, in fact, it is not an exaggeration, is more about women than about men … That singing voice, that power that nurtures an ethnicity. I am not sure my gender has to do with that construction … There is always something personal in what one writes … Right now I recall an aunt I talk about, whom I made a version of in the book, what she would do was a *santera* [believer in Orishas]. She was a woman that wouldn't let anybody mess with her family. Things that later on I would find out about and say 'It's impossible that my dear aunt could have done that!' But she had a conception of 'I am here and nobody is going to mess with my family, and I will do anything to protect my family'. There were many women in my family that, although they had their husbands, they were the ones that made tough decisions. The decisions that dealt with the extremes. Perhaps there is something of that empowerment, that strength of the Afrodescendant woman that is so important to the topic [of Afrodescent]. In the case of Adolfina Villanueva. She was the one who faced the police because her husband was … she was the one who was tough enough to confront them, and she was the one they killed.

JTMIV: I would like for you to talk more about the story 'The Milk Nanny'. I noted similarities with the work of [Luis] Palés Matos and Gilberto Freyre. How do you think the fact of having this second 'mother' or a 'double mother' affects the family and the subconscious?

YDR: Fist of all, 'The Milk Nanny' is very fictional, but it is based on a story that had to do with my great-grandmother, who was a slave. She was the slave that worked with the children of a family that is very well known here in Puerto Rico called the Carrións. They were the owners of the Banco Popular in Puerto Rico, and my aunt and my mom told me, since she was their grandmother, that my grandmother went with my great-grandmother to the Carrión house and she accompanied her in doing the housework. So my grandmother lived on the edge of when my great-grandmother was no longer a slave. My grandmother was alive then. She lived through that process. So she goes and leaves her kids and her family to work with their family. It is a true story. So my grandmother knew the Carrión family and talked about how she lived and helped her mom at that time. 'The Milk Nanny' is, well, is something I made up, but she was the Carrión's slave and she did tend to that family, particularly because that couple, the father is widowed very early, and that is true, and a milk nurse comes in to help him. Beyond that, and to answer your question, I think there are two characters here that, psychologically, are affected more than anyone else: the wet nurse and the [enslaver's] child. Because, from my critical point of view of that historical moment, slavery – since that is the setting of the story – I don't see it, and this might sound a bit unfair – that those masters saw in that nanny, that wet nurse, a human being that was providing something more than the physical, the milk that she could provide. Beyond that there was an affection that was gradually created. And I am not sure that I do not believe that many of those masters were aware of that. At that time, that woman was offering a service to my child. That was the way it was seen. She gives him something because, and the denouement of the story shows just that, this is my position, that causes me to situate them as unappreciated people. Because they forgot what the woman did for their children and, indeed, they completely forgot about her. However, there was, within that child, and this is something psychological, that could not be disconnected from that mother that nursed him, because that mother, that closeness is so intimate, so pure that there is no physical body that could, no mind that could separate itself from that feeling. I believe that the mother as well as the child are definitely the most affected. The biological mother and father, I think they saw that woman as an instrument to satisfy their son because he had physical needs. Beyond that, I see nothing more. It was a tough reality, but it was what they lived through. That is what they were for.

JTMIV: There is an ignorance of oral traditions. You mentioned that regarding your grandmother. Also, you mentioned the Orishas in your work. Can we see them as a primary source or a parallel canon to the literary canon?

YDR: Specifically, that has to do with those marginal focuses. Oral cultures are where poverty prevails. That is one reason we associate orality with the poor, where there were no opportunities, where they could document something in writing, and it is tossed aside. It is a shame, no? Many of our traditions come specifically from orality. That is specifically what I was working on in the past few days with Canal 6 (WIPR, public television) in 'capsules' (short documentaries) on Afrodescendants. We were working on the history of Pura Belpré, who is an Afrodescendent woman, a librarian in the United States. Pura made a book that was based on an oral story, a story for children called 'La Cucaracha Martina' ('Martina the Roach'). It is based on an oral story. The value is that the story, among Puerto Rican children, is very, very important. How can someone dismiss something that goes from one listener to another and that has been transmitted to this day as a story? That orality has allowed me, for example, as you correctly say, to talk about my great-grandmother, orality has allowed many of the people who live in Piñones, for example, of Loíza who are descendants of those Black people who defeated the British in 1797 to continue to celebrate that event in Piñones. There are people who lived, their family lived through that episode of history and repeat the story. If it were not for that orality, for those 'tales from the road' as they call them, we would not have discovered many things. The official history did not include it. Orality is what allows it.

JTMIV: We are writing in a postmodern era. All truths are under scrutiny. Often, we fall into a total relativism. Can we fall into the trap of being able to say everything about a truth that, in official history, has never existed?

YDR: What I am I owe to those people that, nowadays, postmodernity wants to hide or ignore. I come from my origins, my line of ancestors is real. It is not something I came up with, something I felt, beyond the spiritual, of the magical, of my concept of religion. There are ways to confirm that, yes, they existed. The representation of what I am is precisely what makes me claim insistently that yes, it happened. Denying it is to deny human existence itself, the very existence of the history of what we are as a people, of our identity, of our past. I don't go along with that concept of postmodernism. No. There was something before. What there is now, what we are, we owe it to that past. And I can't negotiate that ... Talking about my great-grandmother, to bring her into this century.

JTMIV: You mentioned religion. What role does it have in your texts, your writing process?

YDR: Yes, in my family. I have a late uncle who was a babalawo [AfroDiasporic priest]. My aunt was a *santera* [believer in Orishas]. My mother's side. Santería was very common. It was practised. On my father's side, it was not. My father's family was Black – mulatto, no? – but there was always a closeness to Santería because of that uncle. And I always grew up seeing the altars, seeing rituals, accompanying them to events, and, without a doubt, it has a lot to do with what I have written and I still show it in my writing in a way because it was a way to keep us united. That religion, that inclination, that Santería, that tradition of working to create closeness as a family united us with Africa. My family still follows it ... I cannot say they all practise it, but they respect it. For example, I have cousins that go to the Catholic church, but I don't know, the other day it was raining and we had a birthday and my cousin put a glass of water out and she threw salt and lit a candle. These are the contradictions in my family that are really interesting, but there is respect. See, I don't practise it, but this is in my family. No doubt, in some way, it comes out in my writing. And I like it, I like the subject a lot.

JTMIV: You mentioned the subject of eroticism in *Bufé* [2012]. Would you like to comment more about that?

YDR: It is a subject that interests me a due to the aspect of Black women. And I have exceedingly criticised, like I was telling you, we have eroticised the Black woman with such an incorrect image in literature, and it still is prevalent, it worries me a lot how the Black woman is seen as a hot, sultry woman, and people cannot glimpse beyond that a capable person. We have associated Blackness with eroticism and exoticism, and we keep repeating it, huh? That approach I used in the novel was a way to criticise that other that saw the woman who was Black, elegant, and pretty like the erotic and exotic one that walked in, when it is just another woman who walked in. It is those ideas that they have and it comes, obviously, from slavery. That thought about the other, that which is different, savage, all of that stuff continues in literature written by Afrodescendants and non-Afrodescendants. I always want to point something out. It is a criticism I point out, and I give it to some of my colleagues that approach it from that angle, I criticise them. Because I don't need them to use the image of the Black woman to talk about her virtues. That image of the hot, passionate woman does not give women any benefit at all. Not only the Black woman, but the woman in general. That idea of constant, prevalent sex, I resist that as the main subject of a text. It is not that I don't write on it, but we have associated it in people's minds. It is a set of racist ideas that when they say 'she's a *negrita* [Black girl] but she is beautiful' or 'she's a hot *negrita*', that exhausts me, because it is a way to stereotype us. And perhaps in an unconscious manner, since it has been a habit in Puerto Rico, in this country, it is seen as correct and true and, in many cases, it is the opposite – 'it is wonderful that they find me exotic and hot' – no. What is the point? You know, I can't handle that. It really bothers me. I have said that to colleagues that write like that, 'I don't agree. It shows us as objects'. And it's like repeating exactly the slave times when we were the object of the *hacendado* [enslaver] that wanted something specific from us, right? It is repeating, in literature, precisely what happened [on the plantation].

JTMIV: If the island is in crisis, in economic terms primarily, but also its political status, et cetera, someone could argue that focusing on racism has to be secondary to the general, national issues of the island.

YDR: Well, then. Let's talk about the matter of the colony [Puerto Rico]. We are all in a colony – Black people, whites, mulattos – there is no way for anyone to say 'attend only to the marginalised, the poor and the Black', because for the United States we are Black, we are poor, we are Latinos, we are in a trashcan. We cannot separate one thing from another. We are a colony, we are colonised, and that's it. Socially, here in Puerto Rico, in the day-to-day, without a doubt there is racism towards specific groups ... The subject generates a lot of discussion, and it continues to be controversial among those who work on it ... I resist Palés Matos. I know Luis Palés Matos is one of our most renowned poets. But I cannot accept how Palés Matos presented Black women. There are many who defend him, but I believe he was an excellent poet, an innovative poet, but in particular to me as a Black woman – the treatment he gave Black women, although in that time he wanted to point out what his forefathers had not pointed out, I am not pleased to think that our Black women were dealt with in that manner. That is something I feel. And there is a lot of resistance because he is in the canon, right? He is a very well-known poet, but beyond that there are some images of women that are disrupted, although they were beautiful verses there is an idealisation, some stereotypes, some aspects that he worked with that I cannot accept.

JTMIV: Even in the digital era, literature continues to have a very important role, and I see a continuation of that in your comments, right? This subject of Blackness as it was seen before and in these comments that you just mentioned.

YDR: It is still relevant. People think it is not, but it is. The journalist did not think that talking about racism would generate so much discussion ... We are still dealing with the same debate that Zenón and others lived in the flesh and confronted so much discrimination precisely for defending their Blackness ... In fact, I was at the Afrodescendant Congress that was held last year [2015] and the debate was endless. I think that, like my article said, racism is resistant. There is resistance to leaving the panorama of humanity. I believe slavery is what generated in this century the fact that we keep justifying discrimination like we do, that we keep practising it, that it is alongside us. It has not disappeared.

JTMIV: What are your next projects?

YDR: I have a lot of projects going at once. I have the problem of doing a lot of things at once that I like. That keeps me alive. Right now, I have a project with Canal 6 that I love. We made 'capsules' [short documentaries] designed to highlight Afro-Puerto Ricans, they last three minutes fifty seconds, and we began with Eleuterio Derkes [Martinó, 1836–83], a Puerto Rican playwright ... Also being broadcast is José Celso Barbosa (1857–1921), who was a republican. They call him the father of the Anexionist [Statehood] party, but that is an offence, honestly. And we work on him from the focus of him being Afrodescendant and his contribution to the country. Pura Belpré [1899–1982], Celestina Cordero [Molina, 1787–1862], Rafael Cordero [1790–1868], we did a capsule on him. There is a capsule on Ismael Rivera [1931–87] as well. We did a capsule on the rector of the university. There are several, and they come out this summer. I worked on the scripts and I liked seeing them. I loved the image of Black people from another perspective. Not in folklore, not *alcapurrias* [banana fritters], but important topics. Thanks to that, we have representation. There is another image of Black people that has to be highlighted – their intelligence, too, their contributions on the intellectual level.

Yolanda Arroyo Pizarro
(Original interview in Spanish. My translation.)

13 May 2016
JTMIV: I wanted to start with your book *las Negras*. I wanted to ask why you chose its structure. Why three parts? Why these women? Why this point of view?

YAP: First, what concerns me is writing. We writers are avid readers. And I read so much about heritage, about the ancestors, on who were supposedly our ancestors. I am a visibly Black person. My ancestors, no doubt, in slavery times, were slaves. Very early on, I found out that my last name and almost all the last names of all Black people in Puerto Rico are those of the slave masters. The original one was taken away. It was part of the transition from Africa to the Americas. That was very clear to me. I had what I read on slavery. I was reading Guillermo Baralt, (Roberto) Ramos-Perea, Marcus Rediker, an extraordinary but repugnant history that is called *The Slave Ship* (2008). I read on maroons, *Puerto Rico Negro* (Jalil Sued Badillo and Ángel López Cantos, 1986). If I get general to come back to the specific, the examples I have given you are all men. They are the only ones of their time. First, I thought that, for the matter of women, I had to go to the sexual part, to the sexual abuse that occurred. We all know the evidence is in the writings. And there were people who did not want to deal with that. By its very nature, it involves people at the emotional level. It is as if that rape were happening to them while they are writing. And I understand that. And then these things get silenced. Then, with my readings in Marie Ramos Rosado, with my getting closer to María Reinat[-Pumarejo] and the Cátedra de Mujeres Negras Ancestrales [The Ancestral Black Women's Writing Group of Puerto Rico], Mayra Santos-Febres, of course. I just thought of another author I read, Zaira Rivera Casellas, who taught at the Centro de Estudios Avanzados de Puerto Rico y el Caribe [Centre for Advanced Studies of Puerto Rico and the Caribbean], who wrote a text comparing the literature from slavery times on women with Mayra Santos, my work, and Carmen [María Colón] Pellot. Both Beatriz Berrocal and Carmen Pellot touch on the theme of the enslaved woman – one more than the other – they talk about the matter of how they were sexually abused, exploited. The sexual abuse was not the only kind. I have read, for example, histories of the US South, in which they treated Black women almost like cattle. They experimented on them like they did with cows and calves or horses or other mammals. They had these women raped by many men in one night to see if they would have more than one son at a time. That kind of thing. In that time, there was not much science, so they would try it … I read Toni Morrison. *Sula* [1973], it seems to me, is foundational. It is impressive … I am giving you this explanation because there is another side to it. You have to keep in mind the fact, since we flippantly say that at that patriarchal time sexist men did not describe women. There is a great probability that this happened. But on further reflection, I think there are these other oppositions that I mentioned. In the hegemony of the patriarchy, the penetrated being is almost always the woman. The man is the one who penetrates.

JTMIV: It is something taboo and secret. Is it the case that only today we can break this taboo and talk about these topics in this way? Only today in the new millennium, I believe, we have the freedom to discuss these topics: rape, sexuality, desire, the body. I have noticed in all the writers of recent years that write on women's slavery are talking about these themes in one form or another. That goes along with talking about several taboos at the same time.

YAP: Totally. Yes, that's right. We share the same thoughts. However, they are things that must be discussed. It is uncomfortable, or they are taboo topics that are not so much on the surface. It is easy to identify eroticism as a taboo topic or rape as a taboo topic. I think, for example, of these slave women. They had to negotiate so that they could feel free or achieve freedom. They came to the negotiation of 'I am going to give you this quantity of children: ten kids ... if you give me freedom. I will be a sexual object to you, your brothers, your male children'. They came to negotiations with the body as object, which is related to desire, or non-desire. To me it seems that it must have been difficult at that time to feel desire for a master. To me it seems unthinkable. But it is also a taboo topic. And what if it did happen? In that aspect, I think of Mayra Santos[-Febres], who talks about him kissing her wounds. She uses, in *Fe en disfraz*, the body of the Black woman as an object of eroticism. Of course, the past, the old times, temporality, this idea that I am going to transport myself to another era and, just the same, it is a woman who is raped [*burlada*] versus the [modern] woman who puts on a dress and incarnates it by her own will. So even when we touch on taboo topics, and even when we have these conversations, because we have more freedom now, even when we unveil these taboos, there are still topics that the majority do everything they can to escape. There are topics that are taboo only on the surface. There is religion, eroticism and so on. There are others that are deeper.

JTMIV: Slavery changes how we see rape, right? The enslaved woman has no free will. I wonder what eroticism would be like for an enslaved woman, like in *La cuarterona* or in *Cecilia Valdés*.

YAP: I think human beings, and that includes slave women of that time, had to have gotten their way. They had to create places. You know the phrase 'go to your happy place'? They must have gone to their 'happy place' and had some far off, hidden corner of their minds. That place where it would never enter, where only that place could give them pleasure. We see it today with prostitution. Many prostitutes say, 'I will do anything except this', so they keep it there. For the majority, it is kissing, but there are things they keep for themselves and their loved ones. I am sure that happened. It was not discussed. Rape became a kind of tool of rebellion, of transgression as well. I saw many books in a series that also is about the subject of women under slavery. And the part that it dedicated to the topic of rape is a very 'refined' treatment. Even so, they do not repress it. They do not visualise it. We do that when we go back to write about slavery. We like to repeat the rape scene. There are many people who just decide not to. There are others who say, 'yes, but I am going to give it a different approach'. So in these books, in spite of being a sexually abused object, the conjugal visits they made to their partners, other Black slaves, were really those moments of pleasure. Women during slavery used, in what I have read and what I imagine is that they sought strategies to guarantee that. There were women, like I describe in 'Las Matronas', who would kill the foetuses when they were being born. But there were women who were dedicated to herbalism, the herbs of the earth, to identifying the plants that were abortive or that kept women from becoming pregnant. It was a time of great suffering but also of great creativity.

JTMIV: In what ways do you think these models continue nowadays, those of the master and slave woman in the relationship between white men, Black women, the sensual mulatta – those figures?

YAP: We have internalised all of that too much. So much that we do not even realise it. And we repeat those patterns ... Even in our circle of defenders of Blackness, it is strange if a Black man is married to a Black woman. If a Black woman is married to a white man, if a woman is married to a Black man. I hear it almost every day. It has a very strong effect. I hear that we are supposed to 'improve the race'. I hear it in almost every place in my country. 'Improve the race'. Once I asked my grandmother, 'I have to marry a white man, right'? She said, 'yes. To improve your race'. What is going to happen with the family of the white man who also has to 'improve the race'? It is a constant war.

JTMIV: Are lesbian relationships a form of rebellion against that past?

YAP: Of course. For me, this is a lifestyle. It is the matter of religion. There were men and women who were atheists. There was also ancestral religion. We must embrace ancestral religions. Before, it was thought that before the Saviour, there was nothing.

JTMIV: I noticed the leitmotif of the slaves' doubt in all gods. Is that something you found in the archives or something you suppose must have happened?

YAP: It is something that must have happened.

JTMIV: It is a valid question: how can one believe in a divine being, for example, Changó, who lets something like that happen?

YAP: Changó, or Olodumare or Obatala ... this was their plan that this slavery should occur.

JTMIV: Hegel says the master does not want to destroy the slave – he wanted to destroy his culture, yes – because he has to keep him alive in a certain way. Could you talk about death in your texts?

YAP: I think that, at the root, we are talking about the psyches of several characters, but in my texts, death is not necessarily a radical finality. It can be a perfect solution for a problem. What would have happened if all those Black people jumped overboard? All of them. Not one. All. It is believed that they tried to do that. That is why they started to try to convert them to Catholicism or whatever religion at the ports. It was so they would be afraid of death. Of a God that would punish them. I take all that with a grain of salt because they lived a life convinced that your body reincarnates, so the finality – there is nobody who can convince me, and even less the women of my tribe or my family. But really, it is shown in history that this [suicide as escape] happened. I don't question death much in literature because I understand. I am an intelligent person who reads well, who reasons well, who really enjoys astrophysics ... I think I am a person who understands. How come nobody has been able to explain life after death to me? If there are so many ways to be or not to be, because that is the only way to end, there is no choice. What does that have to do with religion? I have studied several. None was able to explain it to me satisfactorily, life after death.

JTMIV: There are ancestral religions as well, that think of life as cyclical, that we return, that it is not a finality.

YAP: But we come back with no memory. We don't remember anything. There are many cases that have been studied in which people are buried and return. I don't know why they return here. The universe is so big. The notion of religion as a method of control bothers me. The fact that a religion convinces you that death brings you closer to God, unless you are the one that commits the act, that the responsibility falls on you, I say the slave had no life.

JTMIV: Death gave them free will.

YAP: Completely.

JTMIV: Do you believe religion has a special function in the interpretation of history, at least in your fiction?

YAP: For me religion does not work at any level other than controlling people. It is a distraction. Nothing more.

JTMIV: Do you feel that you are part of a circle or group of Black writers? Who is in that circle? Does it have a mission?

YAP: There is not much unity, not as much publication. It doesn't have as much to do with us who write, but with the time, we chose to write it. This time is crazy. Including religion, you see. If you put your trust in a deity, a power, it is to turn the reins over to the wind. Do to me whatever you want. Destiny or whatever. Even within the community of writers, and even within the community of writers that claim Blackness, there is still a lot of fundamentalism, lots of people who I tell 'I am part of this, but I don't believe in God'. Others want us to know they are Catholics or Protestants or Yoruba or Santero or whatever, as if all of a sudden that, in some magic way, filled in all the empty blank spaces. That lack of wanting, that not requiring decisions on anything at all, will always leave you adrift. So it leaves you without cohesion because you think all the problems of life will be solved and that's it. It drains your passion. Like [Frantz] Fanon, I think religion is a distraction. I have been getting together since last year at the Casa-Museo [Dr. Bailey K.] Ashford in Condado with a group we have named Departamento de Estudios de Literatura Afro-Puertorriqueña because, and I am ashamed of it, and perhaps some other friends, none of our universities has a Department of Afro-Puerto Rican Studies or African Studies. There are no universities that have them. So, in a performative way, we adopted that name. Within the works that are done in that 'department', we meet, we read books that deal with the topic. And we take all those texts and we say 'let's change the setting. Let's go to historical archives'. We assign ourselves a male or female slave. We always try to represent her as the woman that was in the original case. So that group that is doing work on women we named the Cátedra de Mujeres Negras Ancestrales ['Ancestral Black Women's Study Group']. So starting with not only the historical archives of slave women – and many of our great and great-great-grandmothers were slaves – we try to construct a memory. We try to establish the basis of a generation [or artistic movement]. And if we cannot find it, we have permission, poetic licence to invent it. That is what we try to do. Starting in 2016, we are going to see more books with more covers with women from slavery times, more books that will be published between 2016 and 2017 – books on history, books that are necessary, poems on slave times, narrative books, because it is sad. It made me sad when I looked at the books that had been written and I realised there were no more than ten that focused on women in slavery times.

JTMIV: Who is in this circle? This study group?

YAP: There are authors who are already well known: Mayra Santos, Moreno Vega ... the interesting part about getting together with that group is when we get together and do writing, narrative exercises, of drama, of all the genres I told you. We get together theatre scenes – monologues – seeking to publish those texts. Within the Cátedra de Mujeres Ancestrales we also have a project ... I don't know if you know that, starting in 2014, the Library of Congress published for free, and it is on the Internet, the first newspaper, *La Gazeta de Puerto Rico*, from the 1700s to 1910–12, I think. It started in 1790 or 1800. All those issues that they have are in digital format. For my students the most important thing is that we take the initiative to study and look in those documents. It is created that way. And we concentrate on the lives of slave women, especially the escapees. We have found a lot in the archives, in history.

JTMIV: Why do you think we look for maroons? What is the maroon, the *palenque* for you, these tropes, these archetypes that are so often repeated in literature about Afrodescendants?

YAP: Why not write about tame slaves? It is because, within us, in 2016, we are seeking freedom. In our lives, we are imprisoned. We face so many things. I think seeking out the maroon, seeking out documents that say 'we have never been sheep, we have never been tame', we have always wanted to be liberated. We've wanted to be recognised and not abused. The Puerto Rican, but not just for the

Puerto Rican, for the Latin American, popular culture has us imprisoned.

JTMIV: This figure has become an object of desire, of many desires.

YAP: It is an ideal.

JTMIV: It is not always an object of erotic desire, like it is for Dahlma Llanos Figueroa and Isabel Allende (*Island beneath the Sea*, 2010), but as an object of desire for freedom and agency.

YAP: Look at what [Queen] Nanny achieved in Jamaica! Nanny was obviously a maroon woman that led a revolt – and one day she is on a banknote! Today there are organisations that have her name. That is the ideal. We aspire to that. I think that is why. We feel trapped in this life. We are not always honest enough to say it, but we do.

JTMIV: Is there a danger in all this of escapism? Of escaping from the sad reality that the majority of slaves did not rebel in such an obvious way?

YAP: Yes, but they had strategies for other forms of rebellion.

JTMIV: Puerto Rico not only is in economic crisis but also in one of identity, of nation, but also a crisis in the humanities. Many people are questioning the value of writing, the value of studying history. Why should one read these texts?

YAP: Judith Butler, in one of her books, answers that question. Literature does not function to explain the world categorically. Its purpose is not didactic or anecdotic or for personal growth. However, all the people I know who prefer literature when they have doubts … The book *The Little Prince*, for example. It is not a dogmatic book, but it is my bible. It could be a kind of religion, and you could use verses from *The Little Prince* like you do the bible. In essence, it is a simple book. I agree the humanities are going through a crisis … Let's look at art. The concept of art has changed an awful lot. It is in crisis. It is difficult because sometimes I think human beings create our own prisons and our own vicious cycles. Let's resist a little bit. And it seems that those who resist, and I tell you this based on experience, are writers, with their compositions. Those who are not in the humanities, not all, are in agreement with being sheep and being part of massification, with being generic. Sadly, that is what is happening ... [L]iterature is daring, because you are writing something down. Writing is dangerous. I'm glad it is. Writing is marronage. It is a great metaphor for rebelling. The simple fact of writing is daring.

JTMIV: What kind of criticism do we need today, especially for the kind of literature you write and the topic of slavery? How do we approach these texts?

YAP: I think that you all, the critics, are another means of rebellion. You can say 'this text is not just the text'. That is what critics do. We are part of a whole. You are the ones that make those connections. You, me and the philosophers are giving meaning to life. Sometimes it is not pretty writing a book or a scene that is based on life, like rape. I am reminded of a historical fact, that in North Carolina, that when slaves would flee they would cut off their big toes so that they would limp when they ran. It was because the owners paid a lot for them, so they only cut off the big toes. Based on cutting off their big toes, a doctor decided they were ill. That is why they ran. Their mental illness was wanting freedom, drapetomania. It was a name he just made up. How does life work in these instances? It is a philosophical question. From me, from my mom, from my grandmother, that thought can be devastating. That desolation can be philosophical as well.

JTMIV: So, you are seeking a truth? A historical truth, a human truth, a truth that has meaning for today in our lives.

YAP: I do not like to say 'truth'. I do not think 'truth' exists. There are so many roots, so many nuances, so many colours. I am sorry to say that the truth for me now, compared to twenty-five years ago, is totally different. It can be painful. It is complicated.

JTMIV: But you are rescuing voices, you are seeking out historical sources. Is there a danger of relativism in postmodernism? It is problematic, since, if you can say just anything about a slave woman, isn't it a struggle?

YAP: It is a constant struggle. For example, you know I recently married a woman here in Puerto Rico when marriages between the same sex were legalised. I thought it was an act of rebellion, of marronage of denouncement. But in the past few months, I feel trapped in heteronormativity due to the fact that marriage is legal between my partner and me. So I don't know if that rupture is innate, if it is programmed, when I stop to reflect on what is happening, what is the truth? It is what you are saying, I can say all this about the slave woman. A chorus of voices might reach a consensus that what you said is not true. You lose verisimilitude. Verisimilitude can be utopian or illusory. Or really what we are looking for is astuteness, like a magician, to fool the reader with a relative verisimilitude. This is getting philosophical, ha, ha! Honestly, I don't think about this when I write. I sit down and I write a (hi)story.

JTMIV: What are you working on now? What books?

YAP: I will be working with the Cátedra de Mujeres Negras Ancestrales ('Ancestral Black Women's Studies Group', the Department of Afro-Puerto Rican Studies). We talk about how we do not have Afro-Puerto Rican Studies. We are trying to make it happen. I think it is high time. The right time would have been the 1960s, 1970s when other departments [in the United States] were creating African-American Studies. Creating one now is anachronistic, not in the right time.

JTMIV: Many barriers are coming down.

YAP: They should be. There are people who think fighting for Blackness, defending Blackness, is ultimately divisive. They do not see that the division was not made by the person defending herself. Which is sad. But many have said it. There is a reading by Judith Butler that says – in fact, it is the epigraph of my book *Transmutados* [*Transmutadx*, 2016] – that is about possibility. It seemed brilliant to me. I feel real freedom. 'Possibility is not a luxury; it is as crucial as bread.' What is possibility? That you are a slave and that you have the possibility and desire to leave that system. Or if you are a cisgender woman and, then, in this moment, be something else. I want to bind my breasts or I want to seem more masculine or non-feminine. It is a possibility. At the moment, as human beings, when they bind our wings, when there is no longer possibility, that's when it all goes to hell. Possibility is necessary.

JTMIV: So you see an intersection between queer theory and the history of slavery.

YAP: Totally. It is a type of slavery. Because of the contradiction in which it is entangled. I am orientated towards A, but heteronormativity says I should not be ... If I have a preference ... right? When I say 'I prefer women', I am also saying 'you prefer women' to the heterosexual. Saying one thing has implications for others ... It is an oppressive system. Sometimes we fall into the trap as well.

1 October 2020
JTMIV: In what I see as the first period of your Black writing, in *Saeta: The Poems* (2011), *las Negras* (2012) and your TEDxUPR talk (2016), it seems that you take on your Black identity without going into your lesbian identity, or at least that you go into it without a lot of detail in *Saeta*. Are they different audiences? Is it possible to separate the Black struggle from the LGBTQ+ struggle?

YAP: I would like to say that it was planned, but the truth is that it just flowed that way. The voice of the Black woman about whom my grandmothers told me, I think it came out before that of the intersection of the Black lesbian woman. I have noted that there are a few hints, pieces, glimmers in some works. For example, in *Los documentados* ('*The Documented*', 2005) and also in *Origami de letras* ('*Letter Origami*', 2005), there is a text in which I pay homage to the English writer Virginia Woolf (1882–1941). There is already a game with why Virginia Woolf commits suicide, why she decides her life is so unhappy that, you know, even though she feels some romances, that in writings by critics and in reviews about the work of Virginia Woolf, that she did have romances with women. But, at least in what I have read, it was always in a tragic way. There was always a lot of sadness. She did not have a full life, be it in her lesbian relationships or in her polyamorous relationships, because she was married, and her husband, from what I have read, according to critics, she did have an affection for women. So, in that book there is a story on Virginia Woolf. And I ask myself today – that was 2004 [when she wrote *Origami*] – sixteen years later, today, if that story was there for a reason. If it was to remind myself, to look back one day and say, even though it was not in the open, I was daring enough to take on the subject, right? Then, the second book, which is the novel *Los documentados*, there is a character who is a lesbian. She is secondary, but she is a lesbian. Even if a character is secondary, the main characters who refer to this secondary character as lesbian – at this time I was a militant Christian, a missionary ... *Saeta* is what you just said: it was a time where being Black, getting that identity out there, was very important to me. To make Blackness known and talk about it. In *Saeta*, for example, I realised due to a student that reviewed it. A professor from Ohio wrote to me and said the student had chosen to write on three poems from *Saeta*. And one of the poems is an enslaved woman telling how her owner asks her 'do the same to me that you do with my husband at night when he sexually assaults you'. I had forgotten entirely I wrote that poem. But there it is. The answer is that, although I was not working on queer or Afro-queer identity, it always comes out. There is always something.

JTMIV: Is it possible to separate Black identity from Puerto Rican national identity for you? I noted that, in all the Black Puerto Rican women writers of this generation, there is a desire to found or re-found in Puerto Rico a nation that gives visibility to Black people, particularly Black women. Not a separate identity or one that is excluded from the nation.

YAP: I think that what you are saying is a correct premise. I think there is an attempt, at least among the Black Puerto Rican women writers I know, to do that. On the other hand, there have been moments when it gets so frustrating trying to be Afro-Puerto Rican and trying to be Afrodescendant.

JTMIV: Is it possible to separate Black identity from Puerto Rican national identity in your opinion?

YAP: It is what you said. Not a separate identity or one that is excluded. I feel tempted to think that the effect of women in Puerto Rico, we are making that intertwined relationship. There are moments of such great frustration when I claim it … On occasions I have to ask myself: what am I going to privilege at this time? At this specific moment? That bind I feel, just like the bind to my homeland, the nationalist bind or the Afro-Puerto Rican national bind that my surroundings inculcate, which is also inculcated by inter-familial surroundings in my case. Because I have a close relationship with my great-grandmothers, my aunts, my great-great-grandmothers. When I get to the great-grandmothers part, my great-grandmother was brought here, and her mother, my great-great-grandmother, was not even from the Caribbean. She was from Africa … If what my heart tells me to do is defend Blackness, it proceeds from that natural nucleus, which is the womb of my grandmothers who were brought here after being kidnapped in Africa. Sometimes that conflicts. On the other hand, having said that, there are moments when, to reconcile that message, what I think is that 'I was born here, I have the right to live here, I have a right to live where I was born, right? Equality and justice'. So, through resistance, I am trying to construct a space where living together and descendance in a country that, although it is where I was born, I feel like it is always trying to expel me. It is almost like, like many Puerto Ricans who have to migrate. They have to go and they say the island pushes them out. I remember that on one occasion I was talking to the Puerto Rican poet Nemir Matos Cintrón (1949–), whom I admire very much – for me, she is the mother of Puerto Rican lesbian poetry … [The island] had expelled her for being so visible. This exile is what Puerto Rican literature calls 'sexilio' ('sex-ile'). They call 'sexiliados' the group of queer people, LGBT people, that, for being so visible, were expelled from the country. They kicked them out of their jobs … And ultimately, they were so cornered that they could do nothing but leave. I have not had that experience. But at times I feel like I am in the vortex, in the midst of that experience. My problem is that that group of *sexiliados*, due to being sexual dissidents, at that moment, the United States was a real possibility to try to live with others and have a life. I feel like I would have nowhere to go if I had to leave, because this historical moment of near civil war that the United States is having against sexual dissidents, against Black people, because of politics, because of the leader the United States has, I would not feel comfortable or at peace.

JTMIV: Could you comment on the impact on the island of the protests against racial injustice provoked by the murder of George Floyd.

YAP: Yes, I want to comment, but I want you to know why I am commenting, because I have participated in many protests, and in political terms, of public policy, they have led to nothing. So that makes me very disillusioned. I feel like it has been a cosmetic, esthetic participation … 'let's get together because the world is doing things and somebody put it on social media so we have to do something'. In terms of public policy, well, as recently as the political debates for governor that we had last Sunday [*Convénceme*,

('Convince Me') 27 September 2020], none of the candidates, none of them, talked about the topic of racism. Nobody asked them. [Questions] didn't even come among the young people, because the debate was for young people so that they decide who to vote for. There was a decisive moment regarding a gender focus, regarding education about gender, because Puerto Rico does not have that, but our femicides are rising, which is very concerning. Femicides and trans femicides. And only two candidates of the five that were there talked about a focus on gender. But not one of the five talked about Blackness. So it's been ... the George Floyd thing was in May. So, since May we have had marches, we have had vigils, we have given talks, we have led seminars, colleges have made agreements to work on curricula with an anti-racist focus ... I have not seen – and I pay close attention – the subject of Blackness. It is disillusioning.

JTMIV: Do you think the events after Hurricane Maria have changed your activism and your literary work? After the protests of 2019?

YAP: Before the Hurricane, I did more performances. I called that – it's a term I invented, I know that it's a term the specialists don't work on – artivism. So I participated in a lot of artivism – we created protest art, we closed highways, we would arrive and do sit-ins so that people couldn't get into the bank that day, or the malls. After Hurricane Maria, that diminished, it went down. And during a pandemic? Forget about it ... It has been hard since Maria. The most significant thing after Hurricane Maria and before COVID was the protests we held to demand dignity for the homes of people who live in the south [of the island]. There was a series of tremors that we have been going through for about a year, earthquakes, and they lost their homes. Then, the Puerto Rican government, the government what it has received – a lot of it has been hidden. It has been given to rich people so that they will sell their support; aid is not reaching poor communities. We have had to do small things in our communities. That is another kind of work we are seeing ... Our protests have not been able to have a larger scope. That is the most drastic change that I have seen.

JTMIV: Would you like to talk about the groups and institutions you have founded?

YAP: The project that consumes most of my attention is rooted in the initiative of the United Nations and UNESCO to celebrate the Decade of People of African Descent. We started a group called the Cátedra de Mujeres Ancestrales ('Ancestral Women's Study Group'). Literary artivism in which we write about Blackness. All aspects of Blackness. Then, more recently, a project birthed out of a dissertation project, for which I was the object of study [through my work], I don't remember the whole title but the title has the word 'Afro-Queer', 'Afro-Queerness in the Work of Yolanda Arroyo Pizarro'. And through that two-year project, I have been starting to observe that other writers are 'Afro-Queer' in literature. There are not many. Very few. So, starting with the pandemic, a grass-roots organisation came up to me, one that does work with the arts as well as with growing crops and defending territory, and they asked me if I could give workshops on Afro-Queerness in literature. At the moment, I have another project. I have to devote my care and attention to the Cátedra de Saberes Afro-Queer ['The Afro-Queer Knowledges Workshop'] and the Cátedra de Mujeres Ancestrales. We go to the archives from the sixteenth, seventeenth and eighteenth centuries in Puerto Rico, and the Cátedra de Saberes Queer, which includes that, but we give relevance to the voices of sexual dissidents within Puerto Rican Blackness.

JTMIV: Could you talk about the Congresos de Afrodescendencia de Puerto Rico at the UPR in 2015 and 2018? And the International Decade of People of African Descent?

YAP: The initiative I work with for the Decade is the Cátedra de Mujeres Ancestrales, recently, we have two campaigns. We have several, but the two we are giving the greatest visibility and amplitude is the Black Curriculum Campaign or, as I call it, #ennegrecetuprontuario. It is a campaign that works to educate teachers, students and tutors or guardians. We do outreach work with educators, outreach for students and an outreach workshop for parents and caretakers of students ... In all subjects. Not only in literature class ... And if it doesn't happen at the level of teacher or student, it might be the parents or caretakers who takes the list of materials for their children and go up to the teacher and tell them 'you have to include people who are my colour, topics related to my colour, historical figures of my colour, *et cetera*', right? ... The other campaign, which is #pelobueno, is an attempt to give mini-workshops, seminars on *afro-auto-estima* ('Black self-esteem'). Little children ... to twelfth grade as well, working on Black self-esteem and anti-racism as such ... Regarding the Conferences of Afrodescent in Puerto Rico you mention, I participated in both. I was a little upset when I left the second one. I felt that the first one, the first time you do something there are always exclusions or blind spots. But the second time you do something, they are no longer blind spots. It hurt me a lot not to see representation of Afro-Queerness, Afro-LGBT in the activities that the conference offered. I left a bit upset, [but] I am collaborating with Marielba [María Elba Torres Muñoz]. We have to see if, at the third conference, they take into account the observations I made and also have representation of sexual diversity in the spaces of Blackness.

JTMIV: This book is about how you and other Black women authors are changing the idea of the 'great Puerto Rican family'. Would you like to comment on that metaphor of the family on the island?

YAP: Seriously, it is a change in paradigm. The work that is being done is good. It is happening here on the island and beyond by writers and scholars like you. That fills me with a lot of hope. What more could I want? That we make a diametrical change to the perception we have of the 'great Puerto Rican family'. The 'great Puerto Rican family' is also a family of two women where one can have an Afro-Queer identity and where they are raising children, like in my case. Regarding identities, in my wife's case, an ironclad defender of Blackness, of anti-racism ... but who defends her Puerto Rican indigenous identity and the hidden history of those first occupants. That, too, is the 'great Puerto Rican family', right? That dichotomy of reconciliations that have happened in the process is something that is really important. Sometimes it is a rupture with those that see in my marriage or that see in my family an attempt to defy the 'great Puerto Rican family'. Defy the critics, regarding the non-monogamy that we practise in our family, let's say, when we try to be decolonial subjects, when we try to go against hegemony, being anti-hegemonic, we come out as anti-patriarchal. One also has to break with that pattern that others defend, even if it is from Blackness and even if they are LGBT. That too, has turned out to be a site of encounters and controversy and resentment, right? We are not always going to agree on many of the positions where the majority of the groups identify – for example, 'I feel

LGBT, my family counts, too, but here we are monogamous and believe in relationships that are similar to the hetero-norm' ... We are always trying to bring that message that the less possession one feels from the other, the easier it is for one to decolonise her thought, to build herself up, to make herself into a more ethical subject. But that goes against many customs that have to do with the religion that was imposed by the coloniser, right? In that aspect, we are also dissidents, because we are not Christians. In my case, I am atheist. Zulma is not atheist but practises alternative religions that are not colonial. And that brings with it, as a consequence, perhaps a lot of confusion and a lot of rejection, including on the part of allies that are fighting alongside you. In summary, I love what you are doing, and I love that you are interviewing me to allow me to tell you what I am doing to break that pattern of the traditional Puerto Rican family, which, when all is said and done, has done us so much harm.

Notes

Introduction

1 All translations are mine unless otherwise noted.
2 Ramos Rosado considers Santos-Febres, Denis-Rosario and Arroyo Pizarro part of an Afro-Puerto Rican corpus of writers born between 1966 and 1970, but my work goes beyond the archipelago (207).
3 While the terms 'mulatto' and 'mulatta' are offensive in some Anglophone contexts, they are very common in the Spanish-speaking world (Maddox and Stephens 373–80). The classification, which includes mixed-race people and can even be used to refer to those with no European descent, is essential to understanding the works I discuss. Those with lighter complexions had more opportunities under slavery, a phenomenon that continues in social norms today. To not use the word 'mulatto' would be to force a Latin American reality into an Anglocentric Black-white binary and limit understandings of the texts.
4 Margaret Shrimpton sees Caribbean identity as constantly 'fluctuante' ('fluctuating') in the author's work, like waves (153).
5 Blanco also idealised the 'great Puerto Rican family' in his *Prontuario histórico de Puerto Rico* ('Historical Overview of Puerto Rico', 1935) and *El prejuicio racial en Puerto Rico* ('Racial Prejudice in Puerto Rico', 1938). He presented the white Creole as the paternalist, Hispanic, Catholic head of the plantation family (Moreno 33). Emilio Belaval and Enrique Laguerre, members of the 1930s generation, evoked the 'great family' myth in their writing on national identity (33). Luis Díaz Soler joined them in the 1950s (Márquez 119).
6 She draws on sociologist Jorge Duany's *The Puerto Rican Nation on the Move* (Moreno 24).
7 He was preceded in less extensive projects by Samuel Betances and Edgardo Rodríguez Juliá in 1972 (Márquez 120).
8 Édouard Glissant (1928–2011) is one of the most influential thinkers of Martinique, a novelist, theorist, poet and dramaturge (Shlensky

353). A postmodernist thinker in the tradition of Deleuze and Guattari, he devised a Caribbean poetics and advocated for recognising (as well as the opacity of) Martinique's Creole language, landscape and culture. An advocate of popular culture, he often wrote on *marronage*, or Black resistance at a personal and philosophical level to oppressive structures created by enslavement (Shlensky 353).

9 Maddox argues for the consideration of intersectionality in Latin America in his introduction to Maddox and Stephens's *Dictionary of Latin American Identities*, a comprehensive study of terms for identity that includes race, ethnicity, gender and sexuality (1–28). The concept of intersectionality of race and gender, among other variables, in scholarly discourse, dates back to the work of Crenshaw.

10 Carlos Gardel (1917–35) was a French-born Argentine singer, songwriter, composer, film producer and movie star. He is a foundational icon of Argentine culture. He grew up singing in Buenos Aires's Abasto neighbourhood, where many immigrants lived (Del Barco). In the 1920s and 1930s, he popularised the tango worldwide and spread the legend of an immigrant who became a self-made man (Del Barco). He added vocals to what had previously been an instrumental genre. His image on screen was that of the 'Latin lover'.

Chapter 1

1 For a full discussion, see Gonzenbach Perkins (53), Maddox ('The Black Atlantic' 156), Schulman (7), and Vieira. Luis states 'Manzano's *autobiografía* is the only slave account written in nineteenth-century Spanish America' (*Literary* 84). Narratives culled from non-abolitionist documents are gathered, for example, in McKnight and Garofalo (ix) and Crespo Vargas (8).

Chapter 3

1 For a full biography, see Sánchez González (1).

Chapter 4

1 While Valdés does not argue in *Daughters* that Morrison adopts a syncretic worldview in her novel, Yeates claims that her iconic character Beloved is a zombie in the Haitian Vodou tradition and that life

and death are permeable realms in the novel, as they are in *Daughters* (518).

Conclusion

1 While writing this book, I learned that Yvonne Denis is finalising her study *El mito literario Yoruba en la mujer negra caribeña: Interdisciplinariedad en obras de Mayra Santos-Febres y Fátima Patterson Patterson* ('*Literary Yoruba Myth in Black Women of the Caribbean: Interdisciplinarity in the Work of Mayra Santos-Febres and Fátima Patterson Patterson*') (Abadía-Rexach and Díaz Torres). It is based on her doctoral research in anthropology. Her approach reaffirms my dialogue with Yoruba faiths in this book of criticism.

Glossary of Terms

1898 – The US occupation of Puerto Rico during the Spanish-American War.

Afro-Boricua – Puerto Rican of the island or diaspora who is self-aware of their Afrodescendant identity and African heritage. Often, the person will be 'visibly black', having African features that mark them in a racialised society.

Afro-Puerto Rican – Afro-Boricua.

afrodescendencia, **Afrodescent** – according to Campos García, awareness of and/or belonging to the African diaspora in Latin America. I extend this definition to include African-Americans and the rest of the African diaspora worldwide (15).

afrodescendiente, **Afrodescendant** – someone who displays *afrodescendencia*, usually a person who is considered Black.

archipelago – a group of islands. Puerto Rico includes the main island, Vieques, Culebra, Mona and smaller, uninhabited islands. Since I am following Santos-Febres's thought, which Benítez Rojo inspired, the notion of the Caribbean as a 'cultural meta-archipelago without center and without limits', a cultural and political unit that is simultaneously scattered and impossible to reduce to homogeneity, is part of my reminder to the reader that Borinquén is not an isolated island but a repeating island that includes its scattered diaspora and connections to the outside world (9).

Atlantic Creole – a person born in the hierarchy of the colonial Americas but retaining elements of Africa. They were often enslaved or indentured servants. In the British colonies, they often had cultural elements of the Spanish and Portuguese colonies from which they were imported (Berlin 39).

Borcua – a Puerto Rican from the island or the diaspora.

Borinquén – the Taíno, or first, name of the island now called 'Puerto Rico'.

El Barrio – also, 'East Harlem' and 'Spanish Harlem', it is the area of Manhattan bounded by Fifth Avenue on the west and Ninety-Sixth Street on the South. It has been the cultural and population centre of the Puerto Rican community in New York, most notably since the 1930s, though other Latinxs and African Americans are an influential population there today (Exploring the Latino Metropolis).

Cangrejos – Santurce, historically, an area of metro-San Juan with a large Black population.

capá prieto – a tree with deep roots common to the Caribbean. It is also the name of a secret nineteenth-century Puerto Rican nationalist society (Ramos Rosado, 'Prólogo' 31).

craft – *techné*.

curandera – a folk healer who often preserves African or indigenous traditions.

Family of choice – fractal family with agency for Black people and other marginalised groups.

filial, filiation – I use these terms in the sense Glissant and Santos-Febres use them (*Caribbean* 73; 'Caribe' 19:04). Plantation-rooted societies, for these theorists, create linear notions of logic and time to ensure the perpetuation of inequalities for the benefit of the Westernised elite: fathers beget sons who inherit their plantation property, for example, and borders are naturalised.

Fractal – a fractal is an irregular shape of which a part is the same shape as another that is larger or smaller than it ('fractal'). The particles of a snowflake are roughly the same form as the full snowflake (m-w.com). Santos-Febres summarises the concept as the '*uno-múltiple*' ('multiple-one') ('Fractal' 25:52). That is to say that an identity can be simultaneously individual and changing yet part of a greater diaspora or repeating fractal. Another example is the shape of coastlines, making the paradigm highly relevant to the Caribbean imaginary ('fractal'). 'Fractal' comes from the word 'broken,' but Santos-Febres shows pride in the Caribbean and Blackness ('fractal'). Shattered Caribbean and Black identities are represented by the families that this book analyses.

fractal Caribbean – a postmodern definition of the Caribbean based on the fractal and the theories of Deleuze, Guattari, Glissant, Benítez Rojo and Santos-Febres.

fractal family – the opposite of the plantation family, the basis for the 'great Puerto Rican family' metaphor. Santos-Febres imagines the family not as bloodline but as a social network that includes allies beyond the island and beyond one's race. It is also a metaphor for the Puerto Rican nation, which is simultaneously insular and diasporic. This nation-family recognises Afro-Boricuas as having experiences conditioned by enslavement and continued discrimination. The diverse, expanding, fractal family should be a 'family of choice'. The term emerged among LGBTQ+ people who had to form new communities after their birth families rejected them. The term recognises the pain and rejection minorities face and establishes an analogy between the African diaspora and the LGBTQ+ people who shaped Santos-Febres and other Afro-Boricuas' thought. These families parallel the communities of Afro-Puerto Rican religions commonly called 'Santería'.

Free Associated State ('Estado Libre Asociado') – the local Spanish name for Puerto Rico's political status, which in English is 'Commonwealth'. Since it was coined in 1952, 'colony' had fallen out of favour, but the relationship between the United States and Puerto Rico is, arguably, different from other postcolonial Commonwealth territories, such as Guam, for example, which has no representation in Congress, to mention one benefit. This liminal status has fuelled heated debate over whether to maintain the status quo, become a US state, or declare independence.

great Puerto Rican family – while the definition varies, the general notion is that the island lives in racial harmony. It can be traced to the late nineteenth century, when liberals on the island sought to create a local identity based on the values of the moneyed white Creole class. Often, it presents a romantic notion of the hacienda or plantation. Commonly, the white patriarch is presented as a benevolent ruler and the basis for future generations. It is associated with Insularist thinkers, particularly Antonio Pedreira. Arguably, it evolved into René Marqués's romantic notion of the patriarchal, white skinned or mestizo *jíbaro*. Today, the 'great family' is considered synonymous with conservative dismissal of the criticisms and affirmations Black, feminist and LGBTQ+ thinkers and activists make.

hacienda, *hacendados* – plantation, enslavers who owned plantations.

hispanophilia – romanticisation of and identification with the Spanish colonial past.

Hurricane Maria (and Irma) – the hurricanes that struck Puerto Rico in September 2017 in a two-week succession. President Trump was widely criticised for his handling of the disaster. Approximately 3,000 people died due to the storms and the long-lasting power outage they caused. Resentment and suspicion stemming from initial reports of few fatalities have led to belief that even more people died due to the series of catastrophes, which intensified discontent regarding a financial crisis that gained international infamy the previous year.

Independentist – someone who supports national independence for Puerto Rico from the United States.

Iupi – the main campus of the University of Puerto Rico at Río Piedras (UPR or 'Iupi' in playful, affectionate Spanglish), the flagship of the university system. The university has been a centre of Puerto Rican nationalism. Pedreira represents a conservative cultural nationalism. Historically, it is the centre of Independentist movements on the island. The campus boasts the first Black Studies programme on the island, called Afrodescendencia y Racialidad, since 2021. The flagship has suffered major budget cuts and serves as a symbol for the nation as a whole for many.

jíbaro, jíbara, jíbare – Puerto Rican peasant, often imagined as white or mestizo and male, the head of a patriarcal family that symbolises the Puerto Rican nation.

loiceños, loiceñas, loiceñes – Residents of Loíza, a historically Black region of Puerto Rico.

Loíza – a northeastern region of Puerto Rico that is considered a major centre of Afro-Puerto Rican population and culture. It is the 'Capital of Tradition' due to practices like the annual Santiago Apóstol Festival in Loíza Aldea (now officially 'Loíza Pueblo'), to which the term often refers. Piñones is a town in the region.

lunfardo – the popular Spanish subdialect of Buenos Aires, Argentina.

maroon – runaway slave.

marronage – Black rebellion.

negrismo, negrista – an avant-garde artistic movement, represented most prominently by Luis Palés Matos in Puerto Rico, which created exoticised representations of local Black people, their speech and customs. Most practitioners were white but recognised the profound impact Afro-Antilleans had on local culture.

negroide – a term used in Palés's time to refer to negrista poetry that is frequently used on the island today. It is now considered demeaning to Black people, since *–oide* implies 'less than human' (Arroyo Pizarro, *Blancoides* 11).

Nuyorican – a Puerto Rican from New York.

Partido Democrático Popular – pro-Commonwealth party Luis Muñoz Marín founded, led, and, in some ways, personified. One of three major parties. The others represent statehood and independence.

performativity, performance – the notion that gender identity is not biologically or otherwise naturally determined but that it is continually created as a structured illusion. A common metaphor for it is drag. Performers do not accept biological determination of gender manifestation but choose to control how gender is presented through clothing, speech and other signs. Since gender intersects with race and sexuality, these other key aspects of identity can, in many ways, be seen as performative. For example, one performs Black identity by protesting the racism that they experience.

pharmakon – Derrida's theory that a catalyst that preserves systems can also destroy them, represented by the fact that 'pharmakon' meant 'medicine' and 'poison' for the Ancient Greeks (70).

Piñones – town in Loíza.

plantation – a system that emerged during the colonial period that is patriarchal, racist and sexist. This political unit is closely associated with the cultivation of sugar, which has historically been a high-profit but labour-intensive monoculture in the Caribbean. Typically, the plantation is led by a white patriarch who controls the inheritance of this property by demanding fidelity from his wife who is, when possible, also white and of his class or higher. The legitimate male heir was expected to perpetuate the system. The basis of the plantation was slave labour, always Black or Afrodescendant, until 1873, which was complemented by wage labour. The ramifications of this colonial system continue today in multiple forms of racism, sexism and phobias against those who challenge the binary notions of gender that justify patriarchy. Benítez Rojo, an influence on Santos-Febres, theorised the 'Plantation' as an oppressive machine that repeated throughout the Caribbean, connecting with other machines or recognisable political, cultural, and economic patterns (i.e., the Spanish Fleet, other languages). Glissant theorised the plantation as an equally oppressive system, but he focused on its role in creating insular, linear political structures: borders, inheritance and monolithic, Eurocentric notions of national identity and thinking. Glissant, Benítez Rojo and Santos-Febres advocate for a postmodern challenge to linear thought and romaniticise the maroon (whom Benítez Rojo called the 'anti-Plantation') as a symbol of Afro-Caribbean identity (Benítez Rojo 42, 242).

Ponce – the largest and most influential city in the south of Puerto Rico. Its Barrio San Antón has a large and famous Afro-Boricua community (Santiago-Díaz 25).

posmodernos, posmodernes – Puerto Ricans who reject the foundational metanarrative that the island and its unique culture are the true bearers of national identity and include the diaspora in the national community (Moreno 44).

puertorriqueñistas – Puerto Ricans who consider the island and its unique culture to be the true bearers of Puerto Rican identity (Moreno 44).

racial democracy – originating in Brazil, it is the often superficial and conservative notion that, in Latin America, there is no racism or little racism due to a less extreme form of slavery, racial mixing and a lack of overtly racist laws, such as Jim Crow (Lloréns, 'Identity' 29; Moreno 13).

raciality (*Racialidad*) – race as a social construct and basis for association (Guanche Pérez 51).

Regla de Ocha – Santería.

Río Piedras – the Iupi (or UPR), the University of Puerto Rico at Río Piedras.

Santería – a syncretic religion that emerged in societies based on the enslavement of Africans. Its deities, or Orishas, originate among the Yoruba of Africa. In Catholic slave societies, the enslaved camouflaged their deities with the names and images of saints.

Taíno – the native people of Puerto Rico, who called it Borinquén.

tano – abbreviation of *napolitano*, someone from Naples. It is used for Italian immigrants to Argentina (Maddox and Stephens 507).

techné – craft. Becoming part of a community through work. Arroyo claims that the Ancient Greeks displayed skill, or *techné*, in their profession, regardless of its prestige (agriculture, medicine) (7). For Socrates and Plato, *techné* means skills of the 'self': self-protection, bettering oneself and contributing to the community (7). One element of *techné*, as I see it, is assuming control over one's body and identity.

transloca – coined by LaFountain-Stokes, the term refers to a translocal identity employed by an LGBTQ+ person (17). I build on this definition as a performance of individual, corporeal, and transnational identity as Afro-Puerto Rican, including a common LTBTQ+ phenomenon, the family of choice.

uno-múltiple – the paradoxical nature of diversity in community. Santos-Febres's use of the term is inspired by Yoruba-based religions, which influence how most Afro-Puerto Ricans shape identity and community.

vejigante – a folk devil represented by ornate masks during the Carnival and Santiago Apóstol festivities in Loíza and Ponce.

white Creole – *criollo*. This term and its cognates have many definitions. Typically, it refers to someone born in the New World. In this case, I use it to refer to the legitimate descendants of Spaniards who retained much of the privilege of the colonies but who experienced a glass ceiling for certain offices and privileges of colonial hierarchy. After Spanish colonialism in Puerto Rico, the white Creole elite became the most powerful local group, second only to the US occupiers, who continue to control certain areas of political power.

Yoruba – an African people from west Africa. Many of them were enslaved during local wars and sold as captives to provide labour for the Hispanic Caribbean.

Zorzal Criollo – 'Creole Thrush', the nickname of the Argentine 'songbird' of the tango, Carlos Gardel.

Works Cited

Abadía-Rexach, Bárbara, *Musicalizando la raza: La racialización en Puerto Rico a través de la música* (San Juan: Ediciones Puerto, 2012).
—— 'Los repiques de la afrodescendencia en Puerto Rico: Salsa, plena, bomba y rumba', *Afro-Hispanic Review*, 37/1 (2018), 14–28.
—— and Mayra Díaz Torres, 'El mito literario yoruba en la mujer negra caribeña', *Negras*, PodCast 210903, Cadena Radio Universidad de Puerto Rico, Apple.com, 7 September 2021, *https://podcasts.apple.com/us/podcast/el-mito-literario-yoruba-en-la-mujer-negra-caribe%C3%B1a-210903/id1502099638?i=1000534585685* (last accessed 22 November 2021).
Agamboue Azizet, Grace Cathy, 'El negro: Un "fantasma" en la literatura puertorriqueña, el ejemplo de *Capá prieto* (2010) y *Fe en disfraz* (2009)', in Nurse Allende (ed.), pp. 262–70.
Allende, Isabel, *Island Beneath the Sea*, trans. Margaret Seyers Peden (New York: Harper Perennial, 2010).
Álvarez, Sonia, 'Introduction to the Project and the Volume/I Enacting a Translocal Feminist Politics', in Álvarez et al. (ed.), pp. 1–18.
—— Claudia de Lima Costa, Verónica Feliu, Rebecca Hester, Norma Klahn and Millie Thayer (eds), *Translocalities/Translocalidades: Feminist Politics of Translation in the Latin/a Américas* (Durham NC: Duke University Press, 2014).
'Ancestro', *Diccionario de la Lengua Española* (2020), *https://dle.rae.es/ancestro* (last accessed 3 May 2022).
Andrews, George Reid. *The Afro-Argentines of Buenos Aires, 1800–1900* (Madison WI: University of Wisconsin Press, 1980).
Arce, Chrissy, 'La Fe disfrazada y la complicidad del deseo', in Celis and Rivera (eds), pp. 226–46.
Arriaga-Arando, Eduard, 'Multiple Names and Time Superposition: No Anxiety in the Electronic Poetics of Yolanda Arroyo and Diego Trelles', in Robbins and González (eds), *New Trends in Contemporary Latin American Narrative: Post-National Literatures and the Canon* (New York: Palgrave Macmillan, 2015), pp. 191–215.

Arroyo, Jossianna, 'Historias de familia: Migraciones y escritura homosexual en la literature puertorriqueña', *Revista Canadiense de Estudios Hispánicos*, 26/3 (2002), 361–78.
—— *Writing Secrecy in Caribbean Freemasonry* (New York: Palgrave Macmillan, 2013).
Arroyo Pizarro, Yolanda, *Afrofeministamente* (Hato Rey: Editorial EDP University 2020).
—— *Afrohistoria* (Self-published, 2018).
—— 'Los amamantados', in Arroyo Pizarro and Cruz Centeno (eds), 21–30.
—— *Blancoides* (Charleston: Boreales, 2018).
—— *Cachaperismos 2010: Literatura lesboerótica* (Carolina: Boreales, 2010).
——*Cachaperismos 2012: Literatura lesboerótica* (Carolina: Boreales, 2012).
—— *Las caras lindas* (Hato Rey: Editorial EDP University, 2018).
—— 'Carne negra', in Arroyo and Cruz Centeno (eds), pp. 31–4.
—— *Los documentados* (Self-published, 2017).
—— *Huracana* (Carolina: Boreales, 2018).
—— Interview with Ana María Fuster Lavín, in Arroyo Pizarro, *Tongas*, pp. 109–22.
—— Interview with David Caleb Acevedo, in Arroyo Pizarro, *Tongas*, pp. 123–42.
—— *Marie Calabó: De niña curiosa a mujer líder* (Self-published, 2017).
—— 'La medalla mágica de Juana Agripina', in *Las caras lindas*, pp. 49–64.
—— *Mis dos mamás me miman* (Self-published, 2016).
—— *las Negras* (Charleston: Boreales, 2012).
—— *Negras: Stories of Puerto Rican Slave Women*, trans. Alejandro Álvarez Nieves (Charleston: Boreales, 2012).
—— 'Las nietas', in *Las caras lindas*, pp. 37–8.
—— *Ojos de luna* (San Juan: Terranova, 2007).
—— *Oscarita: La niña que quiere ser como Oscar López Rivera* (Self-published, 2017).
—— Personal interview, May 2016.
—— 'La piel negra que transgrede: Entrevista por David Caleb Acevedo a la escritora Yolanda Arroyo Pizarro, mayo 2012', *Label Me Latino/a*, 9 (2012), 1–11.
—— 'racismolengua', in Arroyo Pizarro, *Blancoides*, p. 43.
—— 'Río Piedras 2013, sede del Women Warriors of the Afro-Latina Diaspora', in *Afrohistoria*, pp. 113–18.
—— *Saeta: The Poems* (Charleston: Boreales, 2011).
—— 'Las cosas que se cuentan al caer', in Santos-Febres (ed.), *San Juan Noir* (Brooklyn NY: Akashik Books, 2016), 119–30.
—— *Tongas, palenques y quilombos* (Self-published, 2013).
——*Violeta* (Charleston: Boreales, 2013).

—— '"¿Y tu abuela, dónde está?"', TEDxUPR, 20 July 2016, YouTube. https://www.youtube.com/watch?v=EB0hQEvXgDM (last accessed 25 August 2022).

—— and Marlyn Cruz Centeno (eds), *Revista Boreales: Palenque: Antología puertorriqueña de temática negrista, antirracista, africanista y afrodescendiente* (Charleston: Boreales, 2013).

Associated Press, 'Hurricane Cristobal Building Strength as it Moves North,' *Central Broadcasting Station News*, 26 August 2014, www.cbsnews.com/news/hurricane-cristobal-building-strength-as-it-moves-north/ (last accessed 24 October 2021).

Ayala, César, and Rafael Bernabe, *Puerto Rico in the American Century: A History Since 1898* (Chapel Hill NC: University of North Carolina Press, 2007).

Ballesta 9 [José Arturo Ballester Panelli], 'Fractal Caribbean', *Ballesta 9* (n.d.), www.ballesta9.com/artworks-grid/ (last accessed 24 October 2021).

Baquaqua, Mahommah Gardo, 'Biography of Mahommah G. Baquaqua, a Native of Zoogoo, in the Interior of Africa. (a Convert to Christianity,) With a Description of That Part of the World', *Documenting the American South* (2001), https://docsouth.unc.edu/neh/baquaqua/summary.html (last accessed 3 May 2022).

Baralt, Guillermo, *Esclavos rebeldes: Conspiraciones y sublevaciones de esclavos en Puerto Rico (1795–1873)* (Río Piedras: Ediciones Huracán, 1981).

—— *La Buena Vista: Life and Work on a Puerto Rican Hacienda, 1833–1904*, trans. Andrew Hurley (Chapel Hill NC: University of North Carolina Press, 1999).

Barnet, Miguel. *Cimarrón* (Buenos Aires: Del Sol, 1987).

Barnett, Pamela, 'Figurations of Rape and the Supernatural in *Beloved*', *Publication of the Modern Language Association*, 112/3 (1997), 418–27.

Benítez Rojo, Antonio, *The Repeating Island: The Caribbean and the Postmodern Perspective* (Durham NC: Duke University Press, 1997).

Bennett, Herman, *African Kings and Black Slaves: Sovereignty and Dispossession in the Early Modern Atlantic* (Philadelphia PA: University of Pennsylvania Press, 2018).

Berlin, Ira, *Many Thousands Gone: The First Two Centuries of Slavery in North America* (Cambridge MA: Belknap Press, 1998).

Binder, Wolfgang, '"¿Un mundo enfermo?" Manuel Zeno Gandía's *La Charca* and National Puerto Rican Discourse', *Revista Iberoamericana*, 21/3–4 (1997), 56–65.

Black Latinas Know Collective, 'The Collective'. *Black Latinas Know*, 2021, www.blacklatinasknow.org/the-collective (last accessed 23 November 2023).

Bolden, Millicent, 'Yvonne Denis Rosario. *Capá Prieto*', *Afro-Hispanic Review*, 30/2 (2011), 194–200.

Boria, Juan, 'ICP/L-9: Majestad negra en Juan Boria', *Archivo Virtual Instituto de Cultura Puertorriqueña* (2021), *www.archivoicp.com/icpl9-majestad-negra-en-juan-boria* (last accessed 24 October 2021).
Branche, Jerome (ed.), *Black Writing, Culture, and the State in Latin America* (Nashville TN: Vanderbilt University Press, 2015), pp. 149–70.
—— 'Disrobing Narcissus: Race, Difference, and Dominance (Mayra Santos-Febres's *Nuestra Señora de la Noche* Revisits the Puerto Rican National Allegory)', in Branche (ed.), pp. 149–70.
Brown, Kimberly Juanita, *The Repeating Body: Slavery's Visual Resonance in the Contemporary* (Durham NC: Duke University Press, 2015).
Brown, Rachel Jolivette, 'Margaret Garner', *From Slave Mothers and Southern Belles to Radical Reformers and Lost Cause Ladies: Representing Women in the Civil War Era* (2021), *https://civilwarwomen.wp.tulane.edu/essays-3/margaret-garner/* (last accessed 24 October 2021).
Burgos, Julia de, *Obra poética* (San Juan: Instituto de Cultura Puertorriqueña, 2014).
Butler, Judith, *Bodies that Matter: On the Discursive Limits of 'Sex'* (New York: Routledge, 1993).
—— *Gender Trouble: Feminism and the Subversion of Identity* (New York: Routledge, 1990).
C and AL, 'Nuevo programa de la Universidad de Puerto Rico: Primer Programa de Afrodescendencia y Racialidad', *Contemporary and América Latina* (14 February 2021), *amlatina.contemporaryand.com/editorial/primer-programa-de-afrodescendencia-y-racialidad/* (last accessed 3 May 2022).
Cabrera, Lydia, *El Monte: Igbo Finda Ewe Orisha Vititi Nfinda* (Miami FL: Universal, 1983).
Campos García, Alejandro, 'Introducción', in Valero and Campos García (eds), pp. 15–64.
Carpentier, Alejo, *El reino de este mundo* (Barcelona: Seix Barral, 2007).
Casamayor-Cisneros, Odette, 'Cuando las negras se desnudan: La experiencia inasible del cuerpo caribeño y afrodiaspórico en la creación plástica de María Magdalena Campos-Pons y la narrativa de Mayra Santos-Febres', *Cuadernos de Literatura*, 19/38 (2015), 137–58.
Castillo, Debra, 'Anamú: La palabra efectiva de Mayra Santos-Febres' (Introduction), in Mayra Santos-Febres, *Sirena Selena vestida de pena*, pp. xvii–xxvi.
Celis, Nadia, 'Heterotopías del deseo: Sexualidad y poder en el Caribe de Mayra Santos-Febres', in Celis and Rivera (eds), pp. 132–52.
—— and Juan Pablo Rivera (eds). *Lección errante: Mayra Santos-Febres y el Caribe contemporáneo* (San Juan: Isla Negra, 2011), pp. 9–36.
Chamoiseau, Patrick, and Janice Morgan, 'Re-Imagining Diversity and Connection in the Chaos World: An Interview with Patrick Chamoiseau', *Callaloo* 31/2 (2008), 443–53.

Chasteen, John Charles, *Born in Blood and Fire: A Concise History of Latin America* (Chapel Hill NC: University of North Carolina Press, 2001).
Constantine-Simms, Delroy, *The Greatest Taboo: Homosexuality in Black Communities* (New York: Alyson Books, 2001).
Crenshaw, Kemberlé, 'Demarginalising the Intersection of Race and Sex: A Black Feminist Critique of Antidiscrimination Doctrine, Feminist Theory and Antiracist Politics', *The University of Chicago Legal Forum* 1, n.pag.
Crespo, Elizabeth, 'Domestic Work and Racial Divisions of Women's Employment in Puerto Rico, 1899–1930', in Vargas-Ramos, pp. 225–32.
Crespo Vargas, Pablo, 'Ana de Mena: Una bruja caribeña en el siglo XVII', *Revista del Instituto de Cultura Puertorriqueña*, 3/14 (December 2020), 8–17.
Cruz-Malavé, Arnaldo, 'The Anti-Foundational Foundational Fiction of Piri Thomas (1928–2011)', *Centro Journal*, 24/1 (2012), 12–19.
Curete Alonso, Tite, and Rubén Blades, 'Desahuicio', *Sentimiento de Pueblo: Tite Curete Alonso y Rubén Blades*, Consalsa.org, José Massó (ed.) (2 December 1994) *Laesquinaderuben.com* (last accessed 24 October 2021).
Dávila Gonçalves, Michele, 'El universo caleidoscópico de Yolanda Arroyo Pizarro', in Hidalgo de Jesús (ed.), pp. 39–64.
Del Barco, Magdalit, 'Carlos Gardel: Argentina's Tango Maestro', Morning Edition, *National Public Radio* (13 September 2010) *www.npr.org/templates/story/story.php?storyId=129783483* (last accessed 12 November 2021).
Denis-Rosario, Milagros, 'The Silence of the Black Militia: Socio-Historical Analysis of the British Attack to Puerto Rico of 1797', *Memorias: Revista Digital de Historia y Arqueología desde el Caribe Colombiano*, 8/14 (2011), 48–74.
Denis-Rosario, Yvonne, *Bufé*, 2nd edn (San Juan: Isla Negra, 2012).
—— *Capá prieto*, ebook (San Juan: Isla Negra, 2012).
—— *Capá Prieto: Stories*, trans. Marci Valdivieso (San Juan: Isla Negra, 2010).
—— *Delirio entrelazado* (Hato Rey: Editorial EDP University, 2016).
—— *Sepultados* (Hato Rey: Editorial EDP University, 2018).
Derrida, Jacques, 'Plato's Pharmacy', in Barbara Johnson (ed. and trans.), *Dissemination* (Chicago IL: University of Chicago Press, 1981), pp. 63–171.
Díaz, Luis Felipe, 'La narrativa de Mayra Santos-Febres y el travestismo cultural', *CENTRO*, 15/2 (2003), 26–37.
Diegues, Cacá, *Xica da Silva* (Rio de Janeiro: Embrafilme, 1976).
Dieppa, Isabel Sophia, Kari Lydersen and Martha Bayne, 'In Loíza the Fight for Property Rights Has a Long History', *Pulitzer Centre* (3

January 2019) *https://pulitzercenter.org/reporting/loiza-fight-property-rights-has-long-history* (last accessed 24 October 2021).

Duany, Jorge, *The Puerto Rican Nation on the Move: Identities on the Island and in the United States* (Chapel Hill NC: University of North Carolina Press, 2003).

—— 'The Rough Edges of Puerto Rican Identities: Race, Gender, and Transnationalism', *Latin American Research Review*, 40/3 (2005), 177–90.

Eaton-Martínez, Omar, 'Constructing Blackness in "¡Presente! The Young Lords in New York" Exhibition', *Afro-Hispanic Review*, 37/1 (2018), 10–13.

Echeverría, Esteban, *El matadero*, Leonor Fleming (ed.) (Madrid: Cátedra 1995).

Elia, Nada, *Trances, Dances, and Vociferations: Agency and Resistance in Africana Women's Narratives* (New York: Routledge, 2001).

Exploring the Latino Metropolis, 'Latino Neighborhoods and Their Histories: East Harlem', *Exploring the Latino Metropolis: A Brief Urban Cultural History of US Latinos* (23 March 2016) *https://scalar.usc.edu/works/latino-metropolis-a-brief-urban-cultural-history-of-us-latinos---1/east-harlem-1* (last accessed 29 October 2021).

Falconí-Trávez, Diego, 'De cuerpos-territorio y disidentificaciones lesbo-eróticas: Las encrucijadas narrativas en la narrativa de Yolanda Arroyo Pizarro', *Kipus*, 44 (2018), 133–55.

—— 'Puerto Rico erizando mi piel: Intertextos/intercuerpos *lordeanos* en la narrativa de Yolanda Arroyo Pizarro', *Letras Femeninas*, 42/1 (2016), 55–73.

Felluga, Dino Franco, 'Sublimation', *Introductory Guide to Critical Theory*, Purdue University (31 January 2021) *https://cla.purdue.edu/academic/english/theory/* (last accessed 24 October 2021).

Feracho, Lesley, 'Uprising Textualities of the Americas: Slavery, Migration, and the Nation in Contemporary Afro-Hispanic Women's Narrative', in Branche (ed.), pp. 127–48.

Ferly, Odile, *A Poetics of Relation: Caribbean Women Writing at the Millennium* (New York: Palgrave MacMillan, 2012).

Ferré, Rosario, 'Maldito Amor', in *Maldito Amor y otros cuentos* (New York: Vintage Español, 1998), pp. 17–85.

Figueroa, Víctor, 'Desiring Colonial Bodies in Mayra Santos Febres's *Fe en disfraz*', *Ciberletras: Revista de Crítica Literaria y de Cultura*, 38 (2017), n.pag, *www.lehman.cuny.edu/ciberletras/v38/figueroav.htm* (last accessed 24 October 2021).

Figueroa, Yomaira, *Decolonising Diasporas: Radical Mappings of Afro-Atlantic Literature* (Evanston IL: Northwestern University Press, 2020).

Flores, Juan, *The Diaspora Strikes Back: Caribeño Tales of Learning and Turning* (New York: Routledge, 2009).

Fortes, Jorge, and Diego Ceballos (dir.), *Afroargentinos* (New York: Third World Newsreel, 2003).
Fountain, Anne, *José Martí, the United States, and Race* (Gainesville FL: University Press of Florida, 2017).
'fractal', Merriam Webster (2021), *www.merriam-webster.com/dictionary/fractal* (last accessed 24 October 2021).
Freyre, Gilberto, *Casa-grande e senzala* (Recife: Fundação Gilberto Freyre, 2003).
Fuente, Alejandro de la, 'Afterword: Afro-Latinos and Afro-Latin American Studies', in Petra Rivera-Rideau et al. (eds), *Afro-Latin@s in Movement: Critical Approaches to Blackness and Transnationalism in the Americas* (New York: Palgrave Macmillan, 2016), pp. 289–304.
Furtado, Júnia Ferreira, *Chica da Silva: A Brazilian Slave of the Eighteenth Century* (Cambridge: Cambridge University Press, 2009).
García, Ana María, *La operación* (New York: Latin American Film Project, 1982).
—— 'Not Many Options for Contraception', *Jump Cut: A Review of Contemporary Cinema*, 29 (1984), interview with Iraida López, trans. Kimberly Safford, 38–9.
García, Beatriz, 'Magic, Witchcraft and Curanderismo: Let's Talk about Cultural Appropriation', *Al Día* (18 September 2020), *https://aldianews.com/articles/culture/social/magic-witchcraft-and-curanderismo-lets-talk-about-cultural-appropriation* (last accessed 23 November 2021).
García-Crespo, Naida, *Early Puerto Rican Cinema and Nation Building: National Sentiments, Transnational Realities, 1897–1940* (Lewisburg PA: Bucknell University Press, 2019).
Gelpí, Juan, *Literatura y paternalismo en Puerto Rico* (Río Piedras: University of Puerto Rico Press, 2005).
Gilroy, Paul, *The Black Atlantic: Modernity and Double Consciousness* (London: Verso, 1993).
Glissant, Édouard, *Caribbean Discourse: Selected Essays*, trans. Michael Dash (Charlottesville VA: University of Virginia Press, 1989).
—— *Poetics of Relation*, trans. Betsy Wing (Ann Arbor MI: University of Michigan Press, 1997).
González, Aníbal, 'Religión, nación y narración en *Redentores* (1925) de Manuel Zeno Gandía', *Romance Notes*, 50/1 (2010), 67–76.
González, José Luis, *El país de cuatro pisos y otros ensayos* (Río Piedras: Ediciones Huracán, 1989).
—— 'En el fondo del caño hay un negrito', in René Marqués (ed.), *Cuentos puertorriqueños de hoy* (Río Piedras: Editorial Cultural, 2008), pp. 89–94.
González Echevarría, Roberto, *Mito y archivo: Una teoría de la narrativa latinoamericana*, trans. Virginia Aguirre Muñoz (Mexico: Fondo de Cultura Económica, 2011).

González García, María, *El negro y la negra libres, Puerto Rico: 1800–1873, Su presencia y contribución a la identidad puertorriqueña* (Self-published, 2014).

González-Wippler, Migene, *Powers of the Orishas: Santería and the Worship of Saints* (New York: Original Publications, 1992).

Gonzenbach Perkins, Alexandra, 'Un pacto tácito: Escritura y poder en *Autobiografía del esclavo poeta* de Juan Francisco Manzano', *Decimonónica*, 11/2 (2014), 52–69.

Goodman, Elyssa, 'How bell hooks Paved the Way for Intersectional Feminism', *them* (12 March 2019) *www.them.us/story/bell-hooks* (last accessed 13 November 2021).

Guanche Pérez, Jesús, 'Etnicidad y racialidad en la Cuba actual', *Temas*, 7 (1996), 51–7.

Gumbar, Diana, 'Uneasy Talk about Race: Critique of Puerto Rican Race Relations in Mayra Santos-Febres's *Sobre piel y papel*', *Cuaderno Internacional de Estudios Humanísticos y Literatura*, 18 (2012), 55–67.

Gunther Kodat, Catherine, 'Margaret Garner and the Second Tear', *American Quarterly*, 60/1 (2008), 159–71.

Gutiérrez Negrón, Sergio, 'Cruel Dispositions: Queer Literature, the Contemporary Puerto Rican Literary Field and Luis Negrón's *Mundo cruel* (2010)', in Ignacio Sánchez Prado (ed.), *Pierre Bordieu in Hispanic Literature and Culture*, (New York: Palgrave Macmillan, 2018), pp. 157–86.

Helg, Aline, 'Simón Bolívar and the Spectre of "Pardocracia": José Padilla in post-Independence Cartagena', *Journal of Latin American Studies*, 35/3 (2003), 447–71.

Herrera, Cristina, '"Undesirable Women?" Afro-Puerto Rican Mother-Daughter Relationships and Puerto Rican Heritage in Dahlma Llanos-Figueroa's "Daughters of the Stone"', *Chicana/Latina Studies*, 12/1 (2012), 30–78.

Hidalgo de Jesús, Amarilis (ed.), 'Introduction', in *La escritura de mujeres en Puerto Rico a finales del Siglo XX y principios del Siglo XXII: Essays on Contemporary Puerto Rican Writers* (Lewiston NY: Edward Mellen Press, 2012), pp. xviii–xxiv.

—— 'Mujer y Esclavitud en el cuento "Saeta" de Yolanda Arroyo Pizarro', *Letras Hispanas: Revista de Literatura y Cultura*, 7 (2010), 1–7, *https:// gato-docs.its.txstate.edu/jcr:66387439-79d4-44ef-91aa-e87e6aabfbeb/ Hidalgo.pdf* (last accessed 24 October 2021).

hooks, bell, *Ain't I a Woman: Black Women and Feminism* (Boston MA: South End Press, 1981).

Hull, Gloria, Patricia Bell Scott and Barbara Smith, *All the Women are White, All the Blacks are Men but Some of Us are Brave* (New York: Feminist Press, 1982).

Hurtado, Roberta, *Decolonial Puerto Rican Women's Writings: Subversion in the Flesh* (New York: Palgrave Macmillan, 2019).

—— 'Decolonial Resilience, Resistance and Healing in Dahlma Llanos-Figueroa's Fiction', *Label Me Latino/a*, 7 (2017), 1–14.

Irizarry, Guillermo, 'Pasión y muerte de la madama de San Antón: Modernidad, tortura y ética en *Nuestra Señora de la Noche*', in Celis and Rivera (eds), pp. 206–25.

Jaime, Karen, *The Queer Nuyorican: Racialised Sexualities and Aesthetics in Loisaida* (New York: New York University Press, 2021).

Janer, Zilkia, *Puerto Rican Nation-Building Literature: Impossible Romance* (Gainesville FL: University Press of Florida, 2005).

Jáuregui, Carlos, *The Conquest on Trial: Carvajal's Complaint of the Indians in the Court of Death*, trans. Carlos Jáuregui and Mark Smith-Soto (College Station PA: Pennsylvania State University Press, 2008).

Jiménez Román, Miriam. 'Un hombre (negro) del pueblo: José Celso Barbosa and the Puerto Rican "Race" toward Whiteness', in Vargas-Ramos (ed.), pp. 41–60.

—— and Juan Flores (eds), *The Afro-Latin@ Reader: History and Culture in the United States* (Durham NC: Duke University Press, 2010), pp. 1–18.

Jones, Nicholas, 'Casting a Literary Mammy in Diego Sánchez de Badajoz's *Farsa de la hechicera*', *University of Toronto Quarterly*, 88/4 (2019), 323–45.

—— and Chad Leahy (eds), *Pornographic Sensibilities: Imagining Sex and the Visceral in Premodern and Early Modern Spanish Cultural Production* (New York: Routledge, 2021).

Kirschner, Luz Angélica, 'Capá prieto and the decolonial Afro-Latin(a/o) American Imagination', in Kirschner et al. (eds), pp. 223–42.

—— María Herrera-Sobek and Francisco Lomelí (eds), *Human Rights in the Americas* (New York: Routledge, 2021). pp. 1–27.

LaFountain-Stokes, Lawrence, 'Recent Developments in Queer Puerto Rican History, Politics and Culture', *CENTRO*, 30/2 (2018), 502–40.

—— *Translocas: The Politics of Puerto Rican Drag and Trans Performance* (Ann Arbor MI: University of Michigan Press, 2021).

Lam, C. Christina, 'Flipping the Script: Memory, Body and Belonging in Dahlma Llanos-Figueroa's *Daughters of the Stone*', *Label Me Latino/a*, 7 (2017), 1–9.

Laó-Montes, Agustín, 'Afrolatinidades and the Diasporic Imaginary', *Iberoamericana* 5/17 (2005), 117–30.

—— and Mirangela Buggs, 'Translocal Space of Afro-Latinidad: Critical Feminist Visions for Diasporic Bridge-Building', in Álvarez et al. (eds), pp. 381–400.

Lassauze, Raphael, 'Author Provides Voice Where There's Otherwise Silence', *The Riverdale Press* (19 July 2020), *https://riverdalepress.com/*

stories/author-provides-voice-where-theres-otherwise-silence,72210 (last accessed 24 October 2021).
The Latino Author, 'Dahlma Llanos Figueroa', *The Latino Author* (n.d.), www.thelatinoauthor.com/featuredauthors/figueroa-dahlma-llanos/ (last accessed 24 October 2021).
Lawless, Tilly, 'Sex Work is Integral to the Feminist Movement', *TEDxYouth@Sydney* (24 October 2017), www.youtube.com/watch?v=hi_OwpNndo8 (last accessed 13 November 2021).
Lebrón, Luz Nereida, 'El cuerpo femenino como laboratorio en *La amante de Gardel*', *XII Congreso Virtual sobre Historia de las Mujeres (15 al 31 de octubre de 2020)*, (Jaen: Amigos del Archivo Histórico Diocesano de Jaén, 2020), pp. 437–47.
Lebrón Ortiz, Pedro, *Filosofía del cimarronaje* (Cabo Rojo PR: Editora Educación Emergente, 2020).
Léger, Natalie Marie, 'Mucho Woulo: Black Freedom and The Kingdom of this World', in Valdés (ed.), *Racialised*, pp. 89–112.
Llanos-Figueroa, Dahlma, *Daughters of the Stone: A Novel* (New York: Thomas Dunne, 2009).
—— Interview with Brittany Shoot, *Bookslut*, September 2009, www.bookslut.com/features/2009_09_015108.php (last accessed 24 October 2021).
—— 'Q and A with Author Dahlma Llanos-Figueroa', *Los Afro-Latinos* (24 January 2012) https://losafrolatinos.com/2012/01/24/qa-with-author-dahlma-llanos-figueroa/ (last accessed 24 October 2021).
—— *A Woman of Endurance* (New York: Amistad, 2022).
—— 'The World of the Afro-Puerto Rican: An Interview with Dahlma Llanos-Figueroa', Interview with Ivelisse Rodríguez, *Centro Voices E-Magazine* (28 November 2017), https://centropr.hunter.cuny.edu/centrovoices/letras/world-afro-puerto-rican-interview-dahlma-llanos-figueroa (last accessed 24 October 2021).
Lloréns, Hilda, 'Identity Practices: Racial Passing, Gender, and Racial Purity in Everyday Life in Puerto Rico', *Afro-Hispanic Review*, 37/1 (2018), 29–47.
—— *Imaging the Great Puerto Rican Family: Framing Nation, Race and Gender during the American Century* (Lanham MD: Lexington, 2014).
Luis, William, 'Afro-Latino/a Literature and Identity', in Suzanne Bost and Frances Aparicio (eds), *The Routledge Companion to Latino/a Literature* (New York: Routledge Press, 2012), pp. 34–45.
—— 'Latino Poetry and Distinctiveness', in William Luis (ed.), *Looking Out, Looking In: Anthology of Latino Poetry* (Houston TX: Arte Público Press, 2012). pp. xii–li.
—— *Literary Bondage: Slavery in Cuban Narrative* (Austin TX: University of Texas Press, 1990).

—— 'The Politics of Memory and Miguel Barnet's *The Autobiography of a Runaway Slave*', *Modern Language Notes*, 104/2, (1989), 475–91.

Maddox, John, 'The Black Atlantic Revisited: Ana Maria Gonçalves's *Um defeito de cor*', *Callaloo*, 40/4 (2017), 155–73.

—— 'Introduction', in Maddox and Stephens, pp. 1–28.

—— and Thomas Stephens, *Dictionary of Latin American Identities* (Gainesville FL: University of Florida Press, 2021).

Manzano, Juan Francisco, *Autobiografía de un esclavo/Autobiography of a Slave: A Bilingual Edition*, trans. Evelyn Picon Garfield (Detroit MI: Wayne State University Press, 1996).

Marqués, René, *La carreta: Drama puertorriqueño*, 25th edn (Río Piedras: Editorial Cultural, 2013).

—— 'El puertorriqueño dócil', in René Marqués, *El puertorriqueño dócil y otros ensayos (1953–1971)* (Río Piedras: Editorial Antillana, 1977), pp. 207–10.

Márquez, Roberto, *The Poet's Prose and Other Essays: Race, National Identity, and Diaspora in the Americas* (New York: Peter Lang, 2019).

Martín Sevillano, Ana Belén (ed.), 'Prologue', in *Puerto Rico indócil: Antología de cuentos puertorriqueños del siglo XXI* (Sevilla: Algaida, 2015), pp. 7–11.

Massó, Benito (ed.), *Rebelde: La historia de Juana Agripina* (Hato Rey PR: Editorial EDP University, 2016).

McKnight, Kathryn, and Garofalo, Leo (eds), 'Introduction', in *Afro-Latino Voices: Narratives from the Early Modern Ibero-Atlantic World, 1550–1812* (Indianapolis IN: Hackett, 2009), pp. ix–xxii.

Melo, Juan Carlos, 'La boda de ellas, preparativos para la primera boda gay', *Metro* (21 July 2015), www.metro.pr/pr/sin-categoria/2015/07/21/boda-preparativos-primera-boda-gay.html (last accessed 25 October 2021).

Méndez Panedas, Rosario, 'El regocijo del disfraz: Ritual entre presente y pasado en la novela Fe en disfraz de Mayra Santos-Febres', in María Luisa Cerrón Puga (ed.), *Rumbos del hispanismo en el umbral del Cincuentenario de la AIH*, vol. 6 (Rome: Bagatto Libri, 2012), pp. 425–30.

Mendoza, Annie, 'Rescatando voces silenciadas: Reivindicación corpórica e histórica en la obra poética de Yolanda Arroyo Pizarro', *Voces del Caribe*, 11/1 (2019), 1138–67.

Merced, Miranda, *Las esclavas fugadas de Juncos* (Self-published, 2017).

MetroPR, 'Mayra Santos-Febres recibe el Gran Premio Literario en Francia', *Metro* (20 January 2020), www.metro.pr/pr/noticias/2020/01/20/mayra-santos-febres-recibe-gran-premio-literario-francia.html (last accessed 25 October 2021).

Miletti, Luis, 'Poder, imagen e identidad en *Capá prieto*', *Tinkuy*, 18 (2012), 177–86.

Mohr, Nicholasa, *Nilda* (Houston TX: Arte Público Press, 2011).
Mora Pérez, Námesis, 'Las niñas negras también luchan', *Afro-Hispanic Review*, 37/1 (2018), 117–25.
Moreno, Marisel, *Family Matters: Puerto Rican Women Authors on the Island and the Mainland* (Charlottesville VA: University of Virginia Press, 2012).
Moreno Vega, Marta. 'Afro-Boricua: Nuyorican de Pura Cepa', in Moreno Vega, Alba and Modestin (eds), *Women Warriors*, pp. 77–96.
—— *The Altar of My Soul: The Living Traditions of Santería* (New York: One World Press, 2000).
—— 'The Co-Founder's Perspective', *CorredorAfro.org* (2020), www.casaafro.org/en/about-negro-a-x/ (last accessed 25 October 2021).
—— 'Dr Marta Moreno Vega Flash of the Spirit Conference, New Orleans', *YouTube*, uploaded by Michelle Eistrup (20 December 2014), www.youtube.com/watch?v=mXidjf9puyQ&t=640s (last accessed 25 October 2021).
—— *When the Spirits Dance Mambo: Growing up Nuyorican en El Barrio* (New York: Three Rivers Press, 2004).
—— Marinieves Alba and Yvette Modestin (eds), *Women Warriors of the Afro-Latina Diaspora* (Houston TX: Arte Público Press, 2012).
Morrison, Toni, *Beloved: A Novel* (New York: Alfred A. Knopf, 1987).
Muñoz, Sarah, 'El travestismo como metáfora en Sirena Selena vestida de pena de Mayra Santos-Febres', *Cuadernos del CILHA*, 7–8 (2005–6), 71–80.
Nascimento, Abdias, *O Quilombismo: Documentos de uma militância pan-africanista* (Petrópolis: Vozes, 1980).
Negrón-Muntaner, Frances (dir.), *Brincando el Charco: Portrait of a Puerto Rican* (New York: Women Make Movies, 1994).
Nieves López, Edgar, 'Autodefinición y subversión en *Fe en disfraz* de Mayra Santos Febres y *la Negra* de Yolanda Arroyo Pizarro', *Afro Hispanic Review*, 37/1 (2018), 48–61.
Nouzeilles, Gabriella, 'La esfinge del monstruo: Modernidad e higiene racial en "La charca" de Zeno Gandía', *Latin American Literary Review*, 25/50 (1997), 89–107.
Núñez, Victoria, 'Remembering Pura Belpré's Early Career at the 135th Street New York Public Library: Interracial Cooperation and Puerto Rican Settlement during the Harlem Renaissance', in Vargas-Ramos (ed.), pp. 133–44.
Nurse Allende, Léster (ed.), *¡Negro, negra! Afirmación y Resistencia: Memorias del Primer Congreso de Afrodescendencia en Puerto Rico* (Río Piedras: University of Puerto Rico Press, 2018).
Oliver Velez, Denise, 'Black History Month: Afro-Latina Pura Belpré Gave Children the Precious Love of Books and Stories', *Daily Kos* (25 February 2018), www.dailykos.com/stories/2018/2/25/1737128/-Black-

History-Month-Afro-Latina-Pura-Belpr-gave-children-the-precious-love-of-books-and-stories* (last accessed 25 October 2021).

Omi, Michael, and Howard Winant, *Racial Formation in the United States*, 2nd edn (New York: Taylor and Francis, 1994).

Oquendo-Villar, Carmen, 'Del griego, flor: Mayra Santos-Febres, *Las espinas del erizo* y la memoria de nuevas escritoras', in Celis and Rivera (eds), pp. 43–52.

Palés Matos, Luis, 'Mulata-Antilla', in Julio Marzán (ed. and trans.), *Selected Poems/Poesía selecta* (Houston TX: Arte Público Press, 2000), p. 82.

Pedreira, Antonio, *La actualidad del jíbaro* (Río Piedras: University of Puerto Rico Press, 1935).

—— *Insularismo* (San Juan: Edil, 1968), *Internet Archive* (21 October 2016), https://archive.org/details/Insularismo (last accessed 25 October 2021).

Peña, Ignacio (dir.), 'Soy de una raza pura: Celestina Cordero', *Vimeo* (24 May 2016), https://vimeo.com/167977940 (last accessed 23 November 2021).

—— 'Soy de una raza pura: Eleuterio Derkes', *Vimeo* (3 February 2016), https://vimeo.com/154099961 (last accessed 23 November 2021).

—— 'Soy de una raza pura: Ismael Rivera', *Vimeo* (25 April 2016), https://vimeo.com/164117195 (last accessed 23 November 2021).

—— 'Soy de una raza pura: José Celso Barbosa', *Vimeo* (4 April 2016), https://vimeo.com/161465531 (last accessed 23 Novemer 2021).

—— 'Soy de una raza pura: Julia de Burgos', *Vimeo* (28 March 2017), https://vimeo.com/210407179 (last accessed 23 November 2021).

—— 'Soy de una raza pura: Juan Boria', *Vimeo* (11 May 2017), https://vimeo.com/217096108 (last accessed 23 November 2021).

—— 'Soy de una raza pura: Pura Belpré', *Vimeo* (5 May 2016), https://vimeo.com/165514352 (last accessed 23 November 2021).

—— 'Soy de una raza pura: Ruth Fernández', *Vimeo* (13 April 2017), https://vimeo.com/213114672 (last accessed 23 November 2021).

Peñaranda-Angulo, Victoria, 'La historia femenina negra o la *herstory* negra: *Fe en disfraz* de Mayra Santos-Febres, lectura y re-escritura de la historia desde y para las mujeres afrodescendentes', *Perífrasis*, 9/18 (2018), 98–116.

Perivolaris, John, *Puerto Rican Cultural Identity and the Work of Luis Rafael Sánchez* (Chapel Hill NC: University of North Carolina Press, 2000).

Quiñones Rivera, Maritza, 'From Triqueñita to Afro-Puerto Rican: Intersections of then Racialised, Gendered, and Sexualised Body on Puerto Rico and in the US Mainland', *Meridians: Feminism, Race, Transnationalism*, 7/1 (2006), 162–82.

Ramos-Perea, Ramón, 'Journal cover', in Arroyo Pizarro and Cruz Centeno (eds), n.pag.

—— 'Lo negro es una causa', in Arroyo Pizarro and Cruz Centeno (eds), pp. 13–20.
—— *Tapia: El primer puertorriqueño* (San Juan: Gaviota, 2015).
Ramos Rosado, Marie, *Destellos de la negritud: Investigaciones caribeñas*, 2nd edn (San Juan: Isla Negra Editores, 2013).
—— 'Foreword', in Arroyo Pizarro, *Negras: Stories*, pp. 17–24.
—— 'Mayra Santos-Febres, Yvonne Denis-Rosario y Yolanda Arroyo Pizarro: Narradoras afrodescendientes que desafían jerarquías de poder', *Tinkuy*, 18 (2012), 203–10.
—— *La mujer negra en la literatura puertorriqueña* (Río Piedras: University of Puerto Rico Press, 1999).
—— 'Prólogo', in Denis-Rosario, *Capá Prieto*, pp. 27–105.
Rangelova, Radost, *Gendered Geographies in Puerto Rican Culture: Spaces, Sexualities, Solidarities* (Chapel Hill NC: University of North Carolina Press, 2016).
—— 'Nationalism, States of Exception and Caribbean Identities in Sirena Selena vestida de pena and "Loca la de la locura"', *CENTRO*, 19/1 (2007), 75–88.
—— 'Writing Words, Wearing Wounds: Race and Gender in a Puerto Rican Neo-Slave Narrative'. *Tinkuy*, 18 (2012), 197–58.
Reinat-Pumarejo, María, 'Del artificio a la transformación del racismo: Procesos y umbrales de crecimiento en el trabajo antirracista', *Revista del ICP*, 3/5 (2017), 67–78.
Rengifo, Alejandra, 'Rompiendo paradigmas y creando nuevos arquetipos: El personaje del negro en la obra de Mayra Santos-Febres', in María Mercedes Jaramillo and Lucía Ortiz (eds), *Hijas del Muntu: Biografías críticas de mujeres afrodescendientes de América Latina* (Bogota: Panamericana, 2011), pp. 507–19.
Richardson, Jill Toliver, *Afro-Latin@ Experience in Contermporary American Literature and Culture: Engaging Blackness* (New York: Palgrave Macmillan, 2016).
Ríos Ávila, Rubén, 'Pájaro Caribe: Puerto Rico y la poética de la relación', in Mónica María del Valle Idárraga and Eliana Milagros Díaz Muñoz (eds), *Cosmografías sutiles del Caribe y Latinoamérica* (Barranquilla: Sello Editorial Universidad del Atlántico, 2017), pp. 51–76.
—— 'Queer Nation', *Revista Iberoamericana*, 75/229 (2009), 1129–238.
—— *La raza cómica del sujeto en Puerto Rico* (San Juan: Callejón, 2002).
—— 'La virgen puta', in Celis and Rivera (eds), pp. 71–80.
Rivera Acevedo, Alejandra, 'La memoria como acto de transformación en *Fe en disfraz*', *Afro-Hispanic Review*, 37/1 (2018), 73–84.
Rivera Casellas, Zaira, *Bajo la sombra del texto: La crítica y el silencio en el discurso racial en Puerto Rico* (Carolina: Terranova Editores, 2016).
—— 'La poética de la esclavitud (silenciada) en la literatura puertor-riqueña: Carmen Colón Pellot, Beatriz Berrocal, Yolanda Arroyo

Pizarro y Mayra Santos Febres', *Cincinnati Romance Review*, 30 (2011), 99–116.

—— and Mayra Santos-Febres. 'Introducción', *Afro-Hispanic Review*, 37/1 (2018), 10–13.

Rivera Clemente, Maricruz, 'Everything Happens at Casa Afro', *Negr@* (2020), casaafro.org/en/casa-afro/ (last accessed 25 October 2021).

Rivera Lassén, Ana Irma, 'Black Girls Ride Tricycles Too: Thoughts from the Identities of an Afro-descendent [*sic*] and Feminist Woman', in Moreno Vega et al. (eds), pp. 67–76.

—— 'Discriminaciones multiples, identidades multiples y otras historias de arañas y telarañas poderosas', in Nurse Allende (ed.), pp. 46–59.

—— 'Negro, negra', in Arroyo Pizarro and Cruz Centeno (eds), *Revista Boreales*, pp. 197–202.

Rivera-Rideau, Petra, Jennifer Jones and Tianna Paschel (eds), 'Introduction', *Afro-Latin@s in Movement: Critical Approaches to Blackness and Transnationalism in the Americas* (New York: Palgrave Macmillan, 2016), pp. 1–30.

Rodó, José Enrique, *Ariel*, ed. Pablo Rocca (Seville: Renacimiento, 2016).

Rodríguez Juliá, Edgardo, *El entierro de Cortijo: 6 de oct. de 1982* (Río Piedras: Huracán, 1982).

—— *La noche oscura del Niño Avilés* (Caracas: Biblioteca Ayacucho, 2002).

Rodríguez López, Miguel, '"La rebelión taína, crónica de una guerra negada". Quinto Centenario de la Rebelión Taína (1511–2011)', *Fundación Cultural Educativa; Instituto de Cultura Puertorriqueña, Centro de Estudios Avanzados de Puerto Rico y el Caribe*, 18–19 (February 2011), 12–21, https://issuu.com/coleccionpuertorriquena/docs/5to_centenario_de_la_rebelion_taina_icp_2011 (last accessed 25 October 2021).

Rosario Natal, Carmelo (ed.), *¡Soy libre! El grito de Agripina, la esclava rebelde de Ponce* (San Juan: Ediciones Puerto, 2013).

Rosenzvit, Miguel, *Fiebre negra* (Buenos Aires: Planeta, 2008).

Russell, Stephen, 'Challenging Homophobia in Schools: Policies and Programs for Safe School Climates', *Educar em Revista, 39 (2011), 123–38.*

Sánchez-Blake, Elvira, 'De *Anamú y manigua* a *Nuestra Señora de la Noche*: Poética errante en la obra de Mayra Santos-Febres', in Celis and Rivera (eds), pp. 187–205.

Sánchez González, Lisa, *The Stories I Read to the Children: The Life and Writing of Pura Belpré, the Legendary Storyteller, Children's Author, and New York Public Librarian* (New York: Centro Press, 2013).

Santiago-Díaz, Eleuterio, *Escritura afropuertorriqueña y modernidad* (Pittsburgh PA: Instituto Internacional de Literatura Iberoamericana, 2007).

—— and Ilia Rodríguez, 'Desde las fronteras raciales de dos casas letradas: Habla Piri Thomas', *Revista Iberoamericana*, 75/229 (2009), 1199–221.
Santos-Febres, Mayra, *La amante de Gardel* (Mexico: Planeta, 2015).
—— *Antes que llegue la luz* (Mexico: Planeta, 2021).
—— 'Caribe fractal y pensamiento afrodiaspórico', *Corredor Afro, YouTube* (streamed live 25 February 2021), *www.youtube.com/watch?v=elQXYpd Nwgk&t=3000s* (last accessed 25 October 2021).
—— 'Confesiones afropoéticas', in Nurse Allende (ed.), pp. 41–5.
—— *Fe en disfraz* (Mexico: Alfaguara, 2009).
—— *Huracanada* (San Juan: Trabalis Editores, 2018).
—— 'Mayra Santos-Febres: The Fractal Caribbean', *UMBCtube, YouTube* (recorded 12 September 2019, uploaded 27 September 2019), *www.youtube.com/watch?v=8tFlLkUSr84&t=2118s* (last accessed 25 October 2021).
—— 'Mayra Santos-Febres: El lenguaje de los cuerpos caribeños', Interview with Nadia Celis, in Celis and Rivera (eds), pp. 247–66.
—— *Nuestra Señora de la Noche* (New York: Rayo, 2006).
—— '¿Qué es la literatura afro? Aproximaciones éticas y estéticas', *Año de la Libertad*, Universidad del Valle, Centro Virtual Isaacs (14 April 2021), live via Zoom.
—— *Sirena Selena vestida de pena*, ed. Debra Castillo (Miami: Stockcero, 2008).
—— *Sobre piel y papel*, 3rd edn (San Juan: Callejón, 2011).
—— *Yo misma fui mi ruta: La maravillosa vida de Julia de Burgos* (Carolina: Municipio Autónomo de Carolina, 2014).
Sarmiento, Domingo Faustino, *Facundo: Civilización y barbarie* (Madrid: Alianza, 1988).
Schulenburg, Chris, '"It Hurts So Good": Resuscitating Female Slave Narratives in *Fe en disfraz*', *Chasqui: Revista de Literatura Latinoamericana*, 48/2 (2019), 116–29.
Schulman, Ivan (ed.), 'Introduction', in Manzano, *Autobiography of a Slave*, pp. 1–30.
Shaw, Lisa, *Tropical Travels: Brazilian Popular Performance, Transnational Encounters, and the Construction of Race* (Austin TX: University of Texas Press, 2018).
Shlensky, Lincoln, 'Édouard Glissant: Creolization and the Event', *Callaloo*, 36/2 (2013), 353–74.
Shrimpton, Margaret, 'El Caribe fluctuante, ¿una metonimia definitoria? Transgresión y desconstrucción en *Sobre piel y papel*', in Celis and Rivera (eds), pp. 153–70.
Sklodowska, Elzbieta, *Testimonio hispanoamericano: Historia, teoría, poética* (New York: Peter Lang, 1992).

Sommer, Doris, *Foundational Fictions: The National Romances of Latin America* (Berkeley CA: University of California Press, 1991).

Spillers, Hortense, 'Mama's Baby, Papa's Maybe: An American Grammar Book', *Diacritics*, 17/2 (1987), 64–81.

Suárez Findlay, Eileen, *Imposing Decency: The Politics of Sexuality and Race in Puerto Rico, 1870–1920* (Durham NC: Duke University Press, 1999).

Sullivan, Laura, 'How Puerto Rico's Debt Created a Perfect Storm before the Storm', *NPR.org* (2 May 2018, 7:10 a.m.), www.npr.org/2018/05/02/607032585/how-puerto-ricos-debt-created-a-perfect-storm-before-the-storm (last accessed 25 October 2021).

Sweet, James, *Domingos Álvares, African Healing, and the Intellectual History of the Atlantic World* (Chapel Hill NC: University of North Carolina Press, 2013).

—— *Recreating Africa: Culture, Kinship, and Religion in the African-Portuguese World, 1441–1770* (Chapel Hill NC: University of North Carolina Press, 2003).

Tapia y Rivera, Alejandro, *Juliet of the Tropics: A Bilingual Edition with an Introduction of Alejandro Tapia y Rivera's* La cuarterona (1867), trans. John Maddox (Amherst NY: Cambria Press, 2016).

Thomas, Piri, *Down These Mean Streets* (New York: Vintage, 1967).

Thompson, Robert Farris, *Flash of the Spirit: African and Afro-American Art and Philosophy* (New York: Random House, 1983).

Torres Muñoz, María Elba, 'El arte como resistencia: Lo afropuertorriqueño', in Vanessa Valdés (ed.), *The Future is Now: A New Look at African Diaspora Studies* (Newcastle upon Tyne: Cambridge Scholars Publishing, 2012), pp. 43–66.

—— Personal interview, September 2020.

Trigo, Benigno, 'From Necrotic to Apoptotic Debt: Using Kristeva to Think Differently about Puerto Rico's Bankruptcy', *Journal of French and Francophone Philosophy*, 26/2 (2018), 15–24.

Truth, Sojourner, 'Ain't I a Woman?', in Paul Halsall (ed.), *Modern History Sourcebook* (New York: Fordham University 1997) https://sourcebooks.fordham.edu/mod/sojtruth-woman.asp (accessed 13 November 2021).

Universidad de Puerto Rico, 'Recinto de Río Piedras de la UPR obtiene la subvención de $700 mil de parte de la Andrew W. Mellon Foundation', *UPRRP.edu* (11 January 2021) www.uprrp.edu/2021/01/recinto-de-rio-piedras-de-la-upr-obtiene-una-subvencion-de-700-mil-de-parte-de-la-andrew-w-mellon-foundation-2/ (last accessed 25 October 2021).

Valdés, Vanessa, *Diasporic Blackness: The Life and Times of Arturo Alfonso Schomburg* (Albany NY: State University of New York Press, 2017).

—— *Oshun's Daughters: The Search for Womanhood in the Americas* (Albany NY: State University of New York Press, 2013).

—— 'Introduction: Centring Haiti in Hispanic Caribbean Studies', in Vanessa Valdés (ed.), *Racialised Visions: Haiti and the Hispanic Caribbean* (Albany NY: State University of New York Press, 2020), pp. 1–26.

Valero, Silvia, 'Afroepistemología y sensibilización en las narrativas históricas afrodescendientes del siglo XXI', in Valero and Campos García (eds), pp. 531–78.

—— and Alejandro Campos García, 'Este libro' in Valero and Campos García (eds), pp. 65-90.

—— (eds), *Identidades políticas en tiempos de afrodescendencia: Autoidentificación, ancestralidad, visibilidad y derechos* (Buenos Aires: Corregidor, 2015).

Valladares-Ruiz, Patricia, 'El cuerpo sufriente como lugar de memoria en *Fe en disfraz*, de Mayra Santos Febres', *Cuadernos de Literatura*, 20/40 (2016), 583–604.

Vargas-Ramos, Carlos (ed.), *Race, Front and Centre: Perspectives on Race among Puerto Ricans* (New York: Centro Press, 2017).

Vasconcelos, José, *La raza cósmica* (Mexico: Porrúa, 2017).

Velázquez Collazo, Edwin, 'The Lost Work of Abolitionist Francisco Oller', *Repeating Islands* (17 June 2019), *https://repeatingislands.com/2019/06/17/the-lost-work-of-abolitionist-francisco-oller/* (last accessed 25 October 2021).

La Verdad, 'Insólito: Las 10 torturas más horripilantes de la Santa Inquisición (2da parte)', *La Verdad* (14 May 2020) *https://laverdadnoticias.com/amp/insolito/INSOLITO-Las-10-torturas-mas-horripilantes-de-la-Santa-Inquisicion-2da-parte-20200514-0151.html* (last accessed 25 October 2021).

Viera-Calderón, Edison, 'Hacia el final del silencio: Más allá de la bomba y plena, la Resistencia y afirmación de algunos pobladores del barrio de San Mateo de Cangrejos', in Nurse Allende (ed.), pp. 165–77.

Vieira, Leonardo, 'Historiadores traduzem única autobiografia escrita por ex-escravo que viveu no Brasil', *Globo*, oglobo.globo.com (27 November 2014), *https://oglobo.globo.com/brasil/historia/historiadores-traduzem-unica-autobiografia-escrita-por-ex-escravo-que-viveu-no-brasil-14671795* (3 May 2022).

Vilches, Vanessa, '*Bufé*, la primera novela de Yvonne Denis', *80grados* (7 June 2013), *www.80grados.net/bufe-la-primera-novela-de-ivonne-denis/* (last accessed 25 October 2021).

Villaverde, Cirilo, *Cecilia Valdés: Novela de costumbres cubanas*, ed. Raimundo Lazo (Mexico: Porrúa, 1986).

Vizcarrondo, Fortunato, '¿Y tu agüela aónde ejtá?', in *Dinga y mandinga: Poemas, Instituto de Cultura Puertorriqueña* (San Juan: Instituto de Cultura Puertorriqueña, 1983), pp. 77–8.

Walker, Alice, 'Everyday Use', *Harper's Magazine* (April 1973), n.pag, *https://harpers.org/archive/1973/04/everyday-use/* (last accessed 25 October 2021).

Wallace-Sanders, Kimberly, *Mammy: A Century of Race, Gender and Southern Memory* (Minneapolis MN: University of Minnesota Press, 2008).

Weldt-Basson, Helene, 'Marginalised Groups and the Mirror Image in the Works of Mayra Santos-Febres', *Revista de Estudios Hispánicos*, 36/1–2 (2009), 165–80.

—— 'Memoria cultural versus olvido histórico', *Hispanófila*, 179 (2017), 187–201.

—— 'The White Male as Narrative Axis in Mayra Santos-Febres's *Nuestra Señora de la Noche*', *Studies in 20th and 21st Century Literature*, 37/1 (2013), 143–60.

Wisker, Gina, '"Your Buried Ghosts Have a Way of Tripping You Up": Revisioning and Mothering in African-American and Afro-Caribbean Women's Speculative Horror', *Femspec*, 6/1 (2005), 71–80.

Yeates, Robert, '"The Unshriven Dead, Zombies on the Loose": African and Caribbean Religious Heritage in Toni Morrison's *Beloved*', *MFS: Modern Fiction Studies*, 61/3 (2015), 515–37.

Zapata-Calle, Ana, 'Yvonne Denis Rosario. *Capá prieto*', *PALARA*, 15 (2011), 141–4.

Zapata Olivella, Manuel, *Changó el gran putas* (Bogota: Educar, 2007).

Zeno Gandía, Manuel, *Garduña* (Río Piedras: Editorial Edil, 1986).

Zenón Cruz, Isabelo, *Narciso descubre su trasero (el negro en la cultura puertorriqueña)*, vols 1–2 (Humacao PR: Furidi, 1974–5).

Zito Araújo, Joel, 'O negro na dramaturgia, um caso exemplar da decadência do mito da democracia racial brasileira', *Estudos Feministas*, 16/3 (2008), 979–85.

Index

1930s generation of writers, 37, 44, 69, 156, 169
1950s generation of writers, 10, 11, 17, 37, 42, 156, 169
1970s generation of writers, 37, 142, 150
Abadía-Rexach, Barbara, 166, 170
Abercromby, Ralph, 110
abortion, 62, 95, 194
Actualidad del jíbaro, La [*The Peasant's Relevance*] (Pedreira, 1935), 9
Act-UP Puerto Rico, 30
Africa, 5, 27, 86, 202–3; Black women's familial bonds with, 78; families destroyed and rebuilt in, 99, 164; as family, 92; idealised, 82; Mina coast, 48; Mother Africa, 140, 185; as 'original maternal home space', 129; return/escape to, 94, 96; 'Slave Coast', 92; *see also* Akan people, of Ghana; Yoruba people/traditions
African-Americans, 19, 28, 40, 120, 176; African American Studies in US academia, 79, 200; homophobia among, 32; matrilineal family structures among, 51
Afroargentinos (Fortes and Ceballos, documentary, 2003), 7, 76
afro-auto-estima ('Black self-esteem'), 205–6
Afro-Boricua. *See* Afro–Puerto Rican (Afro-Boricua) identity

Afrocentrism, 4, 13, 132, 142, 177
Afro-Cuban culture/identities, 15
Afrodescendants, 2, 17, 20, 36, 69, 95; Afrodescendant family, 5; Afro–Puerto Rican family and, 18; death chosen over slavery, 85–6; Haitian Revolution and, 69; hypersexuality and laziness ascribed to, 9; land owned by, 104; in military service of white empires, 110; new generation of women writers, 183; sexualisation of Afrodescendant women, 39; short documentaries on public TV about, 187, 191; strength of Afrodescendant women, 185
Afrofeministamente (Arroyo Pizarro, 2020), 101, 165
Afro-Hispanic Review, 18, 175
Afrohistoria (Arroyo Pizarro, 2018), 78, 89–90, 91, 98, 100, 101
Afro-Latin@ Reader, The (Jiménez Román and Flores, eds, 2013), 106
Afro-Latinas, 41, 45, 163, 169, 181, 182
Afrolatinidad (Afrodescent), 14, 20, 23, 25
Afro-Latino identity, 106, 180
Afro–Puerto Rican (Afro-Boricua) identity, 3, 16, 23, 61, 128, 140; absence in United States, 28; constantly repeating and changing, 156–7; families born enslaved, 35–6; heritage

preserved by, 108; Insularism and, 12; music and, 166; nation-family allegory, 37
Afro–Puerto Rican literature, 2, 127, 150
agency, 22, 36, 91, 155, 161, 198; for Afro-Puerto Ricans, 4; birth control and, 162; feminine, 17; through violence, 86
Agripina, Juana, 58
Ain't I a Woman: Black Women and Feminism (hooks, 1981), 21
Akan people, of Ghana, 29, 158
Albizu Campos, Pedro, 69–70, 184
Allende, Isabel, 198
All the Women are White, All the Blacks are Men, but Some of Us are Brave (Hull et al., 1982), 21
Alonso, Manuel, 13
Altar of My Soul, The (Moreno Varga, 2000), 15
Álvares, Domingos, 84
Álvarez, Sonia, 24
Álvarez Nieves, Alejandro, 77
'Amantados, Los' ['The Suckled'] (Arroyo Pizarro, 2014), 97, 165
Amante de Gardel, La [*'Gardel's Lover'*] (Santos-Febres, 2015), 3, 7, 44, 53, 75–6; as bildungsroman, 67; existential questions for Puerto Rico at end of, 71–5; as family allegory of Borinquén, 161–2; family as daughters of Oshun, 59–63; *Fe en disfraz* compared with, 71–4; medicine and poison in tension with one another, 64–6; narrative, 38; plantation family fractured by, 43; symbiosis of the grotesque and the aesthetic in, 66; white male as 'narrative axis', 76; Yemaya (sea goddess) and melancholy, 66–70; *see also corázon de viento*; Gardel, Carlos; Thorné, Micaela
ancestors, 46, 52, 59, 60, 83, 99; deified, 40; enslaved, 38; female, 60; Oshun's bond with, 131; as

spiritual family, 27; *techné* and, 62; without a nation, 53; worship of, 86
Andrews, George Reid, 76
Anexionist [Statehood] Party, 191
Antes que llegue la luz [*'Before the Lights Come On'*] (Santos-Febres, 2021), 168
Aponte, Nilda, 15
Arce, Chrissy, 53, 57
Argentina, 7, 44, 66–7, 76, 169
Ariel (Rodó, 1900), 8
Arriaga-Arando, Eduard, 78, 82
Arroyo, Jossianna, 29, 61, 64
Arroyo Pizarro, Yolanda, 2–3, 10, 16, 103, 108, 208n2; atheism of, 39, 40, 86, 89, 196, 207; Cátedra de Mujeres Ancestrales de Puerto Rico writing group and, 58, 80, 158, 166, 192, 197, 200, 205; family and biographical elements in poetry and narrative of, 79–81; fractal family and, 26; 'Gabriela Soyna' pseudonym of, 86, 90; on 'great family' myth, 12; interview with, 191–207; new foundational myths based on *cimarronas*, 77; queer eroticism and, 152; Technology Education and Design Talk (2016), 40, 78, 80, 118; Venezuela's anti-imperialism embraced by, 47; writing groups and publishing projects organized by, 58, 166
Arroyo Pizarro, Yolanda, works of: *Afrofeministamente* (2020), 101, 165; *Afrohistoria* (2018), 78, 89–90, 91, 98, 100, 101; 'Los Amantados' ['The Suckled'] (2016), 97, 165; *Blancoides* (2018), 1–3, 78, 100, 101; *Cachaperismos* [*'Dike Stuff'*] (2012), 165; *Caparazones* (2010), 78; *Las caras lindas* (2020), 3, 165, 166; 'Carne negra' ('Black Flesh'), 100; 'Las cosas que se cuentan al caer' ['Things Told While Falling'] (2016), 165; *Los*

documentados ['*The documented*'] (2004), 78, 201; *Huracana* (2018), 168; *Marie Calabó* (2017), 165; 'La medalla mágica de Juana Agripina' ['Juana Agripina's Magic Medal'] (2016), 165; *Mis dos mamás me miman* ['*My Two Moms Spoil Me*'] (2016), 165; *Ojos de luna* [*Moon Eyes*] (2007), 87; *Origami de letras* [*'Letter Origami'*] (2005), 201; '*Oscarita*' (2017), 165; 'Separated from Our Blood', 85; 'Sin raza' ('No race'), 79, 80, 81, 86; *Transmutados* [*Transmutadx*] (2016), 200; *Violeta* (2013), 165. See also *Negras, Las* [*Black Women*]; *Saeta: The Poems*
Ashford, Bailey K., 196
atheism, 40, 86, 89, 164, 194, 207
Autobiografía de un esclavo [*Autobiography of a Slave*] (Manzano, 1996), 173

Baartman, Sarah, 26, 163
Bàbá (Yoruba deity), 86
Báez, Myrna, 15
Baker, Josephine, 76
Ballesta 9, 5, 28
Baquaqua, Mahommah Gardo, 49
Baralt, Guillermo, 91–92, 172, 191
Barbosa, José Celso, 191
Barnet, Miguel, 90–1, 147
Bartman, Saartje, 175
Bataille, Georges, 54
Bathika (Colón Santana, 2016), 172
Belaval, Emilio, 208n5
Beloved (Morrison, 1987), 40, 89, 94, 97, 174, 209n1 (Chap. 4); *Daughters of the Stone* compared with, 137, 139, 144, 145, 155, 168; intergenerational trauma in, 41, 181; mother-daughter relations in, 137; silence in, 136
Belpré, Pura, 41, 104, 121, 126, 166, 167, 191; 'La Cucaracha Martina' ('Martina the Roach'), 187; in Denis-Rosario story, 119–20
Benítez, Jaime, 18, 151
Benítez, Lucecita, 15
Bennett, Herman, 147
Berrocal, Beatriz, 192
Betances, Ramón Emeterio, 102, 125
Betances, Samuel, 208n7
Beverly Hillz, Monica, 34
Binder, Wolfgang, 141
Biografía de un cimarrón (Montejo), 173
Bird, Mary, 15
birth control, 61, 62–3, 72, 73, 74, 162
Black Atlantic, 66, 67
Black consciousness, 19, 20, 38, 99, 132; Afrodescent as political identity and, 160; *marronage* and, 166
Black Curriculum Campaign (#ennegrecetuprontuario), 205
Black feminism, 2, 18, 24, 159; intersectional approach to, 25; postmodern, 4; visibility of marginalised subjectivities and, 25
Black Latinas Know Collective, 42, 170
Black Lives Matter, 29
Blackness, 1, 3, 11, 22, 71, 93, 200; affirmation of, 4, 19, 127; Arroyo Pizarro and, 77; cultural erasure and distortion of, 80; definition of, 4; eroticism and exoticism associated with, 189; Santos-Febres and, 27; as scapegoat for underdevelopment, 13; sexual diversity in spaces of, 206; shame felt for, 61, 65, 74; women labouring in public sphere associated with, 35
Black Power movement, 14, 146
Black Studies, 25, 165
Black women, 68, 89; colonial-era sexual assaults upon, 46; demonised sexuality of, 53–4; enslaved, 35, 90, 185;

fractal family and, 4; Harlem Renaissance and, 68–9; historical record and voices of, 58; mastery over crafts, 29; matrilineal family and, 51; as mothers and caretakers, 122–7; national allegory and, 3; sexualisation of, 56; stereotyped images of, 13; strength of, 31
Blades, Rubén, 113
Blanco, Tomás, 9, 11, 69, 70, 208n5
Blancoides (Arroyo Pizarro, 2018), 1–3, 78, 100, 101
Boca de Cangrejos (Battle of San Juan, 1797), 107, 111, 126, 167
Bodies that Matter (Butler, 1993), 30
Bolden, Millicent, 105
Bolívar, Simón, 6
Bolivarian Wars, 6
bolivarismo, 48
bomba music, 109, 113
boom, Latin American (1960s–1970s), 8
Boria, Juan, 118, 126, 166
Borinquén archipelago, 2, 25, 127, 140, 161; intolerance for 'family of choice' in, 32; origins and history of, 36. *See also* Puerto Rico; Vieques
bozal (African-born, unassimilated woman), 85, 87–8, 99, 139, 141, 164, 169
Branche, Jerome, 17, 18, 51, 70–1
Brau, Salvador, 11
Brazil, 49, 76, 84, 132; 'racial democracy' of, 48; whitening discourse in, 7. See also *quilombos*
Brincando el Charco: Portrait of a Puerto Rican (film, dir. Negrón-Muntaner, 1994), 14
Brindis de Salas, Virginia, 175
brothel, as space of feminine agency, 17
Brown, Kimberly Juanita, 89
brujas ('healers, poisoners, witches'), 55, 63, 138, 178
Bruma, Federico, 118–19

Buenos Aires, 7, 66, 76, 156, 209n10
Bufé (Denis-Rosario, 2012), 103, 168, 188
Buggs, Mirangela, 25
Burgos, Julia de, 11, 26, 166, 175, 184
Butler, Judith, 29, 30, 48, 169, 198, 200

Cabrera, Lydia, 131
Cabrera, Raquel Brailowsky, 166
Cachaperismos [*'Dike Stuff'*] (Arroyo Pizarro, 2012), 165
Caliban, route of, 25
Campos García, Alejandro, 20, 21
Cangrejos (Santurce, San Juan), 13, 40, 108; British invasion of, 110; Campo Alegre slum, 61, 69; history of, 14
Capá prieto (Denis-Rosario, 2009), 40–1, 102, 167, 184; 'Ama de leche' ('Wet Nurse'), 121, 122–5, 126–7, 168, 186–7; 'Calle Felipe Rosario Goyco', 166; 'La cucaracha y el ratón en la biblioteca' ('The Roach and the Rat at the Library'), 119–20; 'Desahucio desde el palmar' ('Eviction from the Palms'), 112–18; 'Periódicos de ayer' ('Newspaper from Yesterday'), 103–7, 118, 126, 167; 'In re: Federico Bruma', 118–19; 'El Silenciamiento' ('The Silencing'), 107, 108, 110–11, 118; 'El turbante del maestro' ('The Teacher's Turban'), 121–2
Caparazones (Arroyo Pizarro, 2010), 78
'Caras lindas (de migente negra), Las' ['The Beautiful Faces (of My Black People)'] (Rivera, 1978), 3
Caras lindas, Las (Arroyo Pizarro, 2020), 3, 165, 166
Cardona, Javier, 33–4

'Caribe fractal y pensamiento afrodiaspórico' ['Fractal Caribbean and Afrodiasporic Thought'] (Santos-Febres, 2020), 28
La Caridad (Black-owned plantation), 128, 143, 148, 168; loss of, 129, 155; Oshun's intervention and, 138; renaming of Las Mercedes plantation, 133; return to, 149–55. See also *Daughters of the Stone*
'Carne negra' ['Black Flesh'] (Arroyo Pizarro), 100
Carpentier, Alejo, 96
Carreta, La [*The Oxcart*] (Marqués, 1953), 69
Carvajal, Miguel, 64
Casa grande e senzala [*The Masters and the Slaves*] (Freyre, 1933), 8
Casamayor-Cisneros, Odette, 46, 48, 55, 56
Castillo, Debra, 30
Castro, Juan Ramón de, 111
Cátedra de Mujeres Negras Ancestrales de Puerto Rico ('Ancestral Black Women of Puerto Rico Writing Group'), 58, 158, 166, 192, 197, 200, 205
Cátedra de Saberes Afro-Queer ('Afro-Queer Knowledges Study Group'), 40, 205
Catholicism/Catholic Church, 40, 47, 86, 95, 96, 119, 195; colonialism supported by, 126; as hegemonic power in Puerto Rico, 115–16; Inquisition, 63, 76, 164; maroons granted freedom in exchange for conversion to, 14; non-Christian practices suppressed by, 138; as rich land developer, 117; *rogativa* ('litany') legend about British defeat (1797) and, 110, 126, 167; Santería and, 188; schools, 31, 50, 81; sense of transgression and, 54; sexual double standard and, 62–3; tyrannical regimes supported by, 112
caudillo, 11
CCCADI (Caribbean Cultural Centre African Diaspora Institute), 15–16
Ceballos, Diego, 7, 76
Cecilia Valdés (Villaverde, 1839, 1879, 1882), 7, 138, 193
Celis, Nadia, 8, 24, 26
Centre for Puerto Rican Studies (City University of New York), 20
Centro de Estudios Avanzados de Puerto Rico y el Caribe (Centre for Advanced Studies of Puerto Rico and the Caribbean), 192
Chamoiseau, Patrick, 51
Changó (deity), 60, 65, 69, 195
Changó el gran putas [*'Changó, The Biggest Baddass'*] (Zapata Olivella, 1983), 96
Charca, La [*'The Pond'*] (Zeno Gandía, 1894), 141
Chávez, Hugo, 47, 52, 58
Chicago, 43, 44, 58, 156
Christianity/Christianisation, 6, 54, 86, 88, 131; *see also* Catholicism/Catholic Church
Cielo de tambores [*Drum Sky*] (Moya, 2002), 76
Cimarrón (Biography of a Runaway Slave) (Barnet, 1966), 90
cimarronas ('female maroons'), 39, 77, 80, 87, 108, 163; qualities of, 90; in slave uprisings and escapes, 89
Cimmarón (Barnet, 1966), 147
'civilisation', as Western concept, 55
class, 12, 16, 22, 25, 34
Cold War, 69
Coll y Toste, Cayetano, 93
Colombia, 169, 171
colonialism, 81, 86, 113, 126, 132
Colón Pellot, Carmen María, 184, 192
'Color de la seducción, El' (Santos-Febres, 2001), 31

'colour blind' society, myth of, 14, 180
colourism, 181
Colour Purple, The (Walker), 174
concubinage, 35, 52, 57, 65, 91, 99; Afro-Boricua family and, 17, 38, 160, 163; Chica ('Xica') da Silva and, 48–49
Conde-Vidal versus Rius-Armendariz (legal case), 77
'Confesiones afropoéticas' ['Afropoetic Confessions'] (Santos-Febres speech), 26
Congreso Afrodescencia Puerto Rico ('Afrodescent Puerto Rico Congress'), 22–3
Conquest, the, 6, 33
Constantine-Simms, Delroy, 32
corázon de viento ('wind heart' plant), 60–2, 63, 65, 72, 73, 162; as alternative to colonial medicine, 75; areas of flourishing in Puerto Rico, 66; as medicine and poison, 39, 64; origins in Colombia, 66
Cordero, Celestina, 166, 191
Cordero, Rafael, 166, 191
Cordero y Medina, Celestina, 121
Cordero y Medina, Rafael, 41, 121
Córdova Escalera, Paxie, 166
Corredor Afro cultural centre, 28
Corregidora (Naylor), 174
Cortes de la Muerte, Las [*'The Court of Death'*] (Carvajal, 1557), 64
'Cosas que se cuentan al caer, Las' ['Things Told While Falling'] (Arroyo Pizarro, 2016), 165
cosmopolitanism, 71
Covid-19 pandemic, 204
craft, 5, 18, 29, 37, 61; in *La amante de Gardel*, 38, 39, 61; in *Fe en disfraz*, 52. See also *techné*
Crenshaw, Kimberlé, 21, 22, 209n9
Creoles, white, 6, 7, 22, 40, 110; defense against US culture, 11; as head of plantation family, 208n5; national identity and, 8; nationalist projects of, 26; romanticisaton of, 10–11; unequal power relations in affairs with Afro-Latinas, 45; *see also jíbaros*
Crespo, Elizabeth, 35
Critique of Black Reason (Mbembe, 2017), 160
Crónica de un mundo enfermo [*'Cronicles of an Inform World'*] (Zeno Gandía five-part novel series), 141
Cruz, Tania, 166
Cruz-Malavé, Arnaldo, 150
'Cuando las mujeres quieren a los hombres' (Ferré, 1974), 142–3
Cuarterona, La [*'Juliet of the Tropics'*] (Tapia y Rivera, 1867), 7, 57, 67, 93, 137–8, 193
Cuba, 6, 7, 9, 47, 49, 106, 118; abolition of slavery in (1886), 147; Humboldt's observations about, 72
Cuban Revolution, 69, 90
curanderas ('healers'), 53, 72, 138
Curete Alonso, Tite, 113
Curet Vega, José, 172

Dahomey, 84
Danubio Azul (LGBTQ+ club), 30
Daughters of the Stone (Llanos-Figueroa, 2009), 41–2, 59, 60, 114, 168–9; Borinquén as fractal family, not filiation, 146–9; corporeal way of knowing in, 145; foundational rape in, 135–40; historical runaway slave villages and, 132–3; Llanos-Figueroa on writing of, 177–9; Morrison's *Beloved* compared with, 137, 139, 144, 145, 155, 168; role of goddess Oshun in, 129–32; surviving traumas in, 143–6; trope of will and testament, 128–9, 138, 141–2; *see also* La Caridad
Dávila, Ángela María, 26, 184
Dávila Gonçalves, Michele, 77, 86, 89

death, 60, 78, 98, 195, 196; in *La amante de Gardel*, 64, 65, 68, 69; in *Capá prieto*, 40–1; in *Fe en disfraz*, 47; Oya as goddess of cemeteries, 73; 'turn towards death' as form of slave rebellion, 85–6
Decade of Afrodescent (Mexico), 23
Delano, Jack, 14
Deleuze, Gilles, 209n8
Delgado, Oscar Colón, 14
Delirio entrelazado ['*Intertwined Delirium*'] (Denis-Rosario, 2015), 168
Denis-Rosario, Milagros, 110, 112
Denis-Rosario, Yvonne, 40, 102, 208n2, 210n1; Cátedra de Mujeres Ancestrales de Puerto Rico writing group and, 158; concern with 'debt never paid', 125; fractal family and, 26; interview with, 183–91; as screenwriter of cultural modules, 166–7
Denis-Rosario, Yvonne, works of: *Bufé* (2012), 103, 168, 188; *Delirio entrelazado* ['*Intertwined Delirium*'] (2015), 168; *Sepultados* ['*Entombed*'] (2018), 168; see also *Capá prieto*
Derkes, Eleuterio, 191
Derrida, Jacques, 64, 162
'De tu lado al Paraíso' (Ferré, 1976), 44
diaspora, 2–4, 9, 102, 105, 128, 156; *Afrolatinidades* and, 20; break with Eurocentric paradigms, 23; as cosmopolitan project, 25; diaspora discourse in academia, 79; excluded by kin on the island, 12; fractal family and, 4, 51; international African diasporic movement, 180; island/diaspora binary, 25; overlapping (Afro and Latinx), 167; Puerto Rican identity and, 24; theorisation of African diaspora, 106; *uno-múltiple* ('multiple-one') and, 37
Diasporic Blackness (Valdés, 2017), 106
Díaz, Doña Isabel, 177
Díaz, Luis Felipe, 30
Díaz Soler, Luis, 208n5
Dictionary of Latin American Identities (Maddox and Stephens, 2021), 209n9
Dieppa, Isabel Sophia, 114, 116, 117
disability, 22, 26
DIVEDCO, 12, 13
divorce, 15, 36, 52, 77
Documentados, Los ['*The documented*'] (Arroyo Pizarro, 2004), 78, 201
Dominican Republic, 6, 7, 30, 83, 118
double consciousness, 154
Down These Mean Streets (Thomas, 1967), 14
drag queens, 30–1
Duany, Jorge, 16, 208n6

earthquakes, 157, 182, 204
Echeverría, Esteban, 7
'En el fondo del caño hay un negrito' ['At the Bottom of the Channel, There's a Little Black Boy'] (González, 1972), 34, 46
English language, 13, 14, 127
Entierro de Cortijo, El ['*Cortijo's Wake*'] (Rodríguez Juliá, 1983), 167
eroticism, 3, 54, 71, 174, 178; body of Black woman as object of, 193; lesbian, 82, 152
Esclavos rebeldes: Conspiraciones y sublevaciones de esclavos en Puerto Rico (1795–1873) (Baralt, 1982), 91–2
Escritura afropuertorriqueña y modernidad ['*Afro-Puerto Rican Writing and Modernity*'] (Rodríguez Torres, 2007), 13

Estudios Afrodiaspóricos y Racialidad ('AfroDiasporic and Raciality Studies') Programme, 5
ethnicity, 16, 22
eugenics, 7, 141
Eurocentrism, 23, 27, 33, 68, 104, 130, 149; atheism associated with, 89; binary oppositions and, 177; history revised to overcome, 132; knowledge and, 174; linearity of, 28; US academia as Eurocentric space, 49
'Euthanasia Law' (1937), 73, 75
'Everyday Use' (Walker, 1973), 54

Facundo: Civilización y barbarie [*'Facundo: Civilisation and Barbarism'*] (Sarmiento, 1845), 7
Falconí Trávez, Diego, 82, 85, 86, 100
Family, *see* filiation; fractal family; 'great Puerto Rican family'; matriarchal/matrilineal family
family allegories, 7, 37, 43, 74, 159, 161
family of choice, 2, 4, 32, 36, 156; artists and, 14; in *Daughters of the Stone*, 155; national, 22; in *Negras*, 77; *see also* fractal family
Fanon, Frantz, 10, 33, 196
Fe en disfraz [*'Faith in Disguise'*] (Santos-Febres, 2009), 3, 18, 77, 161, 193; *La amante de Gardel* compared with, 71–4; *Capá prieto* compared with, 102; Chica da Silva as only historical figure in, 44, 57; colonial Other in, 47–54; Fe as anti-hero not role model, 55–9; fractal genealogy and, 54–5; as historical novel, 44; Martín as patriarchal voice in, 45–7; mirrors in, 46; narrative, 38; plantation family fractured by, 43; Santos-Febres on writing of, 172–5; *see also* Tirado, Martín; Verdejo, Fernanda 'Fe'
femicide, 204
femininity, 37, 71

feminism: Afro-Puerto Rican, 2; Black lesbian, 100; Black women's representation in, 17; bourgeois white, 9, 35; divide between Black and white women in, 140; 'herstory', 47; intersectionality and, 15; white, 38; *see also* Black feminism
Feminist Politics of Translation in the Latin/a Américas (Álvarez et al., 2014), 24
Feracho, Lesley, 129
Ferly, Odile, 25
Fernández, Ruth, 166
Fernández de Oviedo, Gonzalo, 88
Ferré, Rosario, 13, 17, 32, 41, 155, 168; 'Cuando las mujeres quieren a los hombres' (1974), 142–3; 'De tu lado al Paraíso' (1976), 44; 'Maldito Amor' (1986), 142, 143; narrative tradition of sadomasochism and, 44
Festival de la Palabra ('Festival of the World'), 18
Fiebre negra [*Black Fever*] (Rosenzvit, 2008), 76
Fiestas de Santiago Apóstol ('The Feast of St James the Apostle'), 33
Figueroa, Víctor, 56
Figueroa, Yomaira, 128, 170
filiation, 39, 40, 54, 88, 131; failure of family reproduction as literary trope, 137–8; inheritance and, 117; linearity of, 43, 50; masculinist, 26; matriarchal, 41; rejection of, 85
Filosofía del cimarronaje [*'Marronage Philosopnhy'*] (Lebrón Ortiz, 2020), 160–1
Flash of the Spirit (Thompson, 1983), 131, 165
Flores, Juan, 14, 20, 37, 106
Floyd, George, 203, 204
Fortes, Jorge, 7, 76
fractal Caribbean, 5, 28, 39, 57, 131

Index

'Fractal Caribbean, The' (Santos-Febres, 2019), 8, 33
fractal family, 4, 23, 25–9, 82, 208n3; crafts of, 29; disorder and heterogeneity embraced by, 11; fractal genealogy, 54–5; gathering scattered Afro–Puerto Rican family, 103–7; inclusiveness of, 40; independentism of, 38; legacy of, 158; matrilineal structure of Black families, 50–1; as national allegory, 38; non-Black allies included in, 51; performativity and, 31; as postmodern nationalism, 5; in renamed *palenque* plantation, 134; *translocas* and, 34; *see also* family of choice
fractals, as repeating shapes/forms, 5–6, 28, 43
Free Associated State, 25
Freemasons, Afro-Caribbean, 29, 61, 105–6
Freud, Sigmund, 124
Freyre, Gilberto, 8, 186
Fuente, Alejandro de la, 21, 23
Furtado, Júnia Ferreira, 90, 91

García, Ana María, 73
García, Lala, 166
García-Crespo, Naida, 12
García Padilla, Governor Alejandro, 124
García Ramis, Magali, 31, 32
Gardel, Carlos, 38, 60, 64, 76, 162, 209n10; affair with Micaela, 65, 68, 71; death in plane crash, 65, 69; as gigolo or womanizer, 63, 65, 68, 162; syphilis affliction of, 60, 65, 73; voyages of, 66–70; *see also Amante de Gardel, La* [*'Gardel's Lover'*]
Garduña (Zeno Gandía, 1896), 141
Garífunas (Guatemala), 91
Garner, Margaret, 94, 95, 96, 164
Gazeta de Puerto Rico, La (newspaper), 197

Gelpí, Juan, 11, 12, 16, 31, 37, 71, 142, 143; criticism of single heroic figure, 150; on literary 'generations', 157
gender, 11, 16, 25, 29, 175; beyond masculine/feminine binaries, 22; class intersecting with, 34; family and, 35; Insularism and, 78, 99; performative nature of, 22, 30; race intersecting with, 15, 21, 33, 209n9; as series of gestures, 31; *travestismo* and, 29
Gender Trouble (Butler, 1990), 30
genealogy, 20, 21, 34; decolonial, 88; fractal, 54–5
gentrification, 105
Glissant, Édouard, 26–8, 30, 78, 160, 208–9n8; arrow nomadism image of, 88; on centrality of storytelling, 41–2; filiation concept, 85, 117, 131, 150; influence on Arroyo Pizarro, 78, 99; on 'prophetic vision of the past', 173; Rélation concept, 75; transnational theories of, 38
Global North–Global South dialogue, 25
global warming, 117
Godreau, Michael, 135
González, Aníbal, 141
González, José Luis, 11, 34, 46, 51, 134
González García, María, 135
Gorrión family, 121, 122, 123, 125, 186
'Goyita' (Tufiño, 1953), 14
Great Depression, 10
Greatest Taboo, The (Constantine-Simms, 2001), 32
'great Puerto Rican family', 3, 6–16, 70–1, 148, 208n5; Afro-Puerto Rican agency and, 4; changing paradigm of, 206–7; counter-narrative to, 4, 36, 159; defined as racial equality through miscegenation, 129; demonisation of Black women's sexuality, 53–4; dissidents at

dawn of new millennium, 16–18; heteronormative depiction of, 93; heteronormativity and, 31; patriarchal hacienda and, 167; plantation as classic setting of, 34; 'racial democracy' and, 8; revision of, 128, 131; satires of, 12; whitening myth of, 37; *see also* Insularism
Guaracha del Macho Camacho, La [*'Macho Camacho's Beat'*] (Sánchez, 1976), 12
Guattari, Félix, 209n8
Guayama, 19
Guillén, Nicolás, 106
Gumbar, Diana, 43
Gutiérrez Negrón, Sergio, 31

habanera music, 67
hacendados, 6, 8, 10, 134, 189; Insularist narrative and, 43; as a white identity, 176
Haiti/Haitian Revolution, 6, 9, 69, 92, 96, 109
Halloween/Samhain, 45, 47, 55, 63, 174
Harlem, 14, 120; Harlem Renaissance, 20, 68–9, 106; Palladium nightclub, 15
harmony, myth of, 11, 12, 38, 86, 97
Harvey, Sir Henry, 110
Hatuey, Chief, 88
healing crafts, 5, 63, 161
herbalism, 5, 194
Hernández, Rafael, 1
Herrera, Cristina, 129, 133, 153
Herrera, Georgina, 175
Herrero people, women warriors of, 85
heteronormativity, 3, 31, 41; cis-heteronormativity, 32, 125, 156, 164; same-sex marriage and, 199–200
Hidalgo de Jesús, Amarilis, 88, 90, 102, 108, 119, 121, 130
Hispanic Studies, 18
hispanidad (identification with white Spain), 6, 83

hispanophilia, 10, 18, 47, 133, 148
HIV/AIDS, 30
homophobia, 27, 32, 86, 150, 152
homosexuality, 10, 34, 40
hooks, bell, 21
Hughes, Langston, 106
Hull, Gloria, 21
human rights, 20, 21, 22, 88, 97
Humboldt, Alexander von, 72
Huracana (Arroyo Pizarro, 2018), 168
Huracanada (Santos-Febres, 2018), 168
hurricanes, 18, 144–45, 157; *see also* Maria, Hurricane
Hurtado, Roberta, 129, 130, 136, 139, 145, 152

ICP [Instituto de Cultura Puertorriqueña] ('Puerto Rican Culture Institute'), 118
identity, national, 3, 7; Black identity in relation to, 20, 202–3; Creole-defines, 8
identity performance, 55, 71, 160
identity politics, 30
'Identity Practices' (Lloréns), 19
Ifá divination boards, 27
Imaging the Great Puerto Rican Family (Lloréns, 2014), 14
Imposing Decency (Suárez Findlay, 2000), 8
incarceration, mass, 52
Independentism, 38, 102, 115, 116, 151, 156
infanticide, 94, 95, 96, 139, 144, 194
Instituto de Cultura Puertorriqeña ('Puerto Rican Culture Institute'), 12
Insularism, 10, 11, 18, 37, 106, 152; anti-Insularist writers, 32, 70, 77; Christianity and, 86; countryside idealised by, 71; damage done by, 42; enduring influence of, 99; rejection of modernity, 72
Insularismo [*'Insularism'*] (Pedreira, 1934), 9, 11, 12

International Year for People of
  African Descent (2011), 79
intersectionality, 15, 21–2, 38,
  159; 'spiders' and 'webs' of, 22;
  translocal, 33
intersubjectivity, 61
Irma, Hurricane (2017), 18, 23
Island beneath the Sea (Allende,
  2010), 198
Ìyá (Yoruba deity), 86

Jamaica, 95, 99, 198
Janer, Zilkia, 9
Jáuregui, Carlos, 64
Jews, 178
jíbaros ('white peasants'), 104,
  153; Insularist narrative and,
  43; journey of *jíbara* to US
  metropole, 69, 71; as mixed-
  race 'tropical whites', 14; music
  of, 67; as whitening national
  symbol, 118
Jiménez Román, Miriam, 14, 20,
  106, 170
Jones, Nicholas, 122, 124
Jorge, Angela, 150
jouissance, 56

Katrina, Hurricane, 183
Kirschner, Luz Angélica, 21, 88,
  102, 106, 107, 116
Kristeva, Julia, 124
Krudas Cubensi (hip-hop band),
  91

Lacan, Jacques, 34, 46
LaFountain-Stokes, Lawrence,
  32–4, 38, 154, 159–60, 169
Laguerre, Enrique, 208n5
Lam, C. Christina, 129, 130, 133,
  145
Lanzos, Francisco, 108, 111
Laó-Montes, Agustín, 20, 24–5
Las Casas, Bartolomé de, 97
Latin America, 8, 20, 38, 88,
  171; connections to France,
  76; enslaved Africans in, 58;
  Europeanised countries of, 44,
  66; 'great family' image and, 12;
  lack of slave narratives, 7, 49,
  58, 121, 172–3, 209nn1 (Chap.
  1); regionalism and, 23; role of
  Puerto Rico in, 21
Latinx and Afro-Latinx, 23, 40, 42,
  68, 106, 150, 176; Afro-Latinx
  scholars, 169; decolonisation of
  identity and, 151; diaspora, 75,
  102, 167; Latinx studies, 25; as
  victims of Pulse Massacre, 157
Lebrón Ortiz, Pedro, 160–1
Ledru, André Pierre, 66
lesbians/lesbian identities, 22,
  76, 77, 82, 100–1, 142, 163;
  afrolesbiana, 32; in *Daughters
  of the Stone*, 152–3; as form of
  rebellion, 194; lesbian desire,
  100; in *Saeta: The Poems*, 201–2
Lessuck, Jonathan, 182
LGBTQ+ minorities, 2, 22, 31,
  32, 93, 101, 164, 201; break
  with paternalism, 12; families
  of choice, 2, 4; intersecting
  struggles of Black people with,
  100; marginalisation of, 14;
  negative views of, 33; Nuyorican
  poets and, 150; solidarity with,
  152
Liberal Autonomism, 8, 35
liberals, 8–9
Liittle Prince, The (Saint-Exupéry,
  1943), 198
*Literary Bondage: Slavery in Cuban
  Narrative* (Luis, 1990), 7
*Literatura y paternalismo en Puerto
  Rico ['Literature and Paternalism
  in Puerto Rico'*] (Gelpí, 1992), 11
Llanos-Figueroa, Dahlma, 3,
  10, 32, 55, 108, 127, 198;
  Afro-Hispanic transnational
  resistance narratives and,
  129; as decolonial 'artist-as-
  curandera', 129; fractal family
  and, 26; interview with, 177–83;
  subversion of 'great family'
  myth, 41
Lloréns, Hilda, 14, 19, 37, 130, 170

La Loca (Blackface festival performer), 33, 55
Loíza, town of, 15, 16, 19, 28, 92, 126; British invasion defeated in (1797), 107, 108–12, 167, 187; as 'the capital of tradition', 108; Carnival in, 100; Casa Afro, 157; centrality to Puerto Rican nation, 103; Fiestas de Santiago Apóstol in, 33; La Loca mask in, 55; runaway slaves sent to, 117
López, Erika, 34
López, Nieves, 3
López López, Yolanda, 166
Lorde, Audre, 16, 100
Luberza Oppenheimer, Isabel 'La Negra', 17
Lucecita, 166
Luis, William, 7

machismo, 12
Madonna-whore binaries, 50, 59
Majestad negro [*'Black Majesty'*] (Boria, 1978), 118
Malaret, Augusto, 11
'Maldito Amor' (Ferré, 1986), 142, 143
malungaje (Black 'brotherhood' or solidarity), 51
'Mama's Baby, Papa's Maybe: An American Grammar Book' (Spillers, 1987), 51
'Mammy' trope, 54, 97, 121–24, 127, 168
maniguas, 132, 137
Manzano, Juan Francisco, 7, 49, 121, 173, 209nn1 (Chap. 1)
Maria, Hurricane (2017), 18, 23, 27, 163, 168, 204; Blacks disproportionately devastated by, 116; class and racial divides revealed by, 182–3; FEMA repair funds for, 28
Marie Calabó: De niña curiosa a mujer lider [*'Marie Calabó: From Curious Little Girl to a Woman Leader'*] (Arroyo Pizarro, 2017), 165

maroons, 4, 14, 38, 167, 197; masculinist image of, 39; rebellions of, 27; route of the Maroon, 25
Marqués, René, 10, 11, 17, 42, 69, 71, 89; allegories of the national family, 37, 160; figure of docile Puerto Rican, 94; generation of 1950s writers led by, 156, 169
marronage, 64, 85, 92, 94, 209n8; abortion as form of, 95; masculinist violence and, 99; theorisation of, 161; writing as form of, 199
Martí, José, 106
Martinique, 51, 69, 110, 208–9n8
Martín Peña Channel, 117, 119, 126
Martín Sevillano, Ana Belén, 94
Marxism, 132, 134
masculinism, 8, 39, 150, 164; filiation and, 26; 'thing-Zumbi' and, 91, 164; violence of, 99, 164
Massó, Benito, 58
'Matadero, El' ['The Slaughterhouse'] (Echeverría, 1871), 7
Matos Cintrón, Nemir, 203
matriarchal/matrilineal family, 4, 12, 41, 50–1, 82; maternal figures, 38; 'maternal herstory' and, 129; matrilineal structure of Black families, 50–1; Oshun as matriarch, 128
Mbembe, Achille, 28, 160
'Medalla mágica de Juana Agripina, La' ['Juana Agripina's Magic Medal'] (Arroyo Pizarro, 2016), 165
Meléndez, Arturo, 115
Meléndez Muñoz, 108
Méndez, Alma, 15
Méndez Panedas, Rosario, 47, 49, 166
menstruation, 68, 82
Merced, Miranda, 166
Mercy, A (Morrison, 2008), 181
mestizaje, 8, 19, 37

Middle Passage, 51, 78, 81, 146
midwifery, 5, 37, 159
Miletti, Luis, 103, 105, 114, 118
mirror stage, Lacanian, 34, 46, 53
miscegenation, 19, 36, 129, 160
Mis dos mamás me miman ['*My Two Moms Spoil Me*'] (Arroyo Pizarro, 2016), 165
Mohr, Nicholasa, 12, 150–1, 181
Molina, Tirso de, 45
Monte, El (Cabrera, 1954), 131
Montejo, Esteban, 90, 147, 173
Montes Benítez, Cardinal José, 115
Montesinos, Antonio de, 97
Moreno, Marisel, 9, 10, 24, 37, 118, 142
Moreno Vega, Marta, 15–16, 37, 40, 91, 106, 158, 172; Ancestral Black Women's Study Group and, 197; Corredor Afro cultural centre and, 28; on maintaining African consciousness, 129–30; Museo del Barrio and, 150; Santería (Regla de Ocha) and, 165
Morrison, Toni, 40, 41, 89, 94, 146, 174, 209n1 (Chap. 4); *A Mercy* (2008), 181; spirits of ancestors in writing of, 131; *Sula* (1973), 192; universal themes in work of, 181; *see also Beloved*
Moya Ana Gloria, 76
Moynihan Report (1965), 51
Mujer Intégrante Ahora [MIA] ('Women, Unite Now!'), 15
Mujer negra en la literatura puertorriqueña, La ['*Black Women in Puerto Rican Literature*'] (Ramos Rosado, 1999), 13
Mulatresse Solitude (Guadeloupe), 91
mulatto/mulatta, 5, 7, 68, 123, 135, 208n3; Milicia de Pardos ('Mulatto Militia'), 110; Mulatta-Antilles tradition, 70–1, 75; national consciousness and, 11; sensual mulatta trope, 58, 125, 142, 194; 'tragic mulatta' trope, 57, 93
Muñoz, Sarah, 16, 30
Muñoz Marín, Luis, 12
Musicalizando la raza ['*Musicalizing Race*'] (Abadía-Rexach, 2012), 166
Mutis, José Celestino, 72

Namaqua (Namibian indigenous people), 85, 87, 88, 98
Namibia, 169
Napoleon I, 69
Narciso descubre su trasero ['*Narcissus Discovers his Backside*'] (Zenón Cruz, 1974), 10, 34, 47
Nascimento, Abdias, 132
nationalism, 8, 9, 23, 37, 176
Naylor, Gayle, 174
necropolitics, 28
Necropolitics (Mbembe, 2019), 160
Negra Casilda, La, 175
Negras, Las [*Black Women*] (Arroyo Pizarro, 2012), 39–40, 77, 78, 163, 201; Arroyo Pizarro on writing of, 191–2; 'Matronas' ('Midwives'), 78, 82, 85, 94–9, 156, 194; 'Saeta' ('Arrowhead'), 84, 87–94, 135, 156, 164; 'Wanwe', 81–3, 86, 99, 156, 164
negrista poetry, 70, 118
negrito term, 2, 3
'Negro, negra' (Rivera Lassén), 23
Negro flagelado, Hacienda Aurora (1888–90), El [*The Flogged Black Man, Hacienda Aurora (1888–90)*] (Oller painting), 104
'negroid' poetry, 11
¡Negro, Negra!: Afirmación y Resistencia (Nurse Allende, 2018), 23
Negrón-Muntaner, Frances, 14
Negrophobia, 32
neoliberalism, 135
Nereida Lebrón, Luz, 73
New Negro movement, 106
New York, 43, 107, 127, 155, 156, 168–9, 179; El Barrio

(East Harlem), 68, 145, 150, 155; Museo del Barrio, 150; Nuyorican Poets Café, 14, 37, 169; *see also* Harlem
New York Public Library: Denis-Rosario story set in, 119–20; Schomburg Collection, 106, 107, 120
Nieves, E. J., 166
Nigeria, 127, 132, 135, 146, 154, 169
Nilda (Mohr, 1973), 151
nostalgia, 10, 60, 64, 73
nuclear family, 31, 50, 137
Nuestra Señora de la Noche [*'Our Lady of the Night'*] (Santos-Febres, 2008), 18, 51, 54–5, 76, 142, 162–3; 'great family' narrative deconstructed in, 16–17; as part of trilogy of historical novels, 59, 163
Núñez, Victoria, 120
Nurse Allende, Léster, 23
Nuyorican Poets Café (New York), 14, 37, 169
Nuyoricans (Afro-Nuyoricans), 12, 14, 20, 41, 149, 150

'Obea' ['Sorceress'] (Queen Nanny of the Maroons), 95, 198
Obtalá (Orisha spirit), 133, 195
Ojos de luna [*Moon Eyes*] (Arroyo Pizarro, 2007), 87
Oliveira, João Fernandes de, 48
Oliver, Denise, 16
Oliveras Vega, Zulma, 77, 166
Oller, Francisco, 40, 104, 167
Olódùmare (Yoruba deity), 86
Omi, Michael, 6
Operación, La (documentary film, dir. García, 1982), 73
Operación Serenidad ('Operation Serenity'), 11
Operation Bootstrap, 73, 118, 151
Oquendo-Villar, Carmen, 157
oral traditions, 57, 108, 154, 187
Origami de letras [*'Letter Origami'*] (Arroyo Pizarro, 2005), 201

Orishas, 27, 38, 59, 99, 131; in *La amante de Gardel*, 38; binaries resisted by, 159; in *Daughters of the Stone*, 136, 155, 178–9; in *Fe en disfraz*, 38; *santeras* (believers in Orishas), 34, 185, 188; *see also* Santería (Regla de Ocha)
Ortiz, Fernando, 20
Orún (Yoruba deity), 86
'Oscarita: La niña que quiere se como Oscar López Rivera' [*'Oscarita: The Little Girl Who Wants to Be Like Oscar López Rivera'*] (Arroyo Pizarro, 2017), 165
Oshun (Orisha river goddess), 41, 42, 55, 64, 66, 72, 162, 178; creativity and eroticism of, 153–4; debt to, 136, 139; herbal medicine and poison associated with, 138; hidden from Catholic Inquisition, 63; Ibeyi twins of, 148; as matriarch, 128; paternity subverted by, 137; punishment of disobedient daughters, 143–6; redistribution of wealth and, 134; Santería (Regla de Ocha) and, 133; vengeance of, 64–5
Oshun's Daughters: The Search for Womanhood in the Americas (Valdés, 2013), 130–1, 209nn1 (Chap. 4)
Osorio Villarán, Fela, 121, 123
Osorio Villarán, Josefa ('Maíta'), 121–2
Otero, Ramos, 31, 32, 44
Other, becoming, 46, 53, 61, 68, 75
Oya (goddess of death and rebirth), 60, 73, 114

paganism, African, 55
paganism, European, 59, 174
Pagán Sánchez, Eloísa, 166
Pais de cuatro pisos, El [*'The Four-Storied Country'*] (González, 1980), 11
palenques (anti-plantation) communities, 84, 90, 92, 117, 126, 132, 197; harmonious, 134;

as new kind of family, 164; *see also* La Caridad; *quilombos*
Palés Matos, Luis, 11, 70–1, 75, 123, 186, 190
Palmares *quilombo* (Brazil), 132–3
Paréntesis: Ocho Artistas Negros Contemporáneos [*'Parenthesis: Eight Black Contemporary Artists'*] (exhibition, 1996), 15
Paris, Barrio Latino of, 68
patriarchy, 9, 38, 91, 102, 173, 192; matriarchy within, 176; patriarchal family, 4, 8, 10, 12; property inheritance and, 28, 51; white or whitening, 24, 25
Patterson, Fátima, 163
Pedreira, Antonio, 5, 9–11, 18, 42, 67, 69; critics of, 37; generation of 1930s writers led by, 156, 169; notion of nation as child, 55; paternalism of, 130; white Creoles romanticised by, 10–11; *see also* 'great Puerto Rican family'; Insularism
Peñaranda-Angulo, Victoria, 44, 47, 53, 68–9
performance/performativity, 29, 38, 55, 169
Perivolaris, John, 70
phallologocentrism, 16
Picó, Fernando, 172
Pietri, Pedo, 10
Pinet, Carrasquillo, 116
plantation: as classic setting of the 'great family', 34; colonial plantation family, 4, 11, 19, 43; deconstruction of, 128; legacy of racist/sexist abuses and, 15; as literary setting, 78; mythic harmony of, 97, 132; sexual violence of, 87
Plato, 29
Poetics of Relation, A: Caribbean Women Writing at the Millennium (Ferly, 2012), 25
Ponce, city of, 8, 19, 35, 100
Portugal, 6

postmodernism, 44, 105, 173; history and fiction blurred by, 39; *posmoderno*, 38; postmodern national allegory, 28; postmodern turn, 24; relativism and, 188, 199
poststructuralism, 56
Pou, Miguel, 14
Primer Congreso de Afrodescendiencia en Puerto Rico ['First Afrodescent in Puerto Rico Congress'] (2015), 22, 26
Primer Foro Internacional de Afrodescendencia y Descolonización de la Memoria (Caracas, 2012), 79
property inheritance, 28, 51, 64, 141–3, 159
prostitution, 35, 53, 193
Protestantism, evangelical/ fundamentalist, 86, 164, 196
Puerto Rican Nation on the Move, The (Duany), 208n6
Puerto Rico, 21, 94, 99, 179; abolition of slavery in (1871), 7, 35, 41, 122, 129; British invasion repelled by Black soldiers (1797), 40, 103, 107, 108–12, 167; *corázon de viento* herb in, 66; dependency on enslaved Africans in colonial era, 6; European settlers after 1815, 11; extreme debt of, 123, 124; first same-sex wedding (2015), 77; global interactions with, 16; internal migration, 52; migration to US urban centres from, 5, 52, 68–9; musical forms associated with, 67, 109, 113; relationship with United States, 2, 73; US medicine in, 70; *see also* Borinquén archipelago
Puerto Rico Negro (Badillo and Cantos, 1986), 191

queerness, 37, 77, 160
queer theory, 21, 200

Quilombismo, O (Nascimento, 1980), 132
quilombos, 41, 117, 126, 155. See also *palenques* (anti-plantation) communities
Quiñones, Bienmundo, 114, 115
Quiñones Hernández, Doris G., 157
Quiñones Rivera, Maritza, 22, 129, 170

race, 12, 175; 'blood purity' of Spain and Portugal, 6; class intersecting with, 34; family and, 35; gender intersecting with, 15, 21, 33, 209n9; hidden hierarchies and, 16; Insularism and, 78, 99; national identity intersecting with, 38; nation and, 156; as threat to 'great family' paradigm, 20; *travestismo* and, 29
'racial democracy', 8, 10, 48
racism, 3, 7, 56, 78, 125, 189–90; among feminists, 159; among Puerto Ricans, 15; Arroyo Pizarro's experience at school and, 80–1; coded as women's weakness, 91; as individual practice, 20; instituted by Spaniards, 9; internal, 130; recycling of, 2; systematic, 181; traumas of, 28, 156; unconscious, 2; of US medicine in Puerto Rico, 70
Ramos-Perea, Ramón, 7, 24
Ramos-Perea, Roberto, 166, 168, 191
Ramos Rosado, Marie, 15, 33, 56, 76, 184, 192, 208n2; on Arroyo Pizarro's *cimarronas*, 80; on Belpré as *liberadora*, 119; on debt owed to Black wet nurses, 123; on *Las Negras*, 78, 87, 92; on 'patriarchal viewpoint', 91–2; seminar on Afro–Puerto Rican writers taught by, 157; on stereotyped images of

Black women, 13; *uno-múltiple* ('multiple-one') and, 37, 160
Rangelova, Radost, 16–17, 24, 34, 49, 53, 56
rape, 31, 35, 41, 58, 130, 174, 199; *burlador* figure and, 45; in *Daughters of the Stone*, 131, 135–40; in *Fe en disfraz*, 52; homosexual, 40; in 'Saeta', 87, 92–4; slavery and, 193–4; as taboo topic, 192, 193
Reconquest, 6, 33
Recreating Africa (Sweet, 2003), 85
Rediker, Marcus, 191
Regional Conference of the Americas (Santiago de Chile, 2000), 20
regionalism, 23
Reinat Pumarejo, María, 1, 2, 158, 192
Reino de este mundo, El [*The Kingdom of this World*] (Carpentier, 1949), 96
Revista Boreales journal, 24
Reyes, Victorio de los, 111
Rhoads, Cornelius, 70
Richardson, Carmen Belén, 15
Richardson, Jill Toliver, 10
Ríos Ávila, Rubén, 34–5, 54, 71, 88
Rivera, Ismael, 3, 37, 166, 191
Rivera, Juan Pablo, 8, 24, 26
Rivera Acevedo, Alejandra, 43
Rivera Casellas, Zaira, 10, 18, 48, 57, 93, 175, 192
Rivera Clemente, Maricruz, 28, 117, 157
Rivera Lassén, Ana Irma, 15, 19, 22, 37, 140; on Afrodescent as political identity, 38; on Black identity in Puerto Rico, 100; 'Negro, negra', 23
Rivera-Rideau, Petra, 19, 23
Rodó, José Enrique, 8
Rodríguez Juliá, Edgardo, 167, 172, 208n7
Rodríguez Torres, Carmelo, 13, 14, 37, 151, 183

Rojo, Benítez, 27, 38, 51, 132, 159, 160
Rosario Natal, Carmelo, 58
Rose, Ernestine, 120
Roselló, Ricardo, 27
Royal Spanish Decree of Graces (1815), 6
Rozenzvit, Miguel, 76

sadomasochism, 3, 44, 174
Saeta: The Poems (Arroyo Pizarro, 2011), 78, 82, 93, 99, 163, 168; Afro-Boricua identity and, 79; Black and lesbian identity in relation to, 201–2; formation of diaspora in, 81
salsa music, 67
samba, 76
Sánchez, Luis Rafael, 12, 13
Sánchez-Blake, Elvira, 27
San Juan, city of, 50, 79, 121; African-descended population of, 109; Black militias in, 111; migration from countryside to, 52; mothers and we nurses in, 122–3; School of Tropical Medicine, 61, 147; slums of, 69; *see also* Cangrejos; Loíza
sankofa concept, of Akan people, 29, 42, 105, 158
Santería (Regla de Ocha), 27, 34, 61, 111, 165; connection to Africa through, 188; Oshun hidden from Catholic Inquisition, 63; spirits associated with, 133; as stigmatised cultural resistance, 89; as tool to reimagine womanhood, 130–1; *see also* Orishas
Santiago-Díaz, Eleuterio, 13, 14, 19, 46, 50, 108
Santos-Febres, Mayra, 6, 16, 25, 38, 91, 184, 208n2; Afrodescendant notion of, 21; Ancestral Black Women's Study Group and, 197; on Batailles's theories of eroticism, 54; binaries deconstructed by, 69; Black, female identity of, 30; as Black feminist theorist, 4, 18; break with Insularism, 78, 99; Cátedra de Mujeres Ancestrales de Puerto Rico writing group and, 158; extended family of, 26–7; focus on the body, 134; fractal Caribbean concept, 39, 50, 131, 160; international success of, 157; interpretation of Butler's performance concept, 29; interview with, 49, 171–7; LGBTQ+ thinkers and, 22; lived experience of, 35–6, 76; male-centered narratives subverted by, 25; narrative tradition of sadomasochism and, 44; postmodern approach and, 21, 24; Puerto Rican nationalism and, 5; on race and power, 31; racial identity and, 156; Santería (Regla de Ocha) and, 165; secondary bibliography of criticism on, 5; solidarity with Cuba, 47; on *uno-múltiple* of fractal identities, 5, 17, 22, 27
Santos-Febres, Mayra, works of: 'Caribe fractal y pensamiento afrodiaspórico' ['Fractal Caribbean and Afrodiasporic Thought'] (2020), 28; 'Confesiones afropoéticas' ['Afropoetic Confesions'] (speech), 26; 'El color de la seducción' (2001), 31; 'The Fractal Caribbean' (speech, 2019), 8, 33, 158; *Huracanada* (2018), 168; *Nuestra Señora de la Noche* [*'Our Lady of the Night'*] (2008), 16–17, 51, 54, 163; *Sirena Selena vestida de pena* [*'Sirena Selena'*] (2008), 30, 34, 163; 'Sobre cómo hacerse mujer' ['How to Become a Woman'] (2003), 30; *see also Amante de Gardel, La*; *Fe en disfraz*
Sarmiento, Domingo Faustino, 7

Schomburg, Arturo Alfonso, 103, 107, 112, 160, 166, 167; affirmative Black identity of, 37; as cataloguer of Harlem Renaissance, 20; Freemasonry and, 105–6
sea, as liberating space, 12
'Separated from Our Blood' (Arroyo Pizarro), 85
Sepultados ['*Entombed*'] (Denis-Rosario, 2018), 168
sex: in *La amante de Gardel*, 63, 66; in *Fe en disfraz*, 38, 44, 45, 49, 50, 52, 56–7, 59, 174
'sexilio' ('sex-ile'), 203
sexism, 37, 56, 156, 169; continuation of, 13; heterosexism, 25; plantation mentality and, 8
sexual abuse, 35, 52
sexuality, 11, 16, 25, 72, 78, 175; Insularism and, 99; intersectionality and, 33
sexual orientation, 21, 22, 34
sex work/workers, 5, 17, 31, 38, 65; agency and, 91; in *La amante de Gardel*, 67, 73, 162; transnational history and, 18
Shahen, Patricia, 15
Shrimpton, Margaret, 208n4
silence, 56, 74, 86, 91, 101, 156; in academia, 109; 'great family' narrative and, 70; in identity performance, 55; as protection of inner self, 136; silenced voices from history, 4, 28, 83, 107; silencing of women, 9, 10, 116, 140; trauma and, 41
Silva, Chica ('Xica') da, 39, 46, 48–9, 52, 59, 91, 175; 'cursed' dress of, 50, 52–5, 57, 161; descendants of, 49; *Fe en disfraz* and the historical record, 44, 57; rise in hierarchy of plantation system, 134; as slave owner, 74, 161
'Sin raza' ['No race'] (Arroyo Pizarro), 79, 80, 81, 86

Sirena Selena vestida de pena ['*Sirena Selena*'] (Santos-Febres, 2008), 30, 34, 163
skin tone (light skin), 48, 61, 118
slave narratives, 7, 49, 58, 85–6, 89, 121, 172–3; *see also* Manzano, Juan Francisco
slavery, 22, 82, 83, 132; abolition of, 7, 35, 41, 52, 122; Black slave owners, 74, 134; centrality to formation of Cuban national literature, 7; Christianity and, 89; desire for freedom deemed mental illness, 199; diaspora and, 175; enduring legacy of, 190; history of, 3; justification and romanticisation of, 133; left out of education curricula, 151; manumission from, 49, 109, 133, 135, 144, 147; Portuguese-dominated slave trade, 84, 92; sexual violence of enslavement, 87; slave ships, 39, 76, 78, 81; slaves treated as child-like inferiors, 11; as theme in historical fiction, 172; Transatlantic slave trade, 85
Slave Ship, The (Rediker, 2008), 191
'Sobre cómo hacerse mujer' ['How to Become a Woman'] (Santos-Febres, 2003), 30
social justice, 15, 56
Socrates, 29
Sommer, Doris, 7
Soto, Pedro Juan, 17
Spain, 8, 107; abolition of slavery in Puerto Rico (1871), 7; Church marriage under rule of, 36; Golden Age, 6; slavery abolished in Spanish empire, 125
Spanglish, 127
Spanish-American War of 1898 (US takeover of Puerto Rico), 41, 129, 147, 148, 155
Spanish language, 24, 54, 82, 92, 99, 140
Spillers, Hortense, 51

Spivak, Gayatri, 91
'Statement, The' (Black Latinas Know Collective), 169–70
stereotypes, 13, 17, 18, 34, 45, 59, 189; about legitimacy and promiscuity, 38; of Africans as primitive, 154; rooted in plantation sex, 39; trauma and, 129; 'Welfare Queen', 54
Stone, Lucy, 96
Suárez Findlay, Eileen, 8, 35, 36, 52, 140
suicide, 7, 69, 95, 96, 195, 201
Sula (Morrison, 1973), 192
Sweet, James, 84, 85
Symbolic Order, 46

Taíno people, 2, 72, 88, 129
tango dance, 7, 67
Tapia y Rivera, Alejandro, 7, 67, 93, 137–8
techné (skill), 29, 97, 108, 110, 136, 145, 159; in *La amante de Gardel*, 62, 63; as assuming control over one's body, 29; collecting as, 167; in *Fe en disfraz*, 50, 53; wordsmithing as, 118–20
'thing-Zumbi' binomial, 91, 99, 164
Thomas, Piri, 14, 37, 150, 160
Thomas, René, 79
Thompson, Robert Farris, 131, 165
Thorné, Micaela (fictional character), 59, 67, 75–6, 147, 161–2; affair with Gardel, 65, 68, 71; becoming Other with Gardel, 61, 75; death of, 65, 71; family medicinal craft and, 62; Mulatta-Antilles tradition and, 70–1; *see also Amante de Gardel, La* [*'Gardel's Lover'*]
Tibullus (Roman poet), 66
time, fractal versus chronological, 147
Tirado, Martín (fictional character), 44, 52, 55, 58, 67; as not-so-white Creole, 161; patriarchal voice of, 45–7; *see also Fe en disfraz* [*Faith in Disguise*]

Torres Muñoz, María Elba, 22–3, 104, 157, 184, 206
tourism, 95, 104, 107, 113, 115, 119
Toussaint Louverture, François-Dominique, 6
tranformista ('cross-dresser'), 32
translocality, 25
translocas (trans women, drag queens), 10, 24, 30, 113, 159–60; in *Fe en disfraz*, 48; performance and, 33; Villanueva Osorio as, 126
Translocas: The Politics of Puerto Rican Drag and Trans Performance (LaFountain-Stoikes, 2021), 32
Transmutados [*Transmutadx*] (Arroyo Pizarro, 2016), 200
transnational identity, 18
transphobia, 32, 150
trans women, 30
traumas, 28, 58, 125, 174; dismantling of African villages, 39–40; Freudian primal scene and, 123; healing of, 180; intergenerational, 27, 41, 52, 181; of Middle Passage, 84; repressed, 50; rooted in slavery, 42; silenced, 41; of slavery and colonialism, 43, 46, 129, 156; trauma studies, 130
travesti ('transvestite'), 32
travestismo (drag, trans identity), 29–30, 48
Trigo, Benigno, 123, 124–5, 127
Trinidad, British takeover of (1797), 110
Trujillooo, Rafael Leonidas, 6
Trump, Donald, 125
Truth, Sojourner, 21, 38
Tufiño, Rafael, 14
Tuntún de Pasa y Grifería [*Tuntún of Kinks and Nappiness*] (Palés Matos, 1937), 70

UNESCO, 19, 20, 79, 205
Unidos Vencimos en 1797 ('United We Won in 1797'), 108, 109, 112–13

United Nations: Decade for People of African Descent, 166, 171, 205; world conference against racism (Durban 2001), 20
United States, 2, 5, 28, 73, 105, 169; academia in, 49, 57, 79; Boricua population of, 32; Civil Rights and Black Power movements in, 146; Cuban Revolution and, 69; dependency on, 47; effects on families in Puerto Rico, 36; as home of 'real' racism, 8; migrant workers in, 113; Puerto Rican migrants in, 10; 'racial purity' discourse in, 125; US colonialism, 9
uno-múltiple ('multiple-one'), 5, 17, 27, 101, 159, 170; diversity of, 103; island and diaspora in, 37; syncretic Yoruba religions and, 55; of transnational family of choice, 160
UPR [University of Puerto Rico], Río Piedras campus (Iupi), 13, 15, 23, 104, 115, 120, 151, 180; Afrodiasporic and Raciality Studies Programme, 158, 176; budget cuts at, 124; First Afrodescendant Congress (2015), 171, 181, 190; Hispanic Studies at, 18; hispanophilia of, 18; Programa de Estudios Afrodiaspóricos y Racialidad ('Afrodiasporic and Raciality Studies'), 43
Uruguay, 44

Valdés, Vanessa, 20, 41, 106, 130–1
Valero, Silvia, 20, 21
Valladares-Ruiz, Patricia, 48, 57
Vargas-Ramos, Carlos, 20
Vasconcelos, José, 8
Vega, Ana Lydia, 13, 142
Veinte siglos después del homicidio [*'Twenty Centuries after the Homicide'*] (Rodríguez Torres, 1972), 151

Velorio, El [*'The Wake'*] (Oller painting, 1893), 40, 104, 126, 167
Venezuela, 47–8, 58, 79, 161, 169
Verdejo, Fernanda 'Fe' (fictional character), 44, 108, 139; as anti-hero, 55–9; identification with Xica da Silva, 48–50, 52, 161; intergenerational trauma and, 52; as Martín's double, 47; Santos-Febres's identification with, 173–4; sexuality of, 50, 52–3; *see also Fe en disfraz* [*'Faith in Disguise'*]
'Vida ejemplar del esclavo y el señor' (Otero, 1975), 44
Vieques, 13–14, 109–10, 183
Viera-Colón, Edison, 108
Villanueva, Victoriano, 114–15
Villanueva Osorio, Adolfina, 112–17, 119, 120, 126, 184, 185–6; police murder of, 40–1, 112, 126, 167; as *transloca*, 167
Villard, Sylvia del, 15
Villaverde, Cirilo, 7, 138
Violeta (Arroyo Pizarro, 2013), 152, 165
Vives, Carlos María, 177
Vives, Don Salvador, 177
Vizcarrondo, Fortunato, 19, 37, 46, 80, 118

Walker, Alice, 54, 174
'Wanwe' (Arroyo Pizarro), 81–3, 86
Weldt-Basson, Helene, 43, 45, 57, 76
wet nurses, 121–3, 126–7
When the Spirits Dance Mambo (Moreno Vega, 2004), 15
White, Clarence Cameron, 120
white men, 47, 75; enslaved African women as concubines of, 48–9; haunted by Black wet nurses, 104, 126–7; as rapists, 93
whiteness, 1, 8, 14, 15, 47
whitening discourse, 6, 7, 9, 104; of cultural and racial

miscegenation, 160; in Dominican Republic, 83; hair straightening, 19; ICP as promoter of, 118; myth about origin of dark-skinned Puerto Ricans, 129; in Puerto Rico, 10
whites: Black women in service of white families, 121–4; distrust of white schoolteachers, 149–50; killed in revenge, 96–7; population of San Juan during British invasion and, 109; upper-class families, 8, 35, 121; *see also* Creoles, white; *jíbaros*
white women, 35, 48, 53; Catholic school education of, 31; dependence on Black wet nurses, 122–3; straight and educated, 21; white Latinas, 14
Winant, Howard, 6
Woman of Endurance, A (Llanos-Figueroa, 2022), 169, 179
women: as child-like inferiors, 11; empowerment of, 17; as primary storytellers, 130, 149; sexuality used against enslaved women, 178; silencing of, 9–10; sterilisation of, 73, 75; *see also* Black women
Women Warriors of the Afro-Latina Diaspora (Moreno Vega, Alba, and Modestin, eds, 2012), 91

Woodlawn, Holly, 34
Woolf, Virginia, 201
Wright, Richard, 175
Writing Secrecy in Caribbean Freemasonry (Arroyo, 2013), 61

xenophobia, 125

Yemaya (sea goddess), 39, 60, 117, 162, 169, 179; melancholy associated with, 66, 68; as mother of origins, 73
Yoruba people/traditions, 60, 66, 83, 111, 135; gods and goddesses, 86, 130; syncretic religions, 55, 114, 196; Yoruba language, 97
Young Lords, 16, 37, 43, 150, 160, 169

Zapata-Calle, Ana, 102, 104, 123
Zapata Olivella, Manuel, 96
Zeno Gandía, Manuel, 41, 67, 141, 155, 162, 168
Zenón Cruz, Isabelo, 10, 13, 34, 37, 47, 151, 184, 190; as romanticised patriarch, 13
Zenú Indians, 63
Zona de Carga y Descarga (journal), 32
Zumbi, 132